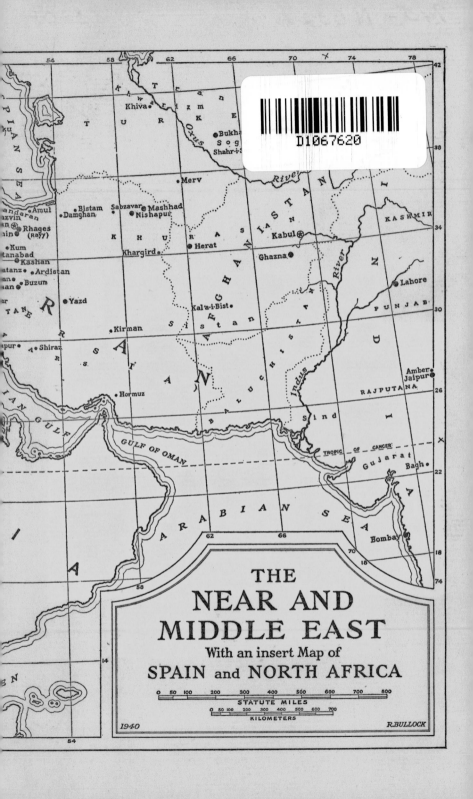

THE
NEAR AND
MIDDLE EAST
With an insert Map of
SPAIN and NORTH AFRICA

STATUTE MILES
KILOMETERS

1940   R.BULLOCK

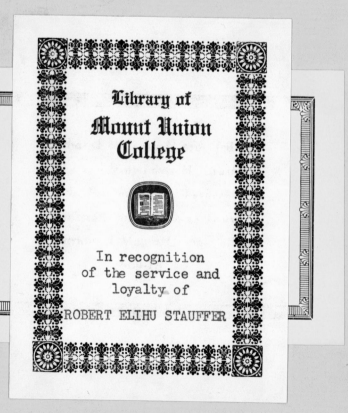

Library of
Mount Union
College

In recognition
of the service and
loyalty of
ROBERT ELIHU STAUFFER

A HANDBOOK OF
MUHAMMADAN ART

A Handbook of Muhammadan Art

By M. S. DIMAND, Ph. D.

Curator of Near Eastern Art

THIRD EDITION

Revised and Enlarged

New York —

THE METROPOLITAN MUSEUM OF ART

NEW YORK

1958

Copyright 1944

by

The Metropolitan Museum of Art

Preface

The first edition of this handbook was issued in 1930 under the title *A Handbook of Mohammedan Decorative Arts*. Since then the Metropolitan's collection of Muhammadan art has been enriched by numerous important acquisitions and today it ranks as one of the foremost in the world. In the present edition the handbook has been revised and brought up to date in the light of recent research and excavations, particularly those at Ctesiphon and Nishapur, undertaken by the Metropolitan Museum. For better understanding of Muhammadan art, a new chapter on "The Origins of Islamic Art," dealing with East Christian (including Coptic), Parthian, and Sasanian art, has been added. Like the first edition, this new one is the only guide to Muhammadan art in the English language and will be useful to students and collectors as well as to visitors to the Museum. Owing to the constant growth of the collection and probable future rearrangements of the galleries, it has seemed undesirable to give this handbook the form of a descriptive "case to case" guide of each gallery.

The representative character of the Museum's collection is evident from the fact that all illustrations in the handbook have been selected from our own material. The foundation of the collection was laid many years ago, in 1891, when the bequest of Edward C. Moore brought to the Museum its first important representation of Near Eastern art, including a magnificent group of enameled glass and a large collection of silver-inlaid metalwork. A notable group of Turkish ceramics was presented by W. B. Osgood Field in 1902. The Persian illuminated books and single miniatures given to the Museum in 1913 by Alexander Smith Cochran greatly enlarged our collection in this field. In 1914 the Altman Bequest brought to the Museum many magnificent rugs and other specimens of Islamic art, and these were supplemented in 1917, through the bequest of Isaac D. Fletcher, by a splendid group of Iranian pottery and fine examples of rugs. The gift of the Morgan Collection in 1917 enriched the Museum with a large and important group of enameled mosque lamps, rare carved ivories, and Indian rugs. Other important miniatures and ceramics came through the bequest of W. M. Grinnell in 1920. Particularly noteworthy was the gift of the James F. Ballard Collection of oriental rugs in 1922. Welcome gifts or bequests have also been received, among others, from Henry G. Marquand, V. Everit Macy, George D. Pratt, Horace Havemeyer, Henry Walters, Edward C. Moore, Jr., and George Blumenthal.

The author wishes to thank Hannah E. McAllister of the Department of Near Eastern Art for her assistance in the preparation of the text and in the reading of the proof and Walter Hauser and Charles K. Wilkinson, also of that department, for many valuable suggestions. The decorative map on the end papers by Randolph Bullock.

M. S. DIMAND

April, 1944

This third edition has been reprinted from the second, with a number of slight revisions of the text and captions and with a thirty-two page supplement of illustrations, which will be found at the end of the volume.

M. S. D.

December, 1957

Contents

Chapter 1

HISTORICAL INTRODUCTION

Throughout this book dates are to be understood as after Christ unless otherwise indicated

Muhammad, the founder of Islam, was born about 570 in Mecca, the heart of Arabia. He belonged to the Banu Hashim, the most distinguished branch of the Kuraish tribe. At the time of Muhammad, Arabia was peopled by various tribes, more or less settled, who worshiped the stars and a number of secondary deities of little importance. The influence of Judaism and Christianity, especially the former, prepared the ground for Muhammad's monotheistic teachings. The personality and genius of Muhammad helped greatly the rapid growth of the new religion, which he founded upon the idea of Allah, the One God, of whom he considered himself the Prophet. In 622 Muhammad migrated with his followers from Mecca to Medina, where he was welcomed with open arms. This year of the Flight, or Emigration (*Hijra*, or *Hegira*), marks the beginning of the Muhammadan era. In 630 Muhammad captured Mecca, where he destroyed all the idols, except a black stone in the wall of the Kaaba, a cube-shaped building which was especially sacred to the pagan Arabs. He made Mecca the center of the new faith and instituted an annual pilgrimage, in accordance with a custom long practiced by the Arabs.

The sacred book of the Muhammadans is the Koran. It contains the collected revelations of Muhammad and is divided into 114 chapters, or *suras*. The fundamental tenets of Islam are expressed as follows: "O believers in Allah, in His Apostle and the Book which He has revealed to His Apostle, and the writings which He had revealed before. Whosoever disbelieves in Allah, His Apostle and His Angels, and His Apostles and the Last Day, errs completely." The essential formula of the Muhammadan faith is: *La ilah illa Allah, Muhammad rasul Allah*—"There is no God but Allah, and Muhammad is His Prophet." Next to the Koran, the

1

Hadith, or "Traditions," are held in great reverence by the Muhammadans.

By proclaiming progressive war on all unbelievers, Muhammad gained strong support from many tribes of Arabia, for these wandering nomads saw in the new creed, besides a moral issue, an opportunity to plunder in foreign countries. Organized by Muhammad and his followers, the Arabs came to believe in a racial superiority, and under the banner of Islam many hostile clans joined interests in a common cause.

At his death in 632 Muhammad left Arabia partly unified. He was succeeded by his father-in-law, Abu Bakr (632-4), who was elected caliph, or representative of the Prophet. To Abu Bakr fell the task of continuing the unification of Arab tribes and of preparing for the conquest of the world. His successors, 'Umar (634-44), 'Uthman (644-56), and 'Ali (656-61), were elected in turn and were known as the Orthodox Caliphs.

The Arab armies of the caliphs invaded Syria, Mesopotamia, Egypt, and North Africa. The rapid conquests that followed were due not only to the strength and organization of the Arabs, but also to the political and economic conditions of the invaded countries. In Syria and Mesopotamia the Arabs found Semitic peoples who in previous centuries had migrated northward from Arabia. Some of them were Christians, some Jews, and others heathens. After the conquest of Irak, 'Ali, the last Orthodox Caliph, made his residence at Kufa, a city founded by 'Umar, and Arabia ceased to be the center of the empire. Kufa and Basra soon became seats of Arabic learning and theology. The Aramaic peasants of Syria greeted the Arabs as deliverers from the foreign rule of the Byzantines, who were hated for the heavy taxes they imposed on the natives of their oriental provinces. Similar conditions were met in Egypt, which for centuries had been used to alien rule; in addition the Copts (or native Christians), who as Monophysites recognized in Christ only a single, composite nature, were in conflict with the official Christianity of the Byzantine empire and thus saw in the new rule a prospect of freedom from the persecution of the patriarch Cyrus.

The conquest of Iran by the Muhammadans was more difficult, for the Iranians were of Aryan race and adhered to Zoroastrianism, a dualistic religion based on the conflict between Good and Evil, or Light and Darkness. The native Sasanid dynasty was defeated, however, at the battle of Nihavand in 642. By 661 the Arab armies had arrived at Herat and soon after reached the Indus. The Iranians, after adopting Islam, were chiefly responsible for the development of the Shi'a doctrine, which maintained that the divine right to the caliphate was restricted to the family of 'Ali and opposed the free election of the caliph as upheld by the Sunnites.

The caliph 'Ali was assassinated in 661, whereupon the caliphate was assumed by 'Ali's great enemy, Mu'awiya, a descendant of Umayya of the tribe of Kuraish and founder of the Umayyad dynasty (661-749). Under the rule of the Umayyads the center of the Muhammadan world was transferred to Damascus in Syria, where the dynasty found the strongest support. The Arab empire now extended over a vast territory, from Spain and the Atlantic coast of Africa to the borders of China, and enjoyed great prosperity. Poetry and science flourished at the court in Damascus, which also became known for its luxury, lax morals, and open ignoring of the laws of the Koran.

In 749 the rule of the Umayyads came to an end. As a result of a revolt against them starting in the province of Khurasan, in eastern Iran, the Umayyads were defeated by their enemies, the Abbasids, who were the descendants of 'Abbas, the uncle of Muhammad.

One of the Umayyads, 'Abd ar Rahman, fled to Spain, where he founded the Western Caliphate. In 1031 the rule of the Umayyads in Spain came to an end and was followed by that of various dynasties from Moorish North Africa. The conquest of Granada in 1492 by Ferdinand and Isabella brought Muhammadan power in Spain to a close.

The alliance of the Iranians with the Arab enemies of the Umayyads was chiefly responsible for the victory of the Abbasids, which in turn brought about the triumph of Iranian culture over Arabic. Iranian ideas and thoughts now invaded the Muhammadan world, hitherto dominated by the Arabs. The Abbasids built a new capital, Baghdad, situated on the Tigris, which became a center of Islamic culture and art. Here was founded a school of Muhammadan jurisprudence, and many works of Greek science and philosophy were translated into Arabic. The caliph Mamun founded an academy known as the "House of Science," with a library and an observatory. Under the caliph Harun ar Rashid, famous from the stories of the *Thousand and One Nights*, Baghdad became one of the most flourishing cities in the world. Sixty miles to the north of Baghdad was the city of Samarra, which was founded by the caliph Mu'tasim. It was an artistic center and the residence of the caliphs from 836 to 892, when it was suddenly abandoned.

The Turks, a non-Semitic people of Central Asiatic origin, made their appearance in the Arab empire during the Abbasid period. Since they were born fighters, they were first employed as body-guards of the caliphs. However, the Turkish chiefs rose steadily in power, until, under the caliph Mu'tasim, they became the actual rulers of the empire, and the caliphs who followed Mu'tasim were deposed or murdered by them at will. As the decline of the caliphate became evident, the empire split up into various states. In 800 the Aghlabid chiefs established a separate government in North Africa. Independent dynasties were founded in 819 in eastern Iran and Transoxiana by the Samanids and in 868 in other parts of Iran by the Saffarids. In 868 Egypt became independent under the Tulunids, a Turkish dynasty, who were followed by the Turkish Ikhshidids and the Berber Fatimids, the period of the Fatimid rule being of special importance in the history of Muhammadan art in Egypt. In 962 the Ghaznavids established dynasties in Afghanistan and the Punjab.

New life was injected into the dying empire by the arrival in Transoxiana of the Saljuks, a people who had migrated from the Khirghiz Steppes of Turkestan. After defeating the Ghaznavid armies, the newcomers conquered Khurasan in 1037 and marched westward. They crushed every dynasty in Iran, Asia Minor, Mesopotamia, and Syria. In 1055 Tughril Beg entered Baghdad and was proclaimed sultan by the caliph.

The end of the political power of the caliphate came in 1258 as a result of the arrival of another Central Asiatic race, the Mongols, who conquered one Muhammadan country after another under the leadership of Chingiz Khan. Before his death Chingiz Khan divided the vast Mongol empire, which stretched from China to southern Russia, among his sons. In Iran, Hulagu established the Il-khan dynasty, which ruled successfully from 1256 to 1353 not only over Iran but also over Mesopotamia and part of Asia Minor. Although the Mongols swept over the Near East in a destructive wave, they soon adopted the superior civilization of the conquered peoples.

The Il-khans accepted Islam, and as converts became generous patrons of Islamic learning, literature, and art. To their courts at Baghdad, Tabriz, and Sultaniya came native and foreign scholars and artists.

The Il-khans were followed by several petty dynasties which fell under the advance of another great Mongol, Timur, or Tamerlane (1370-1404). Like his Mongol ancestor Chingiz Khan, Timur first invaded Iran. In 1403 his armies reached Asia Minor, defeated the Ottoman Turks, and captured the sultan Bayazid I, a defeat which directed the Ottoman advance to the north and west into Asia Minor, Syria, and southern Europe instead of to the south through Iran. Timur's conquests, however, were not so permanent as those of Chingiz Khan. The provinces in which Timur and his descendants, the Timurids (1370-1500), were firmly established were Transoxiana and Khurasan. Under their regime Samarkand and Bukhara grew in importance, and Herat, the capital, became a center of Muhammadan science, literature, and art. Babur, a descendant of Timur, born in Ferghana in 1482, founded the celebrated Mughal dynasty, which ruled India from 1526 to 1857, and it was during his reign and the reigns of Humayun and Akbar, his successors, that Iranian culture gained its influence over the court art of India.

Contemporary with the Il-khans and the Timurids were the Mamluk sultans of Egypt and Syria, who were descendants of the Turkish bodyguard of the Ayyubid sultans. There were two lines of Mamluk sultans, the Bahri (1250-1390) and the Burji (1382-1516). The Mamluks built a strong government which effectively resisted both the Mongols and the Crusaders. They rebuilt Cairo and adorned it with many beautiful buildings. Many works of art known today bear the names of the Mamluk sultans, especially that of Nasir ad Din Muhammad ibn Kalaun, who reigned three times in the period from 1293 to 1340.

Among the many Turkish tribes which populated Asia Minor in the middle and at the end of the thirteenth century were the Ottoman Turks. 'Uthman, the founder of the dynasty, assumed the title of amir in 1299 and he and his followers successfully fought the weakening Byzantine empire. In 1453, under Muhammad II, Constantinople was conquered; in 1516 Selim I took Syria and Egypt from the Mamluks and even received the right of succession to the caliphate. The Ottoman dynasty thus succeeded in gaining not only political but also religious supremacy in the Muhammadan world.

In northwestern Iran there arose at the beginning of the sixteenth century a new and powerful native dynasty, the Safavids (1502-1736). In 1502 Isma'il (1502-24), a descendant of the saint Shaikh Safi ad Din of Ardabil, defeated the White Sheep Turkomans and made Tabriz his capital and residence. Isma'il's great task was the unification of Iran. He conquered each Iranian province in turn and finally took Herat in 1510 from the Uzbeg Shaibanids, who ruled over Transoxiana from 1428 to 1599. The chief kings of the Safavid dynasty were Shah Tahmasp (1524-76) and Shah 'Abbas the Great (1587-1628), who contributed greatly to the development of a national Iranian culture and art. In religious matters the Iranian shahs were the official protectors of the Shi'a sect, whereas the Sunni sect was represented by the Turkish empire.

Chapter 2

THE ORIGINS OF ISLAMIC ART

In the time of Muhammad the Arabs had little or no art of their own, but, in their conquest of Syria, Mesopotamia, Egypt, and Iran they adopted the highly developed art of these countries. It is known from literary sources that the caliphs of the Umayyad dynasty (661-749) requisitioned materials and craftsmen from all the provinces for the construction of new cities, palaces, and mosques. Byzantine and Syrian mosaicists were employed to decorate the mosque at Damascus, for which an Iranian was the chief architect. Artists from Egypt worked in Jerusalem, Damascus, and Mecca. This custom of requisitioning material and workers continued under the Abbasids (749-945). The historian Tabari tells us that at the foundation of Baghdad workers were gathered from Syria, Iran, Mosul, Kufa, Wasit, and Basra.

An Islamic style was evolved gradually and was derived chiefly from two artistic sources, the East Christian and the Sasanian. In early Islamic monuments, such as the mosaics of Jerusalem (691-2), the eighth-century stone façade from Mshatta, and the paintings of the desert palace at Kuseir ʿAmra (about 712), decorative motives derived from East Christian art and from Sasanian art are found side by side.

Christian art of Egypt, Syria, and Mesopotamia furnished models for a number of decorative schemes found in early Islamic monuments. The art of the Egyptian Christians, or Copts, is known to us from sculptures and textiles dating from the third to the seventh century of our era. The Metropolitan Museum has a representative collection of Coptic sculptures, consisting of stone capitals, arches, and slabs of various sizes, which originally decorated churches and monasteries. Capitals from Bubastis, Kharga, Assuan, Sakkara, and Bawit show the evolution of this important architectural element from Hellenistic beginnings to the developed Coptic style of the sixth century. Here we find the naturalistic tendencies so characteristic of Hellenistic art replaced by purely decorative principles

7

Fig. 1. *Carved Stone Arch, Coptic, VI Century*

of Eastern origin. This development was a result of changes in the cultural life of Egypt, in which the Greek element was gradually replaced by the native Coptic. The most popular motives of Christian art in Egypt and Syria were the acanthus and the vine. The Copts borrowed the serrated acanthus scroll from Syria, where it had been used in purely decorative fashion as early as the first century A.D. Often they combined the acanthus and its parts with geometrical motives such as interlacings, thus forming new patterns which had only a remote relation to Hellenistic art. When the Muhammadans adopted the acanthus from Syria and Egypt, this process of disintegration continued.

A fine example of Coptic sculpture is a capital in the Museum which came from the monastery of Saint Jeremias at Sakkara and dates from the sixth or seventh century. The interlacing vine scrolls issuing from several vases form a series of compartments covering the surface of the capital. Another fine example of Coptic sculpture is an arch in the Metropolitan Museum (fig. 1) which is said to have come from Bawit. It is decorated with two scrolls, one bearing palm leaves, the other issuing from two vases and showing a combination of several motives—vine leaves, pomegranates, and figs. Such purely decorative combinations of various plants and fruits were unknown in Hellenistic art but were characteristic of oriental art and became very popular in Islamic ornament. The decoration

8

of the arch reveals other features which are characteristic of Coptic and Syrian sculpture. The ornament, lying in one plane, covers almost every inch of the surface and extends perpendicularly from the receded background. In many reliefs, as in that of figure 1, this method of carving, which replaced the naturalistic modeling of Hellenistic art, produced a highly decorative effect of light and dark. These stylistic features were adopted and further developed by Muhammadan artists.

Islamic art was also influenced by East Christian ivory carvings and jewelry. Well-known examples of the Syrian style are the ivory panels of the chair of Archbishop Maximian in Ravenna. In some of the panels, decorated with vine scrolls enriched with animals and birds, the undercutting produces almost the effect of openwork. Openwork was frequently used in Syrian gold jewelry of the fifth and sixth centuries, represented in the Metropolitan Museum by the Cyprus treasure of the Morgan Collection. The bracelet in figure 2, decorated with vine scrolls in openwork, is a fine example of this jewelry, which, although found in Cyprus, must have been of Syrian manufacture.

In general the decoration of Coptic textiles follows the same stylistic development as sculpture, as may be seen in the fine collection of Coptic textiles in the Metropolitan Museum, which includes complete hangings and garments as well as fragments of tunics and cloaks. For the most part the decoration of these textiles is tapestry-woven in wool and linen, although other techniques, such as loop weaving, lancé weaving, and draw-loom weaving, are also represented. The decoration, in monochrome (usually purple) or polychrome, is in two styles, the Hellenistic and the Copto-oriental, with intermediary stages of development.

Fig. 2. Gold Bracelet, Syrian, V-VI Century

The earliest Coptic textiles belong to the third and fourth cen-

Fig. 3. Tapestry-woven Textile, Coptic, III-IV Century

turies and are decorated with figure subjects or geometrical and floral ornament. The figures and scenes, which are taken from Greco-Roman mythology, are rendered in the naturalistic style of Hellenistic tradition. The modeling and shading of the polychrome textiles were inspired by Hellenistic paintings and mosaics. Coptic weavers of the third and fourth centuries composed floral and geometrical patterns with equal skill. They created a great variety of intricate interlacings (see fig. 3), some of which are forerunners of the geometrical ornament found in Islamic art.

In fifth-century textiles Hellenistic subjects were gradually replaced by Christian scenes and figures of saints and orantes, treated

Fig. 4. Tapestry-woven Textile, Coptic, VII-VIII Century

in a conventional manner, with little or no modeling, as, for instance, on a curtain in the Museum. Textiles of the sixth and seventh centuries show the fully developed Coptic style. Human figures and animals are now schematized in oriental fashion and are rendered in brilliant flat colors, often against a red background. The rich polychromy is one of the most characteristic features of these late Coptic textiles.

Even after the conquest of Egypt by the Arabs Coptic art did not die out. It continued to flourish, and many textiles with extremely stylized Christian scenes and other subjects date from the beginning of the Islamic era (see fig. 4). In a number of these Coptic textiles of the Islamic era, Coptic decoration, including Christian figures, is combined with Arabic writing, as seen in several pieces in the Metropolitan Museum. Because of their skill as weavers Copts were extensively employed in the state manufactories (*tiraz*) established by the caliphs in several Egyptian cities (see p. 249). There

Fig. 5. Fragment of a Rug, Coptic, about 400

were also private factories which made fabrics for the use of the Copts. With the help of material found in recent years in Egypt, we are now able to distinguish several groups of late Coptic textiles, one of the seventh and eighth centuries (see fig. 4), a second group of the eighth and ninth centuries, and a third of the ninth and tenth centuries, in which the figures are stylized in a geometrical fashion. Coptic influence on Islamic art continued for many centuries and is evident as late as the eleventh and twelfth centuries, not only in textiles but also in other Islamic arts and crafts.

Of importance to all students of oriental rugs are fragments of pre-Islamic rugs found in recent years in Syria and Egypt. The excavations of Dura, in the Syrian desert, and of Karanis, in Egypt, furnished us with important evidence that cut-pile rugs were manufactured in these provinces in the beginning of the Christian era. From Egypt comes an important fragment of a woolen rug with a cut-pile surface, said to have been found in Antinoë, a city in Upper Egypt (fig. 5). It had originally a field of four or six rectangles with a geometrical design inspired by Roman and early Christian mosaic pavements. The design of the borders and the rich polychromy are familiar from Coptic textiles. The meander of the inner border encloses various motives, such as squares and rosettes, overlaid with Coptic crosses. The outer border consists of an angular vine scroll bearing leaves and bunches of grapes, treated in a decorative fashion characteristic of Coptic tapestries of the fifth century. The technique of this rug, which may be dated about 400, is different from any known hitherto. The knots of early rug fragments from Central Asia, found in Lou-Lan (II or III century) and Kyzil, near Kutcha (V or VI century), are tied, as are those of Spanish rugs, over one warp. The pile of the Coptic rug is formed by the ends of two knots rather than one, which indicates that the knots were not tied separately as in oriental rugs. This technique is not true rug knotting but a development of the Coptic process of loop weaving, which produced an uncut-pile surface, as may be seen in a number of fine examples in the Museum.

Iranian art of the pre-Islamic era is represented in the Museum by the arts and crafts of the Parthian and Sasanian periods. The style developed under the rule of the Parthian dynasty (248 B.C.-A.D. 226), which dominated Iran proper, Mesopotamia, and parts of Syria, reveals a mixture of Hellenistic and oriental elements. One of the finest pieces of Parthian sculpture known is a relief owned by the Museum, a door lintel from the fortress palace at

Fig. 6. Gold Clasp, Parthian, I-II Century

Hatra, in the Mesopotamian desert, probably dating from the second century of our era. The griffins of the relief, although based on Roman models, show strong oriental influence, which increased

13

considerably under the rule of the Sasanian dynasty succeeding the Parthians. The combination of Hellenistic and oriental features is also apparent in a magnificent Parthian gold clasp (fig. 6) in the Morgan Collection of the Museum. This clasp and a companion piece in the British Museum, found at Nihavand in Iran, both show a medallion enclosing an eagle holding a deer in its claws, probably the eagle of the sun-god Mithra carrying to heaven Homa, the symbol of water and vegetation. The eagle and the deer are cast in high relief, with parts entirely in the round. The whole clasp is enriched with incrustations of turquoise stones. Polychrome stone and enamel inlay was favored by Iranians of all periods and influenced the arts and crafts of the Sasanian and early Islamic eras.

Although in the past several authorities have recognized the influence of Sasanian art on the formation of the Islamic style, its full importance has only recently been realized. Thanks to excavations of Sasanian sites such as Ctesiphon, near Baghdad, Kish in Mesopotamia, and Damghan in Iran, we now have a wealth of material, particularly of decorative sculpture in stucco, in which we find many of the prototypes of early Islamic ornament.

The Sasanian period (226-637) began one of the most brilliant periods of Iranian art. Under royal patronage arts and crafts reached great heights of perfection. The most complete manifestation of the Sasanian style is found in the magnificent rock sculptures glorifying the Sasanian kings and depicting their triumphs over the Romans. Sasanian art must be credited with the creation of a new style of abstract, pseudo-floral ornament based on traditions of Assyrian and Achaemenian art, in which rhythmic repetition and symmetry are the main principles. As it had been in ancient oriental art, the palmette became an important motive in Sasanian ornament. This palmette ornament may be seen in the collection of stucco panels in the Metropolitan Museum which came from the excavations in Ctesiphon conducted jointly by the Metropolitan and the German State Museums. In these stucco reliefs, which date from the fifth or sixth century, we find several combinations and types of palmettes, among them the full and the half palmette, the heart-shaped and the lobed. In the lobed variety, the lobes are usually deeply incised, as seen in figure 7, which shows a band of split palmettes formed by two half palmettes joined together. Here we find already an important characteristic of the Islamic arabesque, namely, the merging of half palmettes with the stem. Sasanian palmette scrolls and palmette devices are direct prototypes of those seen on early Islamic monuments, such as the palace at Mshatta, the mimbar of Kairwan, and the Syrian alabaster capitals (see fig.

Fig. 7. Stucco Relief from Ctesiphon, Sasanian, V-VI Century

51). There was a continuity of artistic development from the Sasanian to the Islamic period. In some cases the Muhammadan artists adopted a Sasanian palmette ornament without any change, in others they developed new, abstract forms which led gradually to a distinctly Islamic style of decoration. Among the motives Muhammadan artists borrowed from Sasanian art were palmette trees, often quite elaborate, showing a combination of heterogeneous motives (see fig. 8). Frequently found in early Islamic decoration is the Sasanian wing motive. In Iran it was used often as an emblem of royalty, enclosing a Pahlavi inscription, as on Ctesiphon stuccoes, or as a base for portrait busts or animal figures. Wing motives are also well known from coins and silver dishes, where they surmount the crowns of several Sasanian kings. In Islamic art the Sasanian wing motive was further stylized so that often it lost its identity, being transformed into an ornament.

Silver vessels of the Sasanian period are among the finest prod-

Fig. 8. Stucco Relief from Ctesiphon, Sasanian, V-VI Century

ucts of Near Eastern metalwork. The favorite decorations on Sasanian silver vessels were hunting scenes, animals, and birds. A magnificent gilded silver dish in the Metropolitan Museum (fig. 9) represents a Sasanian king, Peroz I (457-63), hunting ibexes with a bow and arrow. The king is dressed in rich garments and wears a crenelated crown surmounted by a crescent and celestial globe symbolizing the divinity of the royal person. He is thus, in oriental fashion, glorified as the supreme hunter. The style of the scene shows all the characteristic features of Sasanian art. In spite of a certain approach to realism, some oriental conventions are apparent, including representation of the scene from several points of view at once. Various heights of relief and techniques, such as casting, embossing, engraving, and inlaying are combined with great artistic effect.

Iranians of the Sasanian period held the monopoly of the silk

Fig. 9. Gilded Silver Dish, Sasanian, V Century

trade between China and the West and early established their own looms for the manufacture of silk stuffs, which soon became famous all over the Near East. Important centers of Sasanian silk weaving were in the province of Khuzistan (ancient Susiana), which bordered on Mesopotamia. At Shushtar, Susa, and Gundeshapur, various types of fine silk fabrics were woven, both for home consumption and for export. In the time of Shapur I (241-72), after the conquest of Antioch, Aramaean weavers were brought into Khuzistan. A number of silk textiles preserved in European church treasuries have been definitely established as Sasanian by comparison

17

with designs on garments represented on reliefs at Tak-i-Bustan (near Kermanshah, in Iran) which date from the time of Khusrau II (590-629). Several silks decorated with hunting scenes have also been attributed to Iranian looms of the sixth and seventh centuries.

Sasanian silk weaves have been found in Egypt, chiefly in the cemeteries of Antinoë and Akhmim. Recent research has shown that a group of silk textiles found at Antinoë and long thought to be of local manufacture are of Sasanian origin and date from the third to the sixth century of our era. The decoration of the earlier textiles of this group consists of various lozenge patterns containing geometrical or various stylized plant motives. In other early Sasanian textiles birds, palmettes, and human masks form an all-over pattern or are placed in circular and lobed medallions arranged in rows. Several fragments of such textiles, which were used for garments, may be seen in the Metropolitan Museum's collection. Later silks, dating probably from the sixth and seventh centuries, show the developed Sasanian style, with large circular medallions containing winged horses, hippocampi, and birds, separated by plant devices and other motives. The Museum has one piece of this type, showing within a medallion a duck holding a necklace, a motive which was copied in the wall painting at Kyzil in eastern Turkestan, and in the ninth-century wall paintings of Samarra.

Silk textiles found at Akhmim in Egypt are also frequently attributed to Iran. These textiles are woven in two shades only, buff on green, black, orange-red, red, or purple. The pattern consists of formal plant ornaments, among them palmette trees bearing curved, almond-shaped motives derived from jewelry, which continued to be popular after the Arab conquest (see fig. 168). Some of the Akhmim silks are decorated with figure subjects showing features which point rather to Syria or Mesopotamia as the place of manufacture than to Iran proper. Fabrics found at Dura and Palmyra published by Pfister enable us now to give Syria a more prominent place in the history of textiles.

To Syrian looms should also be assigned a group of silk weaves of the sixth to seventh century with polychrome figure subjects, which Falke attributed to Alexandria. Among the best-known pieces of this "Alexandrian" group is the textile in the Sancta Sanctorum in Rome, with representations of the Annunciation and the Nativity; the so-called Dioscuri textile in the Saint Servatius church at Maastricht; and a silk with hunting scenes (fig. 10). Examples of the last two are in the Metropolitan Museum and various other collections. The hunting silk has an all-over pattern of cir-

Fig. 10. *Silk Weave, Syrian, VI-VII Century*

cular medallions with two huntsmen on horseback, each shooting with bow and arrow at a crouching lion. This silk was formerly regarded as Sasanian because of the subject matter and the arrow wounds on the lions, which were wrongly interpreted as Sasanian royal symbols. However, the style, the figures, and the ornament not only of this textile but of the whole "Alexandrian" group point to Syria as the most probable place of manufacture. Of special interest to students of Islamic art is the ornament of these silk textiles, which is derived from Sasanian art. The "trees" separating the medallions of the hunting silk are composed of various motives, among them large palmette leaves. Several varieties of such palmette trees may be seen in the mosaics of the Dome of the Rock in Jerusalem, dated A.H. 72 (691/2), which were most probably the work of Christian artists of Syria. Cornucopias and conventionalized garlands overlaid with fruits or plants like those seen in the border of the medallion in figure 10 are among the motives the mosaicist of the Dome of the Rock borrowed from pre-Islamic art of Syria.

The evolution of the Islamic style was to a certain extent also influenced by the arts and crafts of Iranian and Turkish nomads from eastern Iran and Central Asia. Through contact with the art of these nomads many new features and techniques were introduced into Muhammadan art which were unknown in East Christian and Sasanian art. The beveled, or slant, carving, for example, which appears in the early Abbasid sculptures in stone, stucco, and wood can be traced back to Scytho-Siberian ornaments in wood, bone, bronze, and gold. These objects belong to different periods, some of them as late as the third century of our era.

The migration of Iranians and Turkish nomads also introduced to the Near East new ornamental forms, such as geometrical scrolls with circular leaves, which appear in the Abbasid stucco decoration of Samarra (see p. 88). The geometrical scroll was at home in Central Asia and the Far East. It appears in wall paintings and wooden objects of the eighth and ninth centuries found in Chinese Turkestan, at Khocho, the capital of the Turkish Uighurs. It is quite probable that objects of gold made by wandering tribesmen introduced this new ornament to the Near East and even further west to Europe, in Albania and Hungary. The Albanian gold treasure in the Morgan Collection of the Metropolitan Museum, which may be dated in the seventh or eighth century, furnishes us with excellent examples of this abstract geometrical ornament which influenced the evolution of the Islamic arabesque.

Chapter 3

WALL PAINTING AND MINIATURE PAINTING

1. Umayyad and Abbasid Paintings (VIII-X Century)

The early history of Islamic painting is still little known to us, but from the few monuments that have been discovered or unearthed in Syria, Mesopotamia, and Iran we can get at least some idea of the richness and splendor of wall decoration under the Umayyads and early Abbasids. The earliest paintings that have been found so far in Syria are preserved in Kuseir 'Amra, a little desert lodge with a bath, built by the Umayyad caliph Walid I about 712 and discovered by Musil in 1898. In 1936 Schlumberger discovered in the ruins of Kasr al-Hair al-Gharbi in Syria an eighth-century palace with two magnificent frescoes, one Hellenistic, the other entirely Sasanian in style.

The growth of Iranian influence under the Abbasids is evident from wall paintings found in a ninth-century palace at Samarra. Of especial interest are the wall paintings of the harem, which show dancing girls, musicians, animals, and birds enclosed by scrollwork or circles. Here the figures and the plant ornament are based on the traditions of Sasanian painting; but wooden boards from the same palace show an abstract, purely Islamic style similar to that of the Samarra stuccoes, the ornament consisting of conventionalized plant motives painted in white, blue, red, and yellow and outlined in black.

Until recently no early Islamic paintings had been found in Iran proper. In 1936, 1937, and 1939, however, the Metropolitan Museum's Iranian expedition unearthed at Nishapur, in eastern Iran, examples of early Abbasid wall decoration which add a new chapter to our knowledge of Islamic art. These paintings come from several buildings and may be roughly divided into two groups, monochrome and polychrome.

The finest example in the monochrome group (now in the Teheran Museum) is painted in black outline and wash. It shows

21

a mounted hunter wearing a rich, belted costume, a helmet, two swords, and a round shield. On his left wrist he carries a hunting falcon, and attached to his saddle is the quarry, probably a hare. The fine drawing of the horse in "flying" gallop and the costume

Fig. 11. Wall Painting from Nishapur, Iranian, Beginning of the
IX Century

recall Sasanian art, whereas certain details, such as the two swords and the helmet, suggest Central Asiatic influences. The painting may be assigned to the end of the eighth century or the beginning of the ninth.

In the polychrome group, which is of approximately the same period, there are fragments of large compositions with human and satanic figures, panels with plant ornament, and plaster niches with "vase" motives and palmette scrolls. The fragments of the figure subjects include portions of male and female heads, busts, and draperies. Here, as in the somewhat later Samarra paintings, we find a mixture of Iranian and Hellenistic elements, the latter especially apparent in the rendering of garments. The colors used are black, white, blue, red, and various intermediate shades and hues. The Museum has a fragment of a haloed female figure with curly black hair recalling figures in some of the Uighur paintings found in Khocho, in Chinese Turkestan.

Of particular importance are the wall paintings from a room in a palace building found on the mound called Teppe Madrasa. These paintings, which may be dated to the beginning of the ninth century, formed a dado, 1.20 meters high, divided into rectangular panels and bordered by a frieze of geometrical motives. The main decoration consists of square panels containing various compositions of plant ornament and abstract motives, which, to a certain extent, recall the Abbasid stucco and paintings of Samarra. These large panels are separated from each other by narrow rectangular panels with marbleized design and a scale pattern. The panel in the Metropolitan Museum (fig. 11) has an interesting design in red, white, blue, and black, in which bands ending in "lotus" motives or hands form a series of compartments filled with large palmette leaves, pomegranates, and pine cones, all motives well known from Abbasid ornament. Like the eyes in the plaster niches (see below), the hands are doubtless of magic character, representing possibly the right hand of Fatima, the daughter of Muhammad.

Equally interesting are the polychrome plaster niches found at Nishapur, of which four are in the Museum. Although the niches vary in size and no two are alike in decoration, they are undoubtedly from a series of multiple squinches, or stalactites, placed under a dome and therefore constitute the earliest known examples of an element which became a highly characteristic feature of later Muhammadan architecture. The decoration consists of composite vase motives and scrolls which send out various palmettes and half-palmette devices (see fig. 12) known from early Abbasid ornament. Some of them suggest elementary features of the arabesque. Great interest in the art of painting existed in Eastern Iran at the courts of Samanid and Ghaznavid rulers. Mahmud of Ghazna (988-1030), a great patron of the arts, established an academy of painting under Abu Nasr. Many rooms of the palace of Ghazna were decorated with wall paintings. Actual Ghaznavid paintings of the early eleventh century were discovered by Schlumberger in a palace at Lashkari Bazar in southern Afghanistan. The audience hall was decorated with forty-four standing figures, dressed in long, belted, richly decorated silk kaftans, representing the Sultan's Turkish guard.

Fig. 12. Polychrome Plaster Niche from Nishapur, Iranian, VIII-IX Century

That another school of Islamic wall painting flourished in Egypt under the Fatimids was established a few years ago by Gaston Wiet, who found fragments of a group of tenth-century frescoes in the vicinity of Cairo. These are now in the Arab Museum at Cairo. The decoration consists of niches with geometrical interlacings, palmette scrolls, arabesques, birds, and seated figures holding cups.

The earliest miniatures extant are fragmentary paintings found in Egypt and dating from the ninth, tenth, and eleventh centuries. For the most part these are now in the Archduke Rainer collection of the National Library in Vienna. Further evidence that a school of book illustration existed in Egypt in the Fatimid period is furnished by Makrizi, the fifteenth-century historian, who tells us that the library of the Fatimid caliphs contained many richly illuminated manuscripts.

Although no actual book illustrations of Syrian or Mesopotamian schools earlier than the thirteenth century have survived, literary sources indicate that illustrated books were in existence in the ninth and tenth centuries. In painting and calligraphy the Muhammadans of this period often employed Nestorian and Jacobite Christians from Syria, who were famous as illustrators and illuminators.

The Mesopotamian school must also have been influenced by

24

the richly illuminated manuscripts of the Manichaeans, adherents of a religion compounded of Zoroastrianism and Christianity by Mani, who was also renowned as a great Iranian painter. Suppressed in Iran, Manichaeism was adopted as the official religion of the Uighurs, a Turkish tribe of Central Asia. Manichaeans immigrated to Mesopotamia in the eighth century, and by the ninth century had become so well established that they enjoyed the favors of the caliph Mamun (813-33). In the tenth century, however, they were persecuted by the Muhammadans, and contemporary historians record that in Baghdad in the year 923 were burnt fourteen sacks of Manichaean books from which trickles of silver and gold ran out. At Khocho, the Uighur capital, fragments of eighth- and ninth-century wall paintings and book illustrations have been brought to light by the excavations of Le Coq and Grünwedel. The book illustrations are painted in the true miniature style, based on Iranian traditions. Survivals of a Manichaean school of painting are apparent in thirteenth-century miniatures of the Mesopotamian school and fourteenth-century Mongol miniatures.

2. *The Mesopotamian School of Painting (XIII Century)*

Several important thirteenth-century illustrated manuscripts and single leaves have been preserved, which are generally attributed to the Abbasid, or Mesopotamian, school. The center of this school of painting must have been Baghdad, which retained its cultural importance in the Islamic world until the Mongol conquest in 1258. For the most part Arabic manuscripts of the thirteenth century are translations of the fables of the Hindu poet Bidpai and of Greek works on plants and animals, physics and medicine. One of the earliest manuscripts known to be of the Mesopotamian school is a book on hippiatry in the Egyptian Library, Cairo, which was written in Baghdad in A.H. 605 (1209). Related in style are a number of illustrations (scattered in various collections all over the world) from an Arabic version of Dioscorides's *Materia Medica*. These have been frequently attributed to 'Abd Allah ibn al Fazl, the copyist of a manuscript dated A.H. 619 (1222/3), but it is more probable that they come from a manuscript of A.H. 621 (1224) in the Topkapu Saray Library, Istanbul. In the illustrations representing such subjects as physicians preparing medicine (fig. 13) or surgeons performing operations, the painters followed a simple narrative style based on East Christian and Sasanian traditions. Landscape is usually indicated by one or two conventionalized trees. The garments and draperies are in most cases treated in a purely decorative manner, in which folds are rendered as ornament

Fig. 13. *Miniature Painting from a MS. of the* Materia Medica *Dated 1222/3, Mesopotamian*

or are covered with an all-over design of rosettes or palmettes. The decorative effect is enhanced by the use of vigorous colors—yellow, red, blue, green, purple—and gold.

A popular book illustrated by painters of the Mesopotamian school is Hariri's *Makamat*, or "Assemblies," which narrates the adventures of al Harith and Abu Zaid. Several copies are known. The earliest, now in the Bibliothèque Nationale in Paris, was written in the year A.H. 619 (1222/3). The illustrations of this manuscript show a strong Syrian influence, some of the figures undoubtedly being direct copies of saints in Christian manuscripts. The most important copy of Hariri's *Makamat*, also in the Bibliothèque Nationale, was written and illustrated in the year A.H. 634 (1237) by Yahya ibn Mahmud of Wasit, known as al Wasiti. The magnificent illustrations, with large figures suggestive of wall paintings, give a realistic account of daily life. We see thirteenth-century Arabs in the mosque, in the field, in the desert, in the tavern, and in the library and engaged in various festivities. Many of the faces, full of expression and highly individualized, are excellent character studies. However, in spite of the artist's realistic approach, the illustrations have a very decorative effect, particularly those with large compositions which follow certain schemes evolved by the Baghdad school of the thirteenth century. Here we find the beginnings of many of the conventions of Iranian paintings of the Mongol and Timurid periods: several rows of closely grouped figures, horses foreshortened in front or rear view, and schematic representation of costumes. The effect is enhanced by a rich palette, which surpasses that of the *Materia Medica* illustrations. Al Wasiti was doubtless a great painter, who, fusing East Christian and Iranian influences, created a new Muhammadan style. Similar in style and of about the same date as the 1237 copy are the illustrations of another manuscript of the *Makamat* in the Asiatic Museum in Leningrad.

A popular subject of illustration in the thirteenth century was the "Kalila and Dimna," a collection of Hindu fables, by Bidpai, translated into Arabic by Ibn Mukaffa. A fine copy of this manuscript in the Bibliothèque Nationale may be assigned to about 1230. The representations of animals are based on Sasanian traditions, but often show a close observation of nature. The various animal scenes form highly decorative ensembles with abstract trees and plants.

It is probable that local schools of painting existed in northern Mesopotamia at the courts of the Saljuk atabegs. In 1181 Nur ad Din Muhammad, the Ortuk sultan of Diar-Bakr (Amida), commissioned al Jazari to write a treatise on his inventions, which included water clocks and various automatic contrivances. The work, known as the *Automata*, was completed in 1206. An illustrated copy written in A.H. 652 (1254), possibly at Mosul or another center of northern Mesopotamia, is in the Topkapu Saray Library in Istanbul. That a North Mesopotamian school existed under Badr ad Din Lulu (1233-59) is evident from a manuscript in Istanbul with four illustrations representing court scenes. Two fourteenth-century copies of the *Automata* belonging to the Mamluk school are in existence. One of them, dated Ramadan, 715 (December, 1315), is now in an American collection and some of its miniatures are in the Freer Gallery in Washington, the Boston Museum, and the Metropolitan Museum. Of the other copy—written in A.H. 755 (1354) for an amir of the Mamluk sultan Salah ad Din Salih—only a few pages remain. These are in Istanbul, in the library of Santa Sophia. The rest of the miniatures are in various European and American museums and collections.

3. Saljuk Painting in Iran (XII-XIII Century)

No Iranian miniature paintings on paper that have been preserved can be authoritatively dated earlier than the Mongol period, although attempts have been made to attribute a number of miniatures to the late Saljuk period. The only known examples of Iranian painting surviving from pre-Mongol times are fragments of wall paintings (among them several with figure subjects) and ceramics with single figures, episodes from legends, and court scenes. Generally attributed to Rhages, or Rayy (see p. 186), and Kashan, these ceramics represent the Saljuk miniature style of the twelfth and thirteenth centuries. Although related to paintings of the school of Baghdad, they show many features which are distinctly Iranian. The figures are more conventionalized than in Mesopotamian miniatures and include types that are plainly Turkish. The subdued color scheme likewise differs from that of the Baghdad school. Pink, olive green, cobalt blue, violet, brown, black, and gold are employed with superb effect on a white or turquoise blue ground.

4. The Mongol School of Painting in Iran and Mesopotamia (Late XIII-XIV Century)

The Mongol invasion of Iran and Mesopotamia was successfully completed in 1258 with the fall of Baghdad, which the Il-khans adopted as their winter residence. Here and to their courts at Tabriz, Maragha, and Sultaniya came artists from all the conquered provinces, but chiefly from Mesopotamia and Iran.

The Il-khan rulers had a great admiration for Chinese culture and art. The Iranian artists were influenced not only by the realism of Chinese landscapes but also by Chinese methods of painting. The earliest known manuscript of the Mongol period is the Iranian copy of Ibn Bakhtishu's famous Manafi al Hayawan, or "Description of Animals," now in the Morgan Library in New York. According to an inscription, it was copied in Maragha at the order of the Il-khan ruler Ghazan Khan (1295-1304). On the last page there are two dates, A.H. 69? (129?) and A.H. 690 (1291). As Ghazan Khan did not begin to rule until 1295, the second date must be a later edition. The illegible numeral of the original date could be 7 or 9, which would date the manuscript 1297 or 1299. The ninety-four illustrations of the manuscript show several hands. A few of

the miniatures are painted in the traditional style of the Mesopotamian school, which continued for some time under the Mongols.
The majority of the miniatures, particularly those with landscapes,
are executed in a summary, impressionistic style with little color,

Fig. 14. Miniature Painting from a MS. of the Manafi al
Hayawan, Iranian, Mongol, Beginning of the XIV Century

imitating the Chinese monochrome ink paintings of the Sung and
Yüan dynasties.

The Metropolitan Museum owns a leaf from another manuscript
of the Manafi al Hayawan, showing two eagles in a landscape (fig.
14); others, with illustrations in a similar style, are in several private collections. These miniatures show clouds, plants, and peony
flowers of Chinese origin painted in subdued colors but in a bolder
manner than those in the Morgan Library copy. We may therefore
conclude that they are somewhat later than the Morgan Manafi al
Hayawan and so assign them to the beginning of the fourteenth
century.

The development of Mongol painting was greatly influenced by
the historian Rashid ad Din, who was also the vizier of the emperors

Ghazan and Uljaitu. His most important work was the *Jami at Tawarikh*, in which he recounted the history of the Mongols in relation to the rest of the world. The first volume he presented to Uljaitu on April 14, 1306. Realizing the importance of this history, Rashid ad Din ordered copies in Persian and Arabic made for his friends and fellow scholars. In the vicinity of Tabriz, he developed a new suburb called Rab-i-Rashidi, which had houses, shops, paper mills, caravanserais, hospitals, and a library of 60,000 volumes—including works on science and art in various languages. Artists and artisans of various nationalities were brought to Rab-i-Rashidi, and there, in the "streets of the savants," were quartered between 6,000 and 7,000 students and numerous professors. The arts of the book were especially favored by Rashid ad Din. Various works, but mainly his own, were copied and illustrated by competent calligraphers and painters. However, of the copies of the *Jami at Tawarikh* made in his lifetime only four fragments have survived. The most important is a manuscript in two parts, one dated A.H. 707 (1307), in the library of Edinburgh University, the other dated A.H. 714 (1314), in the Royal Asiatic Society in London. A characteristic feature of the illustrations is the elongated, almost ascetic type of male figure, which is unlike anything known in Iranian art. The linear style of these minatures, in which color plays a subordinate role, was borrowed from Chinese art.

Two other manuscripts of the *Jami at Tawarikh* copied in the time of Rashid ad Din are in the Topkapu Saray Library in Istanbul. One is dated A.H. 714 (1314), the other A.H. 717 (1317); but only a few of the illustrations belong to the beginning of the fourteenth century. The rest date from the end of the fourteenth century and the beginning of the fifteenth. The first part of the 1314 copy, with forty-nine miniatures, was completed in 1425 under Shah Rukh. A large painting in the Metropolitan Museum, representing Jonah and the Whale (fig. 15), is said to have belonged to one of the copies in Istanbul. Painted in vivid colors recalling those of the Timurid period, it may be assigned to the Tabriz school of the end of the fourteenth century. It shows an interesting mixture of Iranian and Chinese elements. The figures, the colors, and the stylization of the water follow Iranian traditions familiar from the art of the Sasanian period. The landscape and the carp, which is used instead of a whale, are Chinese.

Another manuscript of the *Jami at Tawarikh*, supposed to have
been written in 1318, was still complete in 1926; the leaves have
since been dispersed and the illustrations scattered in various collections. The illustrations are by several hands and for the most

Fig. 15. *Jonah and the Whale, from a MS. of the Jami at
Tawarikh, Iranian, End of the XIV Century*

part are not contemporary with the writing, some of them perhaps
being even modern. Two miniatures from this manuscript are now
in the Metropolitan Museum. One, containing the tailpiece of the
chapter on Ughuz, shows a Chinese figure in a pavilion surrounded
by plants; it is painted in the Mongol Chinese style and may be
assigned to the end of the fourteenth century. The second miniature, which may also be attributed to the end of the fourteenth
century, represents Mahmud of Ghazna before a captured city and
is rendered in brilliant colors which anticipate paintings of the
Timurid period.

A well-known undated copy of the *Jami at Tawarikh* in the Bibliothèque Nationale has been assigned for some time to the fourteenth
century. The figures and colors of the painting, however, indicate
that the illustrations cannot be earlier than the end of the fourteenth century and that they represent the Tabriz school of that
period, which worked for the Mongol Jalairids.

Although of foreign origin, the Il-khan dynasty stimulated the development of a national art in Iran, encouraging their court painters to illustrate copies of the *Shah-nama*, or "Book of Kings," an epic poem completed in A.H. 400 (1010) by Firdausi. This great

Fig. 16. *The Funeral of Isfandiyar, from a MS. of the* Shah-nama, *Iranian, Mongol, about 1320*

work, which served as an inspiration to Iranian artists for centuries, is based partly on history, partly on ancient legends of Iran. One of the earliest copies, generally known as the Demotte *Shah-nama*, was probably written at Tabriz about 1320 and illustrated by several painters. Often one gets the impression that two artists collaborated on a single miniature. The illustrations of this manuscript, about fifty-five in all, most of them large, must be considered among the great masterpieces of the world. They are now scattered among various museums and private collections in Europe and America.

Among the finest are those in the Museum of Fine Arts, Boston, the Freer Gallery, Washington, and the collections of Mrs. John D. Rockefeller, Jr., Edward W. Forbes, Henri Vever, Jean Pozzi, and Charles Gillet. In the Demotte *Shah-nama* Chinese and Iranian elements appear side by side. The landscapes, painted in subdued colors, are Chinese in style, while the figures, costumes, and architecture, rendered in rich colors, are Iranian. The monumental style of many of the miniatures, particularly the battle scenes, recalls the wall paintings of the Turkish Uighurs, known from excavations at Khocho in Chinese Turkestan. The painters have succeeded admirably in depicting the intensity and fury of battles similar to those fought by the Mongols themselves. In some

Fig. 17. *Zahhak and His Priests*, from a MS. of the Shah-nama, Iranian, Mongol, XIV Century

of the miniatures, such as the Funeral of Isfandiyar, in the Museum (fig. 16), the Sino-Mongol linear style is more apparent than in others. This scene, filled with gesticulating mourners, shows a dramatic realism seldom surpassed by later Iranian artists. The mourners are excellent character studies of contemporary Iranian and Mongol types.

Several other large copies of the *Shah-nama* show miniatures painted in a style which is quite different from that of the Tabriz school as exemplified in the Demotte *Shah-nama*. Two complete manuscripts and a number of separate leaves are preserved in libraries and private collections. One of the complete manuscripts, dated A.H. 731 (1330/1), is in the Topkapu Saray Library at Istanbul; the other, (1333), is in Leningrad. Leaves from a third manuscript are scattered in various collections. One of them, in the collection of Henri Vever of Paris, contains an inscription which indicates that the manuscript was copied in A.H. 741 (1340/1) for the library of Kauram ad Din Hasan, Vizier of Fars, most probably in the capital, Shiraz. Five other leaves from the manuscript, two a gift of Horace

33

Fig. 18. Miniature Painting from a MS. of the Munis al Ahrar
Dated 1341, Iranian, Mongol

Havemeyer, are in the Museum. The style of painting of all these
miniatures, which may be attributed to the Shiraz school, is less
elaborate than that of the contemporary Tabriz school. They are
painted in black outline on red or ocher backgrounds with very
little additional color, the palette being limited to blue, red, olive
green, lilac, ocher, and gold. Iranian tradition predominates; Chi-

34

nese influence, so strong in other miniatures of the period, here plays a secondary role.

Another group of manuscripts of the early Mongol period, mostly Shah-namas, are of small size, their illustrations representing the true miniature style of Iran. The best known is a manuscript which is no longer intact, although the majority of the illustrations are in the Chester Beatty collection in London. The Metropolitan Museum possesses one of these illustrations as well as six from a similar manuscript (see fig. 17). These miniature paintings are based on the Iranian style developed under the Saljuks and known to us from Rayy polychrome pottery (see p. 186). The figures are Mongol, and Chinese influence, shown mostly in the landscapes, is less conspicuous than in the Demotte Shah-nama. The delicate color scheme, in which a vivid turquoise is conspicuous, contrasts effectively with the gold background. A number of miniatures from another Shah-nama, similar in style but with emerald green frequently replacing turquoise blue, are in the Freer Gallery in Washington.

Related to the above manuscripts is a small Shah-nama formerly in the Schulz collection and now in a private collection in New York. The miniatures, three of which are on loan in the Metropolitan Museum, are painted in more vivid colors than those just described. Most of the backgrounds are red, a feature which originated in early Iranian painting. Similar in style are the miniatures of a manuscript of the Munis al Ahrar, an anthology of Iranian poetry dated Ramadan, 741 (February, 1341), from which there is a leaf in the Museum (fig. 18). Both sides are decorated with bands of figures and animals having astronomical significance. The figures holding crescents personify the moon, and the various animals accompanying them represent the signs of the zodiac. The painting is executed in tints of blue, green, purple, and yellow, with touches of gold, on a red background.

5. The Timurid School of Painting in Iran (XV Century)

Timur, the successor of the Mongol Il-khans, conquered Tabriz in 1386 and Baghdad in 1401. We know from literary sources that Timur took native artists with him from Baghdad to his new residence in Samarkand, but no existing manuscript can be attributed to the Samarkand school of this period. There are, however, several contemporary manuscripts which were written in other centers, such as Shiraz and Baghdad. To the former school belong three manuscripts of the Shah-nama: one, dated A.H. 772 (1370/1), in the Topkapu Saray Library, Istanbul; a second, dated A.H. 796 (1393/4), in the Royal Egyptian Library, Cairo; and a third, dated A.H. 800 (1397/8), of which part is in the British Museum, part in the Chester Beatty collection in London. As the miniatures of these manuscripts show many features of the Timurid style later developed at Herat, Shiraz is regarded by some as the cradle of the Timurid school. This new style is also apparent in another important manuscript of Timur's time, a book of poems by Khwaju Kirmani (1281-1350) in the British Museum, copied in A.H. 799 (1396) in Baghdad. One of the miniatures is signed by the Iranian painter Junaid Nakkash as Sultani, who was in the service of Sultan Ahmad (1382-1410) of the Mongol Jalairids of Baghdad.

Herat, in Khurasan, was chosen for residence by Shah Rukh (1404-47), Timur's favorite son and successor. Shah Rukh employed many artists in the production of books for his famous library—including the painter Khalil, who was regarded as one of the "four marvels of the age" and second only to Mani. At the library and academy of book arts founded by Shah Rukh's son, Baisunkur Mirza (died 1433), there was a staff of forty painters, illuminators, calligraphers, and binders, with the calligrapher Ja'far Baisunkuri at the head. Among the painters were Amir Shahi of Sabzavar and Ghiyath ad Din, the latter a member of the embassy sent by Shah Rukh to China. Although the court painters continued to illustrate the Shah-nama, they gave more attention to romantic and mystic poems by the famous Iranian poets Nizami and Sa'di. Nizami (1140-1203) wrote five poems known as the Khamsa, or "Quintet," which consists of the Makhzan al Asrar, or "Treasury of Mysteries"; "Khusrau and Shirin"; "Laila and Majnun"; the Haft Paikar, or "Seven Portraits"; and the Iskandar-nama, or "Book of Alexander." Sa'di (1182-1292) wrote two popular poems, the Bustan, or "Fruit Garden," and the Gulistan, or "Rose Garden." In illustrating these poems the Herat school developed a style expressive of their romantic and lyrical content. As a rule the figures are delicately rendered on a small scale and placed in a decorative, truly Iranian landscape with a high horizon and spongy mountains. The color effects are vivid but harmonious, with many new tints added to those of the earlier Mongol period. The school of Herat must be credited with the creation of a national Iranian style of painting which gradually assimilated foreign influences.

A branch of the Timurid school flourished in Shiraz, the resi-

Fig. 19. *Rustam Capturing Rakhsh, from a MS. of the* Shah-nama, *Iranian, Timurid, XV Century*

dence of Shah Rukh's son Ibrahim Sultan, for whom were written the magnificently illustrated Iranian "Anthology" of 1410 in the Gulbenkian collection and the "Compendium" in the British Museum. To the Shiraz school also belong an "Anthology" of 1420 in Berlin and a *Shah-nama* in the Bodleian Library. As Kühnel points out, miniature paintings of the Shiraz school show a cooler and lighter color scheme than those of the Herat school.

A number of fine manuscripts of the Herat school belong to the period of Shah Rukh. A splendid copy of Nizami's *Khamsa*, in the collection of Louis Cartier in Paris, bears the seal of Shah Rukh; while a *Gulistan* in the Chester Beatty collection in London, copied in A.H. 830 (1426) by Ja'far Baisunkuri, bears the mark of the library established by Baisunkur Mirza. In the Gulistan Museum, Teheran, there is a *Shah-nama* copied by Ja'far Baisunkuri in A.H. 833 (1429/30). This masterpiece of Timurid book illustration was unknown in the West until 1931, when it was shown for the first

Fig. 20. Khusrau and Shirin, from a MS. of the Khamsa *by Nizami Dated 1447/8, Iranian, Timurid*

time in the London exhibition of Iranian art. Its twenty-two miniatures represent the height of the Herat school of painting. They are characterized by brilliant colors, a certain formality, and a richness of detail which recall contemporary illuminations. Also of great beauty are the miniatures of a manuscript of "Kalila and Dimna" in the Gulistan Museum, likewise shown for the first time in the London exhibition of 1931.

Twelve important miniatures in the Museum's collection exemplify another variation of the Timurid style. They come from a *Shah-nama* and may be assigned to the same school and period as a manuscript of the *Miraj-nama*, or "Book of the Prophets," written in Herat in A.H. 840 (1436) and now in the Bibliothèque Nationale. Figure 19 shows the popular episode from the *Shah-nama*, of Rustam capturing the horse Rakhsh. The richly colored costumes of Rustam and his follower greatly enhance the composition, while the grandiose landscape, with Chinese trees and flying geese, is fully as important as the figures themselves. Chinese influence is

Fig. 21. *Shirin Carried by Farhad, from a MS. of the* Khamsa *by Nizami Dated 1449/50, Iranian, Timurid*

also evident in another miniature, which illustrates Kai Kaus's attempt to fly to heaven by fastening young eagles to his throne; particularly interesting are the large Chinese clouds, which are more stylized than those in miniatures of the Mongol period.

The developed Timurid style is well exemplified in the Metropolitan Museum by a miniature from a manuscript dated A.H. 851 (1447/8), representing Khusrau watching the beautiful Shirin as she bathes in a pool (fig. 20). The subtle technique, the intimate treatment of the scene, and the small figures are typical of the Herat school of the first half and middle of the fifteenth century.

Different in style are the miniatures of Nizami's *Khamsa* written in A.H. 853 (1449/50). A typical painting is shown in figure 21

39

Fig. 22. Miniature Painting from a MS. of the Diwan by
Jami, Iranian, Timurid, XV Century

which illustrates the episode of Shirin and her horse carried on the shoulders of her lover, the sculptor Farhad. The style of the miniatures and the color scheme suggest the Shiraz school of Timurid painting. The miniatures are more freely drawn and show less detail in the rendering of landscapes and figures than those of the Herat school.

A contemporary work which inspired artists of the Timurid period was the *Diwan*, a collection of mystic and lyric poems by the celebrated Jami (1414-92). In the Metropolitan Museum there is a manuscript copied between 1463 and 1479, in the poet's own lifetime, by the well-known calligrapher 'Abd al Karim of Khwarizm. As this artist worked at the court of Jahan Shah of the "Black Sheep" Turkomans in Tabriz, it is very probable that our *Diwan* was copied there. It is closely related in style to the *Diwan* of 1463 in the British Museum, copied by 'Abd ar Rahim, 'Abd al Karim's brother. 'Abd al Karim and 'Abd ar Rahim were the sons of the famous calligrapher 'Abd ar Rahman, who transformed the style of Nasta'lik writing. The sixteen miniatures illustrating our manuscript are painted in bright, enamel-like colors. The brilliant colors, the conventionalized landscapes, and the special type of turban worn by many of the figures are characteristic of the Timurid style of painting in western Iran. The miniature reproduced in figure 22 is a fine example of the hunting scenes which became so popular in the miniatures of the Safavid school during the sixteenth century.

To the school of Samarkand and the first half of the fifteenth century may be attributed a copy of a treatise on astronomy, now in the Bibliothèque Nationale. This was written for the library of Ulugh Beg, son of Shah Rukh and governor of Transoxiana from 1409 to 1446, who established a famous observatory at Samarkand. The Museum possesses an astronomical manuscript, illustrated with fifty drawings of the constellations, and inasmuch as the style of the drawing and details of the costumes indicate the Timurid period, it is quite probable that it was also written in Samarkand in the time of Ulugh Beg.

6. Bihzad and His School

A new and brilliant period of Iranian painting was inaugurated in Herat under the patronage of Sultan Husain Mirza (1468-1506) and his vizier, Mir 'Ali Shir Nawai, a poet, musician, and painter. The most famous Iranian painter of this time was Kamal ad Din Bihzad of Herat, called the "marvel of the age," who was born about 1440. Of this master, the Iranian historian Khwandamir (1475-1535 or 1537) wrote: "He sets before us marvelous forms and rarities of his art; his draughtsmanship, which is like the brush of Mani, has caused the memorials of all the painters of the world to be obliterated, and his fingers endowed with miraculous qualities have wiped out the pictures of all the artists among the sons of Adam. A hair of his brush, through its mastery, has given life to the lifeless form."

After the defeat of the Timurids by the Shaibanids in 1507, Bihzad remained in Herat working for the Uzbeg sultan Shaibani Khan. About 1510, when Shah Isma'il (1502-24) of the Safavid dynasty conquered Herat, Bihzad moved to Tabriz, thus establishing in western Iran a school which influenced the further development of Iranian painting. The historian 'Ali tells us that in 1514, on the occasion of a battle against the Turks, Shah Isma'il was so anxious for the safety of his court artists that he hid Bihzad and the calligrapher Shah Mahmud an Nishapuri in a cave. After the battle he thanked God that their lives had been saved. In 1522 Shah Isma'il appointed Bihzad director of the Royal Library, in connection with which there was a studio of the arts of the book.

There are extant only a few authentic works bearing Bihzad's signature or showing the characteristics of his style. Some of the works that bear his name are copies (see p. 58), some are contemporary works to which "signatures" were added later. Bihzad's style is best exemplified by the illustrations of two important manuscripts—the British Museum's Khamsa of A. H. 846 (1442), with three miniatures which were painted later than the manuscript, in the year A.H. 898 (1493), and a Bustan in the Royal Egyptian Library, Cairo, dated A.H. 893 (1488). In these paintings the artist reveals himself as a keen observer of nature. He is a fine colorist, using many new shades and creating entirely new color combinations; the illustrations of the Khamsa show a cool color scheme, with blue, gray, and green predominating. The miniatures of the Cairo Bustan represent Bihzad's style at its height. They are masterpieces of composition, full of action and realism, and the figures have decided individuality of expression and gestures.

On the evidence of an annotation by the Emperor Jahangir, six double-page miniatures of a *Zafar-nama*, a history of Timur, in the collection of Robert Garrett in Baltimore, are attributed to Bihzad. The manuscript was copied by the calligrapher Shir 'Ali in A.H. 872 (1467) for Sultan Husain Mirza, and in all probability the miniatures were inserted later. Although the color scheme is somewhat brighter than is usual in paintings by Bihzad, the style is his, and many of the figures and facial types can be duplicated in miniatures by him and his pupil Kasim 'Ali.

There is on exhibition in the Museum a fine painting, from a manuscript of Jami's *Diwan* (fig. 23), representing dancing dervishes, which may be attributed to Bihzad or his school. It is a painting worthy of Bihzad's brush, bearing all the characteristics known from the authentic work of this master. The circular composition of the dancing dervishes recalls the battle scene in a *Nizami* in the British Museum painted in 1493. Other features of Bihzad's style are the delicacy of execution, the lively action, the individualization of the faces and the suppression of detail seen in later work, the variety of the flesh tints, and an unusual combination of colors—pink, vermilion, dark red, brick red, and various shades of yellow, green, and blue, placed against the dark green of the lawn.

Many of the book illustrations painted in the style of Bihzad are doubtless the work of his pupils, several of whom are known. His closest collaborator and pupil was Kasim 'Ali, celebrated as a painter of faces, whose work is known to us from several manuscripts containing miniature paintings bearing his signature. Seven miniatures in another *Khamsa*, dated A.H. 899 (1494/5), in the British Museum, are signed by Kasim 'Ali, while several others may be attributed to Bihzad himself or to some other pupil. Other miniature paintings attributed to Kasim 'Ali are found in two manuscript works by Mir 'Ali Shir Nawai, in the Bodleian Library, dated A.H. 890 (1485). Two of the miniatures are signed by this artist, who reveals himself just as fine a colorist as Bihzad, although his compositions are less pleasing than those of his master. The Museum possesses a miniature from a manuscript of a work of Mir 'Ali Shir Nawai which shows many characteristics of Kasim 'Ali's style, like the golden meadow and the large plane tree with realistic rendering of the autumn leaves. Such trees were introduced by the

43

school of Bihzad and were often copied by Safavid painters of the sixteenth century. The effective color scheme, in which blue, grays, and greens predominate, appears also in several paintings by Bihzad and Kasim 'Ali.

7. The Safavid School of Painting (XVI Century)

At the beginning of the sixteenth century, under the new Safavid dynasty, the center of Iranian painting shifted from Khurasan to Tabriz in western Iran, although Herat, a seat of the governors, continued as an art center for some time. Several early sixteenth-century manuscripts written in Herat and other cities of Khurasan were most probably illustrated there. Bihzad's influence continued to be the dominating factor both in Herat and in Tabriz. In Herat Bihzad's pupils followed the traditions of their great master, who had been in Tabriz since 1510 and who may be regarded as the founder of the Safavid school of painting. Several miniatures are attributed to Bihzad's Tabriz period, but the most authentic seems to be a roundel with two figures in a manuscript of specimens of calligraphy of the year 1524, now in a private collection in New York.

Several manuscripts from the period of Shah Isma'il and single miniature paintings may be attributed to the Herat school. Three miniatures in the Metropolitan Museum, two in the Louvre, and two others in the Bibliothèque Nationale in Paris come from a manuscript of Amir Khusrau Dihlavi's *Khamsa*, copied at Balkh in A.H. 909 (1503/4). The miniatures, painted probably in Herat after the conquest of Khurasan by the Safavids in 1510, show many features of Bihzad's style and were no doubt the work of one of his pupils. Two miniatures and the title page of a manuscript of 'Arifi's *Guy u Chawgan*, or "The Ball and Polo Stick," written at Herat in A.H. 929 (1522/3) by the celebrated calligrapher 'Ali al Husaini and now in the collection of Louis Cartier, Paris, represent the early Safavid style of the Herat school. In all these miniatures some of the figures wear the turban with a pointed cap (kula) which originated with the Safavids and is a characteristic feature of many Safavid paintings. An interesting early sixteenth-century manuscript is a *Diwan* by Hafiz in the Cartier collection; it contains five miniatures of great importance, one signed by Shaikh-zada and two by Sultan Muhammad. Shaikh-zada of Khurasan was a pupil of Bihzad and as such continued many conventions and characteristics

44

Fig. 23. Dancing Dervishes, Style of Bihzad, from a MS. of the
Diwan by Hafiz, Iranian, End of the XV Century

of the style developed by the master. The paintings of Sultan Muhammad, which are discussed below, show a style totally different from that of Shaikh-zada.

Related to the miniatures of the Cartier Hafiz are the illustrations in a magnificent manuscript of Nizami's *Khamsa* in the Metropolitan Museum, copied in A.H. 931 (1524/5) by Sultan Muhammad Nur, poet and calligrapher, the son and pupil of Sultan 'Ali al Mashhadi. This manuscript, which was in the possession of the shahs of Iran until 1908, contains fifteen superb miniatures. One, representing the marriage of Khusrau and Shirin, bears the date Rajab, 931 (April, 1525). The miniature painting representing Khusrau surrounded by his courtiers (fig. 24) is a typical example of the early Safavid style which was evolved in Herat. The types of figures closely resemble those in miniatures by Shaikh-zada in the manuscript of the Cartier Hafiz, and as was suggested recently by Kühnel, the paintings may be attributed to this master, representing a further development of his style. There is more ornamental detail apparent in architecture and costumes. The design is enhanced by the use of new color combinations as seen in the miniature depicting Laila and Majnun in school (pl. 1). One miniature (fig. 25) in this manuscript, different from the rest, is by another artist of the Tabriz school. It shows Alexander received by the *khagan*. The figures and the way in which the cloth of the turban is tightly twisted around the cap are familiar to us from paintings of court artists working for Shah Tahmasp. The light color scheme, the stippled grass, and the types of the faces recall the early work of Sultan Muhammad.

There is a close resemblance between the miniatures in the Metropolitan Museum Nizami of 1525 and those of a *Diwan* of Mir 'Ali Shir Nawai in the Bibliothèque Nationale, Paris, copied in Herat in A.H. 933 (1526/7). The majority of the miniatures in the *Diwan* are painted in the same style as those of Nizami and can be also attributed to Shaikh-zada. As in the Nizami, one of the miniatures in the *Diwan* of 1526 is most probably by Sultan Muhammad. The majority of the illustrations of both manuscripts, as well as those of the Cartier *Diwan*, were made most likely in Herat and then brought partly unfinished to Tabriz for the library of Shah Tahmasp, where they were completed by Sultan Muhammad. A pupil of Mirak, he was the chief painter at the court and the director of the

Fig. 24. Khusrau and His Courtiers, from a MS. of the Khamsa *by Nizami Dated 1524/5, Iranian, Safavid*

school of painting. Both were intimates of Shah Tahmasp, who himself took painting lessons from Sultan Muhammad. Manuscripts written and illustrated in Tabriz for Shah Tahmasp are among the most sumptuous ever produced. The developed style of his court artists is preserved in a copy of Nizami's *Khamsa* in the

Fig. 25. Alexander Received by the Khagan, by Sultan Muhammad, from a MS. of the Khamsa by Nizami Dated 1524/5, Iranian, Safavid

British Museum written for Shah Tahmasp between 1539 and 1543. By Sultan Muhammad are probably some of the miniatures in the richly illustrated *Shah-nama* of 1537 in the collection of Baron Maurice de Rothschild in Paris. It contains two miniatures signed by Sultan Muhammad, and others by Mirak, Muzaffar 'Ali, Mir Sayyid 'Ali, and Mirza 'Ali. All these miniatures have many common features, developed probably by Mirak and Sultan Muhammad under the supervision of Bihzad, who was a teacher of Mirak. The style is characterized by a great elegance of design, decorative richness, and refinement of technique. The figures are usually highly sophisticated and reflect the splendor of Shah Tahmasp's court.

In addition to illustrations for manuscripts, Sultan Muhammad and several other artists are credited with separate miniatures, mostly portraits of elegant, sophisticated youths and drawings of court ladies and princes, some of them perhaps representing Shah Tahmasp himself, such as the painting in the Boston Museum signed by Shah Muhammad. Another portrait painter was Mir Nakkash, who collaborated with Sultan Muhammad in Tabriz. To Sultan Muhammad may be attributed Cartier's equestrian portrait of a prince accompanied by a servant, which is one of the finest known single paintings of the Safavid era.

The style of Shah Tahmasp's court painters is exemplified by several fine miniatures in the Metropolitan Museum. One is a garden scene, probably from a Nizami of the first half of the sixteenth century. Two others are from a *Shah-nama* and illustrate episodes in the life of Zal, father of Rustam. Both miniatures may be assigned to the second half of the sixteenth century.

A great but little-known painter of the second half of the sixteenth century was Ustad Muhammadi, probably a son and pupil of Sultan Muhammad. There are several tinted drawings and paintings with signatures of this master, some of which seem to be authentic. The best-known is a tinted landscape drawing in the Louvre bearing his signature and dated A.H. 986 (1578). Other signed works of importance are in the Bibliothèque Nationale in Paris, the Hofer collection in Cambridge, and the Boston Museum of Fine Arts. The Metropolitan Museum possesses two tinted drawings and a painting in the style of Ustad Muhammadi. The latter (fig. 26), probably from an album, represents a hunting party and is very similar to a miniature in the Boston Museum painted about 1583. These miniatures and the drawings show the characteristic features of Ustad Muhammadi's style—elongated figures with small, round faces, realism in landscapes, and scenes of everyday life in the

*Fig. 26. Miniature Painting, Style of Ustad Muhammadi, Iranian,
Second Half of the XVI Century*

country. Several drawings in the George D. Pratt collection are also
in his style.

In the second half of the sixteenth century the artists of Tabriz,
Shiraz, and other cities of western and southern Iran continued in
the tradition of Shah Tahmasp's court, but their works reveal a

decline in technique and a lack of originality. The compositions are overcrowded, and the painting is careless. The Museum possesses several manuscripts and single miniatures illustrative of this period. A manuscript of Jami's "Yusuf and Zulaikha," copied by Muhammad Kiwam of Shiraz, contains four miniatures painted probably about 1580 by an artist of Shiraz.

8. *The School of Bukhara (XVI Century)*

A contemporary school of painting flourished at Bukhara, which since 1500 had been under the rule of the Shaibanids, an Uzbeg dynasty. About 1535 many artists and calligraphers of the Herat school moved or were exiled to Bukhara and there continued the traditions of the Timurid school, particularly those of Bihzad. Among the artists who had come to Bukhara before that time was the painter Mahmud Muzahib (Mahmud the Illuminator), a pupil of the famous calligrapher Mir 'Ali. Several signed works by Mahmud are known, some of which are assigned to his Herat period—for example, the love scenes in an album in the shrine at Mashhad. This album also contains paintings by his pupil 'Abd Allah which are entirely in the style of the Bukhara school. Mahmud's Bukhara style appears in a double miniature, dated A.H. 953 (1546), in the Bibliothèque Nationale manuscript of Nizami's *Makhzan al Asrar*, or "Treasury of Mysteries," which was copied in Bukhara by Mir 'Ali in A.H. 944 (1537/8).

The Metropolitan Museum possesses three manuscripts and several miniatures of the school of Bukhara. One is a manuscript of Jami's "Yusuf and Zulaikha," copied by Mir 'Ali al Husaini in the year A.H. 930 (1523/4); the accompanying miniatures seem to be of somewhat later date, probably around 1540. The influence of the school of Bihzad is quite evident in the landscape and in the figures, which wear characteristic Bukhara turbans. The same types may be seen in the miniatures of the second manuscript, a copy of Sa'di's *Bustan*. The scene in figure 27 represents a sultan of Syria interviewing two dervishes in a garden. It is painted in the vivid, enamel-like colors, including a brilliant vermilion red, which are characteristic of the sixteenth-century Bukhara school. The third is a copy of Muhyi Lari's *Futuh al Haramain*, or "Description of Holy Cities," with sixteen illustrations.

Fig. 27. The Sultan of Syria Conversing with Dervishes, from a
MS. of the Bustan by Sa'di, Iranian, Bukhara School, XVI Century

9. Safavid Painting of the Shah 'Abbas Period and Later (Late XVI-XVIII Century)

Toward the end of the sixteenth century there was a marked decline in the production of fine books. Manuscripts were still illustrated, especially Firdausi's Shah-nama, but genre scenes and separate portraits of dervishes and princes, often in the style of Ustad Muhammadi, were more popular. Elegantly dressed young nobles were the favored subjects in both western and eastern Iran. Large turbans with feathers and flowers became fashionable at the time of Shah 'Abbas, who was a great patron of the arts.

Shah 'Abbas made Isfahan his capital, endowing it with many imposing palaces and mosques and founding there an academy of painting, where Iranian artists copied the works of earlier masters. The Chihil Sutun, or "Hall of Forty Pillars," and the garden pavilion 'Ala Kapi, or "Sublime Portal," were decorated with wall paintings in the style of Riza-i-'Abbasi, into which the figures of Dutchmen and other Europeans were introduced.

Fig. 28. Drawing by Riza-i-'Abbasi, Iranian, Beginning of the XVII Century

In the Museum are two Shah-namas dating from Shah 'Abbas's period and illustrated with many miniatures. One, dated A.H. 996 (1587/8), has forty full-page miniatures of good quality. The other, dated A.H. 1014-16 (1605-08), contains eighty-five large miniatures revealing many of the features found in works by Riza-i-'Abbasi, the outstanding painter and calligrapher at the courts of Shah

53

'Abbas (1587-1628) and Sufi (1629/42). Riza-i-'Abbasi left a considerable number of signed paintings and drawings dating from 1598 to 1643. His genre scenes and portraits are characterized by close observation of life. His drawings are rendered in a calligraphic

Fig. 29. Tinted Drawings by Riza-i-'Abbasi, Iranian, Safavid, Beginning of the XVII Century

manner, consisting of sure, undulating curves combined with short strokes. This technique was perhaps originated by Aka Riza, who was active in the latter part of Shah Tahmasp's reign as well as in that of Shah 'Abbas and whose work we know through signed drawings in the Boston Museum, the Louvre, and the Bibliothèque Nationale. The Metropolitan Museum also possesses several drawings by Riza-i-'Abbasi and his followers. One, from a sketchbook, represents a man sewing (fig. 28). Two others, in which touches of color are introduced, show a youth holding a wine bottle and a cup, and an old man leaning on a staff (fig. 29); both figures are signed: "Drawn by the humble Riza 'Abbasi."

During the second half of the seventeenth century and through-out the eighteenth, Iranian painting felt the dominating influence of Riza-i-'Abbasi. His style and manner of drawing were imitated by many painters, including Muin, Yusuf, and Muhammad Kasim, but all lacked the master's talent. In the Museum's collection there is a drawing by Muhammad Kasim dated A.H. 114, evidently a con-traction for A.H. 1114 (1702/3). It represents the chastisement of a pupil.

In the eighteenth century Iranian painting began to sink to a low level, both in wall decoration and in miniature painting, owing partly to European influence and partly to the absence of any real creative power in the nation.

10. Turkish Miniature Painting

The history of miniature painting in Turkey is very little known, since the rich libraries of Istanbul are for the most part still unex-plored by scholars. From literary sources, however, we know that Iranian and European artists were employed by Turkish sultans. Among the famous European painters summoned to Constanti-nople by Sultan Mehmed II (1451-81) in 1480 was Gentile Bel-lini, who was commissioned to paint the portrait of the sultan which today hangs in the National Gallery in London. Among the Iranian artists working in Constantinople were Shah Kuli, foremost painter at the court of Sulaiman the Magnificent (1520-66), and Wali Jan of Tabriz, who arrived in 1587 and also became a court painter. Shah Kuli is known as a painter of the large curving leaves called saz. Wali Jan, a pupil of Siyawush, was praised by the his-torian 'Ali for his "magic brush" and the delicacy of his work. Both artists favored as subject matter the houris, winged maidens of the Muhammadan paradise. Examples of their work are preserved in European and American collections, particularly the Bibliothèque Nationale in Paris and the Freer Gallery in Washington. Iranian artists employed at the Turkish court illustrated some of the manu-scripts of the "History of Ottoman Sultans" and of the Sulaiman-nama, a collection of anecdotes written by Firdausi of Brusa for Sultan Bayazid II (1481-1512).

A fine Turkish painting (from a manuscript of a Diwan by Baki) in the Metropolitan Museum is illustrated in figure 30. The style is Iranian, but the costumes and the huge turbans and other headgear

Fig. 30. Miniature Painting, Turkish, XVI Century

are Turkish, and some of the colors, particularly a bright yellow-green, are peculiar to Turkey. Essentially Turkish in style are paintings in the Chester Beatty collection in London, which come from a large manuscript of the *Sulaiman-nama* dated A.H. 987 (1579).

The names of several famous Turkish painters from the fifteenth to the eighteenth century are known: Ossman, who illustrated the *Hunernama*, Nigari (1494-1572), and Levni (1703-1730).

11. Indian Painting: The Mughal School

The conquest of Hindustan by Babur, a descendant of Timur, brought the Muhammadan civilization to India. Although an Indo-Iranian style was evolved at the Mughal court, the native school carrying on the indigenous tradition ·continued to flourish, especially in Rajputana, in northern India.

A. PERIODS OF BABUR (1526-30), HUMAYUN (1530-56), AND AKBAR (1556-1605)

Little is known of the paintings produced at the court of Babur, although we learn from literary sources that this emperor was a patron of the fine arts as well as a learned philosopher, a wide traveler, a hunter, and a lover of nature. Very few miniature paintings may be attributed to his time. Kühnel assigns to this period a painting of a sea fight in an album of paintings once owned by the Emperor Jahangir and now in the State Library, Berlin. This painting shows clearly the influence of Bihzad and the school of Bukhara.

Babur's successor was Humayun, who was forced into exile in 1540 by the Afghan prince Shir Shah and did not return to power until 1555. Humayan spent his years of exile in Iran, where he was entertained by Shah Tahmasp. At the court of the Iranian shah, Humayun became acquainted with the work of some of the greatest Iranian painters. In Tabriz he met Khwaja 'Abd as Samad of Shiraz and Mir Sayyid 'Ali. In 1549 these two masters were invited to Humayun's court at Kabul to illustrate the Iranian romance *Amir Hamza*, a fantastic narrative of adventure. Thus they became the actual founders of the Mughal school of painting. The surviving illustrations of the *Amir Hamza*, which originally numbered fourteen hundred large paintings on cloth, are now scattered in several collections, the greatest number being in the Industrial Museum in Vienna and the Victoria and Albert Museum in London. In the United States there are about fifteen paintings from this manuscript, of which five are in the Metropolitan Museum. The majority of these illustrations were painted in the time of

Akbar, Humayun's successor, by Mir Sayyid 'Ali and 'Abd as Samad with the help of Hindu painters.

Like his father, Humayun, Akbar was a great lover and patron of the arts, especially painting. In 1569 he built a new city, Fathpur-Sikri, for his residence. His palaces there and elsewhere were sumptuously decorated with mural paintings, executed by Iranian and Indian artists. In order to develop a native school of painting, Akbar established a state academy, where about a hundred artists, mostly Hindus, were employed, working under the guidance of Iranian painters. According to the Ain-i-Akbari, or "Institutions of Akbar," written by the historian Abu'l Fazl, these artists painted illustrations for manuscripts of Iranian prose and poetry. For the instruction of native artists there were not only Iranians working at the court, but also magnificent manuscripts illustrated by Bihzad, Mirak, and Sultan Muhammad available in the imperial library. Akbar's court painters copied some of the finest of these works, and of these there is an example in the Museum's collection. It is a copy of Nizami's Haft Paikar, or "Seven Portraits," made for the Emperor Akbar and bearing the date A.H. 988 (1580/1). It contains five miniatures signed with Bihzad's name. However, these signatures cannot be regarded as authentic, as the style of the miniatures is not that of Bihzad but is distinctly early Timurid. The range of the colors and certain details of the drawing indicate that they were copied in the time of Akbar from a fifteenth-century manuscript.

The illustrations of the Amir Hamza were probably executed between 1556 and 1575 and give us an excellent idea of Mughal architecture and customs. The realistic landscapes and some of the types of men and women are Indian, but, as one would expect in paintings of this time, the colors, drawing, and ornament are strongly Iranian in character. A typical example, representing a battle scene, is reproduced in figure 31.

Toward the end of the sixteenth century, Mughal painting became more distinctly national in style as a result of the influence of Hindu traditions introduced by Indian artists from Kashmir, Gujarat, and the Punjab. Among the manuscripts illustrated by the court artists were a number of historical works on the lives of Timur, Babur, and Akbar. A fine though incomplete copy of the Akbarnama, in the collection of Chester Beatty in London, contains miniatures by Dharam Das, Sanwlah, Shankar, Lal, Sur Das, Nar Singh,

Fig. 31. Illustration from a MS. of the Amir Hamza, Mughal, *about*
1556-1575

Farrukh Beg, Mukund, and Govardhan. The style of some of these
famous artists can also be studied in our large and representative
collection of Mughal miniatures. A typical painting of Akbar's
period is a miniature from a manuscript of a *Timur-nama*, representing Timur receiving two noble Turkish prisoners (fig. 32). This
painting, which has been attributed to Dharam Das, shows all the
qualities of the new Mughal style—a mixture of Iranian, Hindu, and
European elements. Iranian tradition is still evident, but the fig-

59

Fig. 32. *Timur Receiving Turkish Prisoners, Attributed to Dharam Das, from a MS. of the Timur-nama, Mughal, Period of Akbar (1556-1605)*

ures and landscapes are rendered in a way unknown in Iranian art
Under the influence of European art, the Mughal painter intro

Fig. 33. Muslim Pilgrim Meets a Braham, from a MS. of
the Khamsa by Amir Khusrau Dihlavi, Mughal, about 1595

duced atmospheric landscapes and perspective, together with modeling in faces and costumes which produced the effect of roundness.
Akbar greatly admired European paintings, several of which he
received from Jesuit missionaries. In March, 1580, a Jesuit mission
arrived in Fathpur-Sikri and presented Akbar with a copy of Plan-

tin's Bible, illustrated by Flemish artists, and two beautiful paintings representing Christ and the Virgin Mary.

Basawan, Lal, and Daswanth ranked foremost among the Hindu painters at Akbar's court. Basawan was a pupil of 'Abd as Samad, but his style was entirely free from all Iranian conventions. Abu'l Fazl wrote of him: "In backgrounding, drawing of features, distribution of colours, portrait painting, and several other branches, [Basawan] is most excellent, so much so, that many critics prefer him to Daswanth." The Metropolitan Museum has a charming miniature by Basawan (fig. 33), with pastel colors and soft outlines. The aerial perspective and the roundness of the figures undoubtedly reflect European influence.

The Museum possesses several other fine miniature paintings of the period of Akbar, including signed works by Farrukh Beg, Nar Singh, Manohar, and Kham Karan. Especially noteworthy are three miniatures from a manuscript of the *Razm-nama*, the Iranian version of the Hindu epic *Mahabharata*. One of the finest of these represents Krishna lifting Mount Govardhan.

B. PERIOD OF JAHANGIR (1605-28)

Jahangir, the son and successor of Akbar, also was a great patron of the arts. In general, miniatures of his time are distinctively Mughal, but Iranian influence is still evident. Jahangir's tastes inclined less to book illustration than to paintings representing events in his life and realistic studies of plants and animals, in which as a devoted naturalist he took great interest. On his travels the emperor always had with him two or three court painters to record events of importance. Mansur, Murad, and Manohar were all skilled painters of birds and animals. Mansur was also a flower painter, and we find several references to his ability in Jahangir's memoirs: "[Ustad Mansur] has become the Nadiru'l 'Asr [Wonder of the Age], and in the art of drawing is unique in his generation. . . . The flowers that are seen in the territories of Kashmir are beyond all calculation. Those that Nadiru'l 'Asr Ustad Mansur has painted are more than one hundred." The only signed flower study by Mansur is in an album in the Habibganj Library in the Aligarh district, India. The Metropolitan Museum possesses a fine study of a pheasant, with a landscape and flowers of several varieties in the background, which may be attributed to some skilled pupil of the master. The painting is mounted on the back of a portrait of Shah Jahan.

During the reign of Jahangir, portrait painting became extremely popular. The emperor himself was constantly portrayed, either alone

Fig. 34. *Fighting Elephants, Mughal, Period of Jahangir (1605-1628)*

or with his courtiers, and his example was followed by the nobles who surrounded him. The chief portrait painters at the court whose names are known were Bishandas, Manohar, Muhammad Nadir, Abu'l Hasan, and Govardhan. Jahangir's favorite portrait painter was the Iranian Abu'l Hasan, the son of Aka Riza, upon whom

Jahangir bestowed the title Nadir az Zaman, or "Wonder of the Times." Among the portraits of Jahangir's period in the Museum is a fine miniature representing the emperor watching a fight between two elephants (fig. 34). The faces, particularly that of Jahangir, painted with infinite care, are masterly examples of portraiture in the mature style of the Mughal period.

The representation of Hindu ascetics and hermits conversing with princes and nobles was also a popular subject with Mughal painters. A characteristic scene of this

Fig. 35. Portrait of Shah Jahan, Mughal, Period of Shah Jahan (1628-1658)

kind in the Museum's collection is signed by Manohardas. Another one, by Hunhar, represents Jahangir visiting a hermit.

C. PERIODS OF SHAH JAHAN (1628-1658) AND AURANGZIB (1658-1707)

Under Shah Jahan, the art of Mughal portraiture reached its climax, and the brilliant court life was splendidly reflected in single portraits and ceremonial groups. In the Metropolitan Museum are two famous portraits of Shah Jahan. One represents him seated in state upon the peacock throne (fig. 35); the other shows him on horseback in all his regal splendor. The colors are brilliant and the faces are delicately modeled, some of them with microscopic details. Among the foremost artists of the period were Muhammad Fakhirullah Khan, Mir Hashim, Hunhar, Bichitr, and Anup Chhatar. By the last is a portrait drawing of Sayyid Amir Khan in the Museum's collection.

Dara Shikoh, Shah Jahan's eldest son, was, like his father, a collector of pictures and a patron of the arts. There are several portraits of this prince, who never reigned as emperor, the throne having been usurped by his younger brother, Aurangzib. One in the Metropolitan Museum shows the prince on horseback, surrounded by his retinue.

Under Aurangzib very few painters worked at the court, but nobles and high officials began to employ painters of their own; several portraits in the Museum's collection may be assigned to this period. This loss of royal patronage, combined with other factors, led to the decline of Mughal painting in the eighteenth century.

12. *Indian Painting: The Rajput School*

Contemporary with the Mughal school of painting, several native schools flourished in northern India, in Rajputana, Bundelkhand, and the Punjab. Coomaraswamy divides these Rajput paintings into two main groups, Rajasthani (Rajputana and Bundelkhand) and Pahari. The latter is subdivided into Kangra, Basohli, Guler, and Jammu.

Rajput paintings, of which the oldest known specimens date from the late sixteenth century or the beginning of the seventeenth, differ in style from those of the Mughal school. Based on the traditions of the native schools of wall painting which produced the famous frescoes at Ajanta and Bagh, they have many of the characteristics of folk art. The subjects also differ from those of the Mughal school. The latter was concerned mainly with portraiture and the recording of historical events, while the Rajput school derived its subjects chiefly from folklore and the great Indian epics.

The best examples of the Rajasthani school are the Ragmala paintings illustrating the thirty-six Ragas and Raginis, or musical modes, and assigned by Coomaraswamy to the late sixteenth century. Two paintings of this kind are in the Metropolitan Museum's collection, one of which, illustrating the mode Sadh Mallara Ragini, is seen in figure 36. The broad technique and vivid colors are quite unlike Mughal painting. Another type of Rajput painting is represented by a miniature in the Museum's collection from a manuscript of the Krishna series, showing Krishna visiting Radha.

To the Rajput school of the eighteenth century are attributed several cartoons for the mural paintings in the Jaipur Palace Library.

Fig. 36. A Musical Mode. Indian, Rajasthani,
XVI-XVII Century

Two such cartoons are in the Museum, one of them representing several female musicians, the other, a beautiful head of Krishna.

To the Jammu branch of the Pahari school belong large illustrations, in the Boston Museum and in the Metropolitan Museum's collection, representing the siege of Lanka, an episode from a Hindu epic, the *Ramayana*. The style of these paintings may be characterized as mural.

The paintings of the Kangra school belong mainly to the eighteenth century. Scenes from the *Krishna Lila* and romantic poems such as "Nala and Damayanti" were popular. A beautiful example of this school in the Museum's collection is the painting representing Krishna quelling Kaliya, whose wives plead for his life.

Chapter 4

CALLIGRAPHY AND ILLUMINATION

The art of calligraphy, or beautiful writing, was cultivated by the Muhammadans from earliest times and was more esteemed than that of painting. There are two principal styles of Arabic writing: a formal style with angular letters and a cursive style with rounded letters. The first type of writing is known as Kufic, from the town of Kufa in Mesopotamia, where it was probably first put into official use; the second type is known as Naskhi. Both types of script were known in the seventh century, the beginning of the Muhammadan era.

Kufic characters were used during a period of about five hundred years for inscriptional purposes and for copying the Koran. The earliest Koran, and the only eighth-century copy with a *wakfiya* date (perpetual endowment of property), A.H. 168 (784/5), is in the Cairo library. Most of the Abbasid Korans are of the ninth century. They are written on parchment, either natural, blue, violet, or red, in black or gold ink, and show thick and rounded Kufic letters with short verticals and exaggerated horizontals. This Kufic was used in Egypt, Syria, and Mesopotamia during the ninth century and part of the tenth. The Metropolitan Museum possesses a section from a small Abbasid Koran and separate leaves from a number of larger ones. The former comprises most of the second chapter of the Koran, entitled "The Cow," which states the fundamental principles of Islam. Of especial interest are the four illuminated pages of interlacings, foliate forms, and palmette scrolls. The design, outlined in brown ink, is painted in liquid gold with touches of red, green, blue, and ocher. Frequently illumination also extended to the text, as seen in a fine leaf from a larger parchment Koran in the Museum's collection (fig. 37). The highly decorative chapter heading shows the usual arrangement of the title within a rectangular panel from which extends a stylized tree. The ornaments of this chapter heading and other Korans of the ninth century are typical of the Abbasid style, in which many of the motives

67

of Sasanian art, as, for example, wing palmettes, are still apparent.

In the eleventh century the use of Kufic script became less frequent in Korans. It was gradually replaced by Naskhi script, although it continued in use for chapter headings even at a much later date. Naskhi reached the height of its development in the first half of the twelfth century, toward the end of the Fatimid rule.

Korans of the Mamluk period, of which there are magnificent examples in the Royal Egyptian Library at Cairo, show different types of rounded script written with great care and decorative sense.

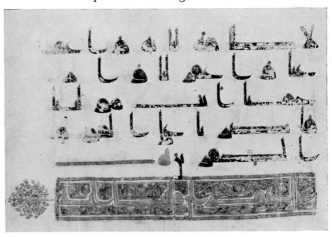

Fig. 37. Leaf from a Koran, Mesopotamian, Abbasid, IX Century

The large Korans are written in Tumar script, a bold variety of the Naskhi. A very fine Koran of the thirteenth or early fourteenth century, written in gold ink with diacritical signs in red and blue, is in the Museum's collection. Some of the pages, as seen in figure 38, show highly ornamental patterns composed of Naskhi script and arabesques in gold and blue, while chapter headings contain titles written in Kufic.

In Korans of Spain and North Africa, we find a distinctive form of writing, known as Maghribi (Western). This script, occasionally called Andalusian or Cordovan, is characterized by the very round forms of its letters (see fig. 39). It was developed in Spain after the center of the Maghrib had been shifted from Kairwan in North Africa to Andalusia. Several leaves of Korans in Maghribi

68

dating approximately from the twelfth and thirteenth centuries are in the Metropolitan Museum. In Maghribi Korans of the fourteenth and fifteenth centuries, copied in Granada and Fez, the writing is less careful, but the polychrome decoration is often very rich.

In Muhammadan Iran, writing as well as methods of book illumination were adopted from the Arabs. But Iranian calligraphers used a variation of the Abbasid Kufic script in which the verticals were more emphasized than the horizontals. Several leaves of a small parchment Koran of the early tenth century are known to be in various collections. The leaf in the Metropolitan Museum has a chapter heading with a composite palmette similar to those in the Abbasid Korans. From this type of Kufic evolved another one, in which the letters are rendered more angularly. In Saljuk Korans of the eleventh and twelfth centuries the Iranian type of Kufic is fully developed and the illumination is richer. A Koran in the British Museum, containing several fine illuminated pages with the interlacings and arabesque scrolls typical of Saljuk art, was written and illuminated by Abu'l Kasim ibn Ibrahim and is dated Jumada 1, 427 (March, 1036).

Fig. 38. Leaf from a Koran, Egypto-Arabic, Mamluk, XIII-XIV Century

Two leaves from a Saljuk Koran of 1054 are in the Metropolitan Museum. Written in Iranian Kufic, both leaves show interesting decorative features typical of Saljuk style. One of the leaves has a chapter heading in gold and polychrome, the other in gold only. Some of the passages of the text, as seen in figure 40, are written in highly decorative Kufic in which the verticals end in arabesques. The background of this Kufic is enriched by rosettes and scrolls in gold. Such decorative Kufic is known to us from Saljuk architecture and from wall paintings, for instance, in the interior of the tower of Pir-i-'Alamdar at Damghan, completed in 1026.

Fig. 39. *Leaf from a Koran, Moroccan, about XII Century*

Several twelfth-century Korans also bear dates: a copy in the Bibliothèque Nationale, written in Sistan in A.H. 505 (1111); another in the University Museum, Philadelphia, written in A.H. 559 (1164); and a third in the Chester Beatty collection, dated Jumada 1, 584 (July, 1188). There are portions of other fine Saljuk Korans in the Chester Beatty collection, the National Museum in Teheran, the shrine of the imam Riza in Mashhad, and the Metropolitan Museum. Three leaves in the Museum (see fig. 41) show a highly decorative combination of fine writing and ornament, consisting of palmette scrolls, painted in brown ink. Another type of Kufic, so-called Kufic fleuri, in which the letters are adorned with arabesquelike palmettes, was frequently used in Iran during the eleventh and twelfth centuries under the Saljuks and was also popular in Egypt under the Fatimids (969-1171).

Sometime during the thirteenth century there developed in Iran a form of writing known as Ta'lik, in which the characters show a tendency to slope downward from right to left, but the more rigid Naskhi continued in use for religious texts. Under the rule of the Il-khans the art of calligraphy and illumination reached a new height. A number of fine Mongol Korans, some of them made at the order of the Il-khan ruler Uljaitu Khudabanda Muhammad, are in several museums and collections. The best-known ones are the Koran in Leipzig, written in Baghdad in A.H. 706 (1306/7) and the Koran in the Royal Egyptian Library in Cairo, written by 'Abd Allah ibn Muhammad in Hamadan in A.H. 713 (1313). The latter has several fully illuminated pages which are masterpieces of abstract ornament. In most cases the field is divided into compartments containing arabesques or rosettes in gold and blue, occasionally with the addition of green. The geometrical compositions are enhanced by the use of contrasting background colors, such as gold and blue—the favorite color combination of Iranian illuminators of all periods. A fine Koran in the Beatty collection written by 'Abd Allah as Sairafi, dated Muharram, 728 (November, 1327), has illuminated chapter headings with arabesques and Kufic

Fig. 40. Leaf from a Koran Dated 1050, Iranian, Saljuk

script in vivid colors, such as red, turquoise blue, green, and white on a gold ground. This polychrome trend of the fourteenth century had a decisive influence upon the future development of Iranian illumination. Another fine Koran, one section of which is in the Beatty collection, the other in the Boston Museum of Fine Arts, was written by 'Abd Allah ibn Ahmad in Maragha and dated Shawal, 738 (April, 1338). Its pages show the extraordinary ability of Iranian illuminators to combine calligraphy and ornament into a decorative pattern.

Fourteenth-century illumination was not confined to Korans alone. Gradually ornament invaded illustrated manuscripts, forming either separate end vignettes or frames for the miniatures themselves, as may be seen in the manuscript of al Hariri's *Makamat* of

Fig. 41. Leaf from a Koran, Iranian, Saljuk,
XII Century

A.H. 734 (1334) in the National Library, Vienna.

In the fifteenth century, under the rule of the Timurids, the arts of the book reached their height. Calligraphy attained the importance of a great art, as the work of many illustrious calligraphers of the fifteenth century bears witness. One of the most famous masters of the fifteenth century was Mir 'Ali of Tabriz, who is credited with the invention of Nasta'lik. This is a highly developed, more elegant form of cursive writing, with features of both Naskhi and Ta'lik, which came into general use with the fifteenth century. A beautiful example of Mir 'Ali's early work is a copy of Khwaju Kirmani's love story, "Humay and Humayun," dated A.H. 799 (1396/7), in the British Museum.

One of the most celebrated calligraphers of the fifteenth century was Sultan 'Ali al Mashhadi, who worked in Herat at the court of Husain Mirza. There is a manuscript from his hand in the Metropolitan Museum, a copy of Mir 'Ali Shir Nawai's *Diwan* dated A.H. 905 (1499/1500). Other well-known calligraphers were Ja'far Baisunkuri of Tabriz, 'Abd al Karim of Khwarizm, and Ibrahim Sultan ibn Shah Rukh [ibn Timur Gurgan]. 'Abd al Karim, whose work is also represented in the Museum's collection by a copy of Jami's *Diwan*, was one of the two sons of the calligrapher 'Abd ar Rahman of Khwarizm. The father and sons worked at Tabriz and are reputed to have introduced many innovations in the style of Nasta'lik writing. Ibrahim Sultan was a great patron of letters and was renowned for his ability to write in six different styles. A fine Koran written by him in A.H. 827 (1424) is in the shrine of the

Fig. 42. Title-page from "Marvels of Creation" by Kazwini,
Iranian, Timurid, XV Century

imam Riza in Mashhad, and in the Museum's collection there is a
Koran with the date Ramadan 4, 830 (June 29, 1427).

Timurid illumination developed a distinctive style in which naturalistic plant ornament, with the frequent addition of birds and

animals of Chinese origin, played an important role. There are several varieties of Timurid illumination. In one the ornament is painted in gold and outlined in black; in another the design is in gold alone placed on a dark blue ground. Both types of illumination were most probably developed by the artists of the Shiraz school, best known from two important Shiraz manuscripts, the Gulbenkian "Anthology" and the British Museum "Compendium" of A.H. 813 (1410). A fine example of this early Timurid illumination of Shiraz (fig. 42) is in the Metropolitan Museum. It is a double title-page from Kazwini's "Marvels of Creation," with Iranian "angels" and Chinese dragons and birds painted in two shades of liquid gold, white, red, and green and outlined in black. Great technical skill and a keen sense of decoration are revealed in the border, which has fine animal grotesques intertwined with a delicate scroll in blue. As may be seen in the cartouches of the title-page and on the reverse of the leaf, the sketchy plant design is in gold against a blue ground.

The illuminated title-pages of several Timurid manuscripts, particularly those made for Shah Rukh and Baisunkur Mirza, are among the most sumptuous ever produced and represent the Herat style of decoration. One of the finest manuscripts of the Herat school is the Shah-nama of 1429 in the Teheran Museum, which has polychrome illuminations created by court artists. The intricate interlaced arabesques and floral scrolls of these illuminations show an astounding richness of detail and brilliancy of color comparable only to those found in enamels.

The arts of calligraphy and illumination developed by the Timurid artists continued to flourish in the sixteenth century under the Safavids. Mir 'Ali of Herat, who was probably a pupil of Zain ad Din Mahmud, was a famous calligrapher of this period. In 1534 Mir 'Ali went from Herat to the Uzbeg court at Bukhara, where he continued the great tradition of Herat calligraphers. From his hand we have a manuscript of Jami's "Yusuf and Zulaikha," dated A.H. 930 (1523/4), which was doubtless written in Herat although it was illustrated in Bukhara.

A great calligrapher at the Safavid court at Tabriz was Sultan Muhammad Nur, the son and pupil of Sultan 'Ali al Mashhadi. The beautiful Nizami of 1524 in our collection is by him. Shah Mahmud an Nishapuri, who wrote the famous Khamsa in the

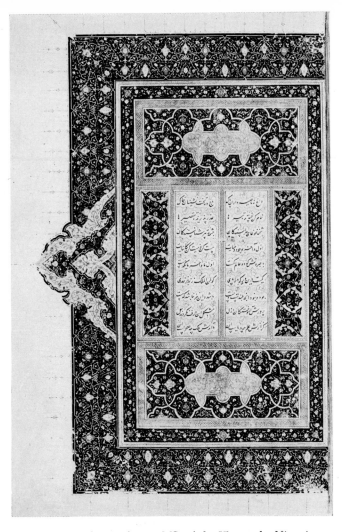

Fig. 43. *Title-page from a MS. of the* Khamsa *by* Nizami
Dated 1525, *Iranian*

British Museum between 1539 and 1543, was a famous calligrapher
of the time of Shah Isma'il and Shah Tahmasp. He was the favorite
calligrapher of Shah Isma'il.

Mir 'Imad, whose name even today is synonymous among the

75

Persians with beautiful writing, was a celebrated calligrapher in the time of Shah 'Abbas. Mir 'Imad settled in Isfahan in A.H. 1008 (1599/1600), where he copied many manuscripts for Shah 'Abbas. His rival was 'Ali Riza 'Abbasi, who sometimes is confused with the painter Riza-i-'Abbasi.

The illuminations of Safavid sixteenth-century manuscripts are as rich as those of the Timurid era. The color scheme and the ornament of the Herat illuminations of the early sixteenth century differ only a little from those of the fifteenth century, as may be seen on the title-page (fig. 43) of the Nizami of 1524. The background is usually blue, although occasionally there are smaller compartments in gold or black, and the ornament is painted in white, yellow, pink, vermilion, red, blue, and green. An interesting feature is the gold tooling. An important innovation of Safavid painters was the introduction of intricate ornament into the miniatures themselves, which enhanced their decorative quality.

Illumination painted in gold was further developed by Safavid artists. Several names of illuminators or workers in gold (muzahib) are known. The well-known Bukhara painter Mahmud (see p. 51) added to his signature the cognomen muzahib. The author Iskandar Munshi, who deals with the life of Safavid painters, mentions Mawlana Hasan Baghdadi as incomparable, unsurpassed, and unique in his time in the art of gilding. "In short he brought the art of gilding almost to a miracle, and all the masters of this art recognized his high attainment in it, and the gilding of Mawlana Bari, who had reached the greatest height in this art, cannot bear comparison with his minute and fine work." Many manuscripts of this period have page borders with floral scrolls, landscapes, animals, and human figures (see fig. 44), painted in liquid gold, in shades of green and yellow, which are as fine as the miniatures themselves. The Metropolitan Museum possesses a number of leaves of a copy of a collection of poems by Sa'di and Hafiz, with illuminations in gold. In several cases silver is added for contrast (see fig. 44). The style of illumination practiced at the court of Shah Tahmasp continued through the sixteenth and seventeenth centuries. In the seventeenth century the colors became more vivid, and large palmettes and lanceolate leaves were often used in the ornament.

Several other techniques practiced by Safavid artists, but known since the Timurid period, must be classified under the head of

Fig. 44. Leaf from a MS. of the Diwan of Hafiz, Iranian, Safavid,
XVI Century

Fig. 45. Tughra of Sulaiman the Magnificent (1520-1566), Turkish

illumination. One is stenciling, in which the design appears as a light or dark silhouette. Another is the so-called *découpé* work, in which the design is cut out and pasted on a colored ground, generally blue. The latter technique was also used by calligraphers of the fifteenth and sixteenth centuries and is exemplified in our collection by an incomplete sixteenth-century manuscript of Nizami's *Khamsa*.

Turkish calligraphy and illumination are represented in the Museum by two large tughras, or calligraphic emblems (fig. 45), which formed headings of imperial edicts of Sulaiman the Magnificent (1520-66). The ornament in gold, blue, and black, with the addition of other colors, is characteristic of the Turkish art of the sixteenth century, known from faience and textiles.

Chapter 5

BOOKBINDING

The work of the calligrapher and the painter in the production of books was complemented by that of the binder, to whom fell the responsibility of protecting the pages from injury and of giving to the exterior of the book an appearance worthy of its contents. Decoration was not confined to the exterior of the covers and the flap that closed over the front edge of the book. It was also lavished on the interior faces of the covers, and these doublures, or linings, are often elaborately ornamented. For bookbinding, leather is the ideal material. In the late period of Muhammadan art lacquered papier-mâché came into favor, but leather was used exclusively by the early binders and never was wholly discarded. Various processes were employed in the decoration of bookbindings. The leather was tooled or stamped, either with or without gold. Cut-out work in gilded leather or paper over a colored ground was a more elaborate technique frequently used for the doublures.

The earliest known book covers of the Muhammadan period come from Egypt and may be dated from the eighth to the eleventh century. Their decoration recalls the geometrical ornament of certain Coptic bindings of the eighth and ninth centuries. Typical of the Egypto-Arabic bindings of the Mamluk period, that is, from the thirteenth to the fifteenth century, are the all-over patterns of geometrical interlacings in blind tooling, enhanced by gold-tooled dots, seen in a binding in the Metropolitan Museum (fig. 46). In two Mamluk bindings in the Museum's collection the intervening spaces are further decorated with stamped rosettes and guilloche patterns. Other Mamluk bindings show central medallions with arabesques of fine cut leather on colored backgrounds. The doublures of the Mamluk book covers usually show a stamped design of arabesques, sometimes with the addition of floral motives, which came into vogue in the beginning of the fourteenth century. Bookbindings of the same period made in the Maghrib, or Muham-

Fig. 46. Book Cover, Egypto-Arabic, Mamluk, XIII-XV Century

madan North Africa, were also decorated with geometrical interlacings and gold tooling.

Iranian bookbindings of the Timurid period are among the finest
ever produced. Technical skill and fine design characterize the bindings made at the Herat academy, where the art of leather filigree
reached a high level of perfection. The exteriors show usually a
stamped decoration, while the doublures have cut-out patterns
against a blue background. Notable fifteenth-century bindings decorated with typical Timurid landscapes and Chinese motives are
found on manuscripts dated A.H. 841 and 849 (1437 and 1445) in
the Topkapu Saray Library at Istanbul. A cut-leather design on
the doublure of the manuscript dated A.H. 850 (1446) is very simi-

lar to one on the binding of a copy of Nizami's *Khamsa* dated A.H. 853 (1449) in the Museum's collection. The decoration (fig. 47) is composed of two Chinese phoenixes in combat against a background of Timurid floral scrolls within a medallion. It shows fine detail work, which we find in all Timurid bookbindings.

In the sixteenth century, under the Safavid dynasty, book covers were elaborately ornamented and gold was used more abundantly than in the fifteenth century. In some cases the decoration covered the entire surface; in others it was confined within medallions or other compartments. A fine example of Iranian bookbinding of this period may be seen on a *Bustan* in the Museum's collection. The exterior (fig. 48) is decorated with stamped and gilded arabesques interlaced with delicate floral scrolls and Chinese cloud bands. On the interior (fig. 49) the ornament consists of arabesques in delicate leather filigree on backgrounds of blue, pink, and green.

Another type of sixteenth-century Iranian bookbinding is exemplified by the magnificent cover reproduced in figure 50. The stamped and gilded decoration of

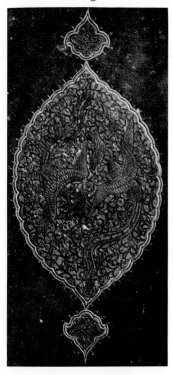

Fig. 47. *Interior of a Book Cover with Cut-Leather Decoration, Iranian, Timurid, XV Century*

the exterior, representing birds and animals in a landscape, reflects the naturalistic style of Safavid painting. Safavid bookbinding decoration, differing in technique from that of the Timurid era, is not hand-tooled and stamped but is pressed with large engraved matrices of copper or steel. The processes of pressing and gilding were usually combined, but sometimes the leather was gilded before being pressed with the hot matrix. The interior of the above book cover is decorated with gold paper filigree, which replaced the cut-leather work of the Timurid period. This paper filigree is placed on backgrounds of red, blue, green, black, and lavender.

Painted and lacquered bookbindings came into vogue in the time of Shah Tahmasp. Although at first leather was used, the covers to be painted were usually of papier-mâché, which was covered with

Fig. 48. Exterior of a Book Cover (Detail), Iranian, Safavid,
XVI Century

a coat of fine plaster or gesso and then with a thin layer of lacquer. Upon this background the design was painted in water colors. For protection the painting was covered with several layers of lacquer. The paintings, which represent landscapes, hunting and garden scenes, and bouquets of flowers, are in the style of contemporary miniatures. According to the Turkish historian 'Ali, the famous Ustad Muhammadi was among the artists who painted lacquer book covers. A number of lacquered bookbindings of the sixteenth century with figure subjects are known. The finest examples are those in the Musée des Arts Décoratifs and the Cartier collection in Paris, the Sarre collection in Berlin, and the Royal Asiatic Society in London, and one in a private collection in London (formerly in the Düsseldorf Museum).

Fig. 49. Interior of the Book Cover Shown in Figure 48

The decoration of seventeenth- and eighteenth-century bookbindings follows the Safavid style of the sixteenth century, but the lacquer technique was used more frequently. The ornament is usually of a naturalistic floral character rendered in light colors.

Beautiful bookbindings were also made in Turkey, the craft following much the same stylistic development as in Iran.

It may be of interest to note that Near Eastern bookbindings were freely imitated in Italy, particularly in Venice, in the late fif-

Fig. 50. Exterior of a Book Cover, Iranian, Safavid, XVI Century

teenth and sixteenth centuries, and through this means many decorative motives of oriental origin became current in European designs. Italian trade with the East was also responsible for the introduction of morocco and the use of gold tooling in the decoration of book covers.

84

Chapter 6

SCULPTURE IN STONE AND STUCCO

1. Umayyad and Abbasid Sculpture in Syria, Mesopotamia, Egypt, and Iran (VIII-X Century)

The sculpture of the early Islamic era is known to us from the decoration of a number of palaces, private houses, and mosques in Syria, Mesopotamia, Iran, and Egypt, built under the rule of Umayyad and Abbasid caliphs. These monuments and occasional finds of architectural elements, such as capitals and prayer niches, reveal the great decorative splendor of both stone and stucco sculpture in the early Islamic period. One of the most important monuments of the eighth century is the Umayyad winter palace at Mshatta, situated in the Syrian desert beyond the river Jordan. The richly carved stone façade of this palace is today in the Islamic collection of the German State Museums in Berlin. The decoration, in deeply undercut relief, may be roughly divided into two main groups. In the triangles at the left of the entrance gate appears a decoration of animals, birds, and human figures amid vine scrolls derived chiefly from the Christian art of Syria. In the triangles at the right there are no representations of living beings, and the vine scrolls are treated in abstract fashion based on artistic traditions of the East. Here the sculptor avoided the use of large stone surfaces, accentuating the decorative effect of light and dark suggesting openwork. A careful analysis of the ornament reveals not only traditional Syrian and Sasanian motives, but a new oriental style, which may be called Umayyad. As Herzfeld has suggested, Mshatta must have been built, and left unfinished, in the time of the caliph Walid II (743/4). Other Umayyad monuments with richly carved decoration are the palaces at Kasr at Tuba and Rabat Amman in Syria and the palace of the caliph Hisham (724-43) at Khirbet el Mefjer in the Jordan Valley.

The Umayyad style of carving in stone, stucco, and wood continued in the second half of the eighth century under the rule of the Abbasid dynasty. Many of these early Abbasid sculptures in stone and stucco, as well as wood carvings (see chapter VII), are of great interest to all students of Islamic ornament, as they show the beginnings of the arabesque, which did not appear in its ulti-

Fig. 51. Alabaster Capital, Abbasid, about 800

mate form until the eleventh century. Of special importance is a series of alabaster capitals found in Rakka and the region between Rusafa and Deir az Zor. Three of these capitals are in the Metropolitan Museum; others are in museums in Berlin and Istanbul. They may be divided into several groups, illustrating the gradual evolution of the true Islamic style. Some of the capitals, derived from earlier pre-Islamic types, show distinctly the disintegration of Syrian acanthus forms; in others, as, for example, two capitals in our collection (figs. 51 and 52), the acanthus has been entirely eliminated. But in most of these richly carved capitals the ornament is based on palmettes combined to form scrolls or various other decorative devices. The principal decoration is carved in low relief

86

and as a rule consists of wavy scrolls formed by half palmettes, split palmettes, and full palmettes. The half palmettes do not form final motives, but, as may be seen in figure 51, merge with the scrolls, their ends developing into other palmettes. The half and full pal-

Fig. 52. Alabaster Capital, Abbasid, about 800

mettes show several incised and grooved lobes, usually rounded, the lowest of which are often carved into volutes. Such palmettes, unknown in East Christian art, were derived from Sasanian art (see p. 14). From Sasanian prototypes the Islamic artists developed new, abstract ornament, which is characteristic of the Abbasid style. The capital shown in figure 51 belongs to a group which may be assigned to the period of the caliph Harun ar Rashid (786-809).

The great artistic activity of the Abbasid period is closely connected with the rise of Baghdad and the temporary residence of the caliphs in Samarra on the Tigris. Excavations conducted at Samarra by German archaeologists under Sarre and Herzfeld revealed a city of great splendor and luxury. It was founded in 836 by the caliph Mu'tasim and was built, enlarged, and abandoned within the short period of forty-seven years (836-883), during which time it was the residence of eight caliphs. The city had wide streets, fine mosques, palaces, bazaars, playgrounds, and special quarters for the Turkish army, officials, and citizens. The palace and private houses were furnished with baths and fountains, and the walls of the principal rooms were decorated with paintings and, to the height of about forty inches, with stucco dadoes. Except for a few original pieces, nearly all the stucco panels exhibited in Berlin are casts made by the expedition at Samarra from the same material as the originals. Four such casts, acquired from the Berlin Museum, are in the Metropolitan Museum's collection.

Fig. 53. Cast of a Stucco Wall Panel from Samarra, Mesopotamian, Abbasid, IX Century

The ornament of the Samarra stuccoes shows three different styles. In two of them, the second and third, the ornament was cut on the wall itself or on separate panels affixed to the wall; in the first style (fig. 53) it was cast in molds. In the third style, which may be regarded as the earliest, the ornament consists of vine scrolls, pine cones, palmettes, and vase motives within geometrical compartments and hexafoil medallions. Although the ornament is based on Umayyad traditions, Abbasid artists created entirely new patterns of great decorative beauty. Characteristic features of the Abbasid style are elaboration of motives and variation in the height of relief, which occur also in an important wooden mimbar from Kairwan and a Takrit panel in the Museum's collection (see fig. 61).

In the second style of Samarra the ornament is of an abstract character, consisting of vase motives and geometrical scrolls bearing

88

circular leaves or various types of palmettes. It is cut in flat relief and the motives are covered with dense lozenge diapers. Many of the forms used here recall Iranian metalwork with stone inlay; others, such as the geometrical scrolls with circular leaves, are of Central Asiatic origin. The Islamic principle of covering every inch of the space to be decorated is fully developed in the first style of Samarra. Here the background is wholly eliminated or reduced to a narrow line by an entirely new method of decoration, in which the sloping surfaces of the motives meet at an oblique angle (see fig. 52). This decoration was also used in stone and wood carving (see fig. 62) and the technique is generally known as beveled or slant cutting. The abstract pattern is composed of a variety of motives based on arabesque scrollwork and palmette devices and completed by the addition of a few notches, short lines, and dots. Many traditional Islamic motives were included but were adapted to this new technique, in which details are suppressed. This style of carving came into vogue with the Abbasids, being already known in the time of Harun ar Rashid, and is represented in the Metropolitan Museum by the fine alabaster capital shown in figure 52. The technique was probably introduced into the Near East by Iranian or Turkish artists employed by Abbasid rulers. It can be traced back to Central Asia, where its prototypes are found in Scytho-Siberian animal ornament in wood, bone, bronze, and gold, some of which dates from the Han period (206 B.C.-A.D. 220).

It was the custom of Muhammadan rulers to requisition the best artists and craftsmen from the various provinces for the construction of their cities, palaces, and mosques. At the foundation of Baghdad, as has been already noted (p. 7), workers were gathered from Syria, Iran, Mosul, Kufa, Wasit, and Basra. This custom must also have been followed in the building of Samarra, the ornament of which shows several styles and the various decorative tendencies prevailing in the Abbasid period.

The Abbasid style of decoration in stucco and stone was adopted in all the provinces of the Muhammadan East. It was introduced into Egypt from Mesopotamia in the time of the Turkish Tulunids, the second and third Samarra styles being evident in the stucco ornament of the mosque of Ibn Tulun (876). The slant carving of Abbasid decoration was also popular in Egypt. In Iran the Abbasid style is exemplified by the rich stucco decoration of the mosque

of Nayin, near Yazd, which shows a vine ornament related to the
third Samarra style. In Nayin, however, there is a palmette ornament, in which occurs a new tendency toward overelaboration of
the surface. Stylistic evidence, therefore, indicates that the Nayin

Fig. 54. Stucco Panel from Nishapur, Iranian, Samanid, X Century

ornament is probably later than that of Samarra and should be
assigned to the beginning of the tenth century. A similar ornament
appears in Egypt in the stucco decoration of a Coptic monastery,
Deir es Suryani, which may also be assigned to the early tenth
century.

The excavations of the Metropolitan Museum at Nishapur, in
the province of Khurasan, have recently brought to light important
new material for the history of Islamic stucco decoration in the
ninth and tenth centuries. The greater part of the stucco decoration
found at Nishapur comes from several buildings in the mounds
known as Teppe Madrasa and Sabz Pushan. The most complete
panels, found in a building at Sabz Pushan, formed the dado of an
iwan, or niche, on the southwest side of a courtyard and an adjoin-
ing domed room. These panels (see fig. 54), originally painted
white, yellow, blue, and red, show a rich decoration of palmette
scrolls and palmette devices, some of which are placed within
quatrefoil or hexafoil medallions similar to those found at Samarra.
The scrolls are purely abstract and bear four or six offshoots, usually
describing circles around a central motive or arranged in a whorl
movement. The offshoots end in palmettes, which may be divided
into several types. There are half palmettes of the Sasanian type and
simplified half palmettes without lobes, placed on top of larger
ones with a ribbed surface. There are also trilobed palmettes and

composite palmettes, five of which may be seen in figure 54.

The Nishapur stuccoes also throw an interesting new light on the survival of the Iranian animal style in Islamic art. Some of the offshoots (seen in the two outside medallions of fig. 54) end in birds' heads and half palmettes, an abbreviated representation of the birds holding palmettes in their beaks that are seen on various Sasanian silver vessels. Among the other decorative forms borrowed by Abbasid art from traditional Iranian art are Sasanian ribbons, which in Samarra and Nishapur were transformed into triangular lotuslike motives attached to birds or palmettes.

The Nishapur stuccoes are stylistically related to those of both Samarra and Nayin but reveal motives and decorative principles characteristic of a later phase of Islamic ornament. The surface elaboration so typical of Nayin is further advanced in Nishapur. Most probably the Nishapur stuccoes belong to the last period of rebuilding, that is, between 961 and 981, when Muhammad ibn Simjur was Governor of Nishapur under the Samanid rulers Mansur I and Nuh II. They thus form an important link between the Abbasid and Saljuk styles of Iranian stucco decoration.

2. Saljuk Sculpture in Iran (XI-XIII Century)

Sculpture in stone and stucco played an important role in the exterior and interior decoration of the Saljuk period. Although different styles of ornament and figure subjects were developed by artists working for the Saljuk princes in various provinces, common features are apparent in all. The arabesque, the true Islamic ornament, and monumental inscriptions in Kufic or Naskhi writing became essential parts of the decoration. The new decorative forms seen in Saljuk stone and stucco decoration probably originated in the Eastern provinces, being influenced by the brick and cut-terracotta ornament of Ghaznavid monuments, for example, the tower of Mahmud (998-1030) in Ghazna and the mosque at Kal'a-i-Bist in Afghanistan. The Kufic letters ending in arabesque motives and placed on a background of arabesque scrolls constitute a type of decoration found fully developed on the tower of Mas'ud III (1099-1114) at Ghazna; it was also used in the province of Khurasan, as we know from ruins at Nishapur and Merv. In Merv, the residence and capital of the Saljuk rulers, there still stand the ruins of the tomb of

Sultan Sanjar (1118-1157), decorated on the inside with panels of fine arabesques and inscriptions, both Kufic and Naskhi, in cut terracotta. One of the most beautiful Kufic inscriptions of the Saljuk period is known from a ruined madrasa, or theological seminary, at Khargird in Khurasan. It contains the name of Nizam al Mulk, the grand vizier of Sultan Alp Arslan, and may be assigned to a period between 1063 and 1092. The use of two or more decorative planes, seen here, was characteristic of many Saljuk reliefs and continued in later periods under the Mongols and Timurids (see the Koran stand in fig. 66).

The developed Saljuk style of decoration in stone and stucco is known to us from a number of twelfth-century monuments, including the Masjid-i-Jami in Kazvin, dated A.H. 509 (1116), and the mihrab of the Imam Zada Karrar at Buzun, dated A.H. 528 (1134). The Masjid-i-Jami at Ardistan (1160) has three mihrabs which rival one another in richness of stucco decoration. Several systems of arabesques are intertwined or placed one above the other, the heavy, or "baroque," arabesque in high relief usually forming the background. Prototypes of arabesques found in thirteenth-century Mamluk woodwork (see fig. 65) may be seen in some of the intricate arabesque patterns of these Saljuk mihrabs.

Stucco was used extensively in the Saljuk era not only for the decoration of mosques but also for that of palaces and houses of nobles. The compositions were often quite elaborate, consisting of hunting scenes or court scenes with princes surrounded by musicians, entertainers, and courtiers. Occasionally the relief of the figures is so high that it approaches sculpture in the round, as may be seen in several complete figures in the museums of Berlin and Detroit. An unusually well-preserved example of figural stucco is the head of a prince (fig. 55) in the Metropolitan Museum. Only the essential features of the face are indicated, but these are skillfully modeled, and the locks of hair are strongly stylized in oriental fashion. The jeweled headdress was originally enhanced by polychromy, which is often found in Saljuk stuccoes. As in other sculptures of the twelfth and thirteenth centuries, the racial type represented by the head is Turko-Mongolian. Also in the Museum's collection are two Saljuk medallions with figure subjects, one representing a court scene, the other a falconer on horseback. Such medallions were modeled separately and rows of them were probably set into walls,

Fig. 55. Stucco Head, Iranian, Saljuk, XII-XIII Century

possibly in combination with wall paintings in which a similar color
scheme was used. Other Saljuk stucco reliefs, found in Iran, chiefly
in Rayy and Sava, are decorated with animals or birds combined
with arabesque patterns, as on a cornice in the Museum's collection. The panel illustrated in figure 56 was a part of an all-over pattern consisting of highly stylized lions, back to back, their joined
tails ending, in Saljuk fashion, in arabesque devices.

The Saljuk style of decoration seen in architecture is also apparent in tombstones from various cemeteries, mostly from Nihavand
and Yazd. The majority are of the twelfth century and are inscribed

with verses from the Koran and the name of the deceased. Frequently they bear dates, and some are inscribed with the name of the sculptor. The Museum has three such tombstones, one in the shape of a small sarcophagus, the other two in the form of a stele, which is the most common type of Muhammadan tombstone. The

stele of Abu Sa'd ibn Muhammad bears the date Muharram, 545 (May, 1150) and the name of the sculptor, Ahmad ibn Muhammad. The decoration consists of a central prayer niche and several bands of inscriptions, in both Kufic and Naskhi. Arabesques fill in the tympanum and spandrels, and palmettes form the background for the highly ornamental writing which played such an important role in Saljuk art.

Fig. 56. Fragment of a Stucco Frieze,
Iranian, Saljuk, XII-XIII Century

3. Saljuk Sculpture in Mesopotamia, Syria, and Asia Minor (XI-XIII Century)

The conquest of Mesopotamia, Syria, and Asia Minor by the Turkish Saljuks brought about a considerable stylistic change in the sculpture of these provinces, which under the Abbasids had been based almost entirely on abstract ornament. Under the Saljuks representations of human figures and animals became frequent on the buildings, bridges, and gates erected in various cities, such as Diar-Bakr (Amida), Mosul, and Baghdad in Mesopotamia, and Konia in Asia Minor. Interesting examples of Saljuk sculpture are preserved in Amida, which was ruled by the Marwanid dynasty from 990 to 1085/6, then by the great Saljuks. Dated monuments in Amida reveal the great progress made by Islamic sculpture and decorative arts under the Saljuks. Inscriptions in the typical Abbasid style of Kufic writing have a plain background without any ornament, while the Marwanid inscriptions of Amida, dated A.H. 426, 437, 457, 460, 476 (1034/5, 1045/6, 1065, 1067/8, 1083/4), show letters ending in arabesque scrolls. In the magnificent inscription of Sultan Malikshah, dated A.H. 484 (1091/2), on the north façade of the Great Mosque of Amida, bands of elegant foliated Kufic with braided letters are placed on a background of finely drawn linear arabesques.

The inscriptions in Amida are frequently accompanied by reliefs of animals and birds, which were used not only as decoration but also as symbols or emblems, personal or dynastic, by Saljuk princes. In Amida, as in Saljuk art in general, figures of animals and birds play an important role, partly as a result of Turkish influence.

Another great artistic center of Mesopotamia under the Saljuks was Mosul, the residence of the atabegs of the Zangid dynasty. The mosques, palaces, and churches of Mosul reveal a rich decoration in stone or stucco carved in the characteristic Saljuk style. In the Great Mosque, which bears the name of Nur ad Din, are two beautiful stone mihrabs with arabesque decoration. The earlier mihrab, made in September or October, 1148, by Mustafa (?) of Baghdad, is decorated with intricate arabesques and inscriptions. The later one, standing in the courtyard of the mosque, belongs to the period of the atabeg Badr ad Din Lulu (1233-59), a great patron of the arts. This prayer niche shows several types of arabesques in low or high relief, often carved in several planes.

Other important Mosul buildings of the period of Badr ad Din Lulu are the Kara Saray, or "Black Palace," and the tombs of the imam Yahya and the imam Aun ad Din. The interior stucco decoration of the palace shows several interesting features, among which figure subjects and birds, so popular in the art of Mosul, play an important role. In some of the panels and one of the friezes birds form integral parts of the arabesques themselves. One band of inscription has a background of scrolls ending in the heads of beasts, a feature most probably originating in Central Asia. Saljuk arabesques appear in other thirteenth-century Muhammadan buildings in Mosul and Sinjar, and in Christian churches as well. The presence of identical ornament in Islamic and Christian buildings suggests the possibility that Christian stonecutters were employed by the Saljuk rulers. In the stone decoration of the church of Mar Ahudamma in Mosul appear purely Muhammadan figure subjects, such as a sultan on a throne, a falconer, and typical Saljuk lions with tails ending in dragons' heads.

The Saljuk style of sculpture spread to all parts of Mesopotamia and to Syria and Asia Minor. The now destroyed Talisman Gate of Baghdad, inscribed with the name of the Abbasid caliph an Nasir and dated A.H. 618 (1221/2), had an arch with a relief which was one of the finest examples of Saljuk sculpture known. It represented a seated figure of the caliph flanked by two dragons with knotted bodies carved in high relief on a background of graceful arabesques forming a lacelike pattern.

After the conquest of Iran, Mesopotamia, and parts of Syria, a branch of the Saljuks established themselves in Asia Minor (Rum), adorning Konia, their capital and residence, with many fine mosques, palaces, and gates. In the decoration of Saljuk buildings, both exterior and interior, sculpture played an important role. Animals were often placed on buildings, city walls and gates, towers, and bridges, probably as talismans against enemies or evil powers. Mosques in Konia erected between 1220 and 1270 show interesting examples of Saljuk ornament, including inscriptions. The mosque of Sultan Han, dated A.H. 626 (1228/9), gives the earliest example of a richly decorated Saljuk marble façade. One of the most beautiful buildings in Konia, the Sirchali madrasa, dated A.H. 640 (1242/3), is decorated with geometrical interlacings which characterize the earlier group of Saljuk buildings in Asia Minor. In the second half of the thirteenth century, ornament developed a rich arabesque design with numerous palmette forms, sometimes resembling rug or textile patterns. Here and there naturalizing tendencies were introduced, probably as the result of Armenian and Western influence, which was to be expected in Asia Minor.

Of great interest are a number of stucco reliefs which, according to Sarre's reconstruction, come from a pavilion of a palace built in Konia by Sultan 'Ala ad Din Kai Kubad (1219-36). Most of the decoration probably dates from a later period, that of Sultan Kilij Arslan IV (1257-67). Ruins of the two-story pavilion were still in existence in 1907, but were gradually disintegrating. The interior of the palace was sumptuous. The walls were decorated with a dado of tiles, above which were placed bands and friezes of stucco relief. Among the larger reliefs with figure subjects is one now in the Chinili Kiosk at Istanbul, which represents two horsemen, one attacking a dragon, the other a lion. The lively composition and excellent rendering of the animals indicate that the Saljuks of Asia Minor were great sculptors.

4. Stone Sculpture of the Caucasus

From remote antiquity the Caucasus was subject to strong influences from the East, being often invaded by Iranian and Turanian tribes. The Arab conquest of the Caucasus was gradual and particularly slow in the province of Daghestan. By the tenth century only

Fig. 57. Stone Relief, Caucasian, Daghestan, XII-XIII Century

Derbend, the principal town, and a few neighboring castles were in Arab hands. In 1049, the Saljuks invaded Armenia, Georgia, and other parts of the Caucasus, and their influence was soon apparent in all provinces. The coins of the Georgian kings, made at first in imitation of Byzantine ones, began to bear legends in Arabic. The influence of Saljuk art extended also to various arts and crafts. Sculpture produced during the twelfth and thirteenth centuries in the province of Daghestan bears an interesting relation to that of the Saljuks of Asia Minor. In the villages of Amusga, Itzari, and Kala-Koreish, and particularly in Kubatchi (from the Turkish *kobeci*, "coat of mail"), were found numerous stone reliefs which had evidently been salvaged from the ruined castles of local princes and later built into the houses of peasants.

The reliefs are in the shape of arched tympanums and rectangular or round slabs and are decorated with figure subjects, groups of animals, fabulous creatures, arabesques, and Arabic inscriptions. Most of these houses have now been destroyed or torn down and

97

the sculptures removed to Russian museums. Two fine tympanums are in this country, one in the Freer Gallery in Washington, the other in the Metropolitan Museum. Both came from the house of Ahmad and Ibrahim in Kubatchi, which was destroyed about 1924. The relief in the Freer Gallery is decorated with a symmetrical composition of two lions bordered by a frieze of running animals against a background of arabesques. The main decoration of the Museum's tympanum (fig. 57) consists of a figure of a warrior on horseback, wearing a tight-fitting coat with a belt, from which are suspended a quiver and a bracer. The archivolt is carved in low relief with a fine arabesque scroll forming circular compartments with trefoiled palmettes. Many of the reliefs with figure subjects and animals are clearly related to Saljuk art of the twelfth and thirteenth centuries. As a group the Daghestan sculptures have a distinctive style, in which Turkish elements are combined with various local ones. The same mixture of motives appears on Caucasian metalwork, particularly on bronze braziers of the twelfth and thirteenth centuries.

5. Mongol Stone and Stucco Sculpture in Iran (Mid-XIII— XIV Century)

As in other fields of art, the techniques and ornament of Saljuk sculpture continued for some time after the establishment of the Il-khan dynasty in 1256. The style of stucco decoration evolved in the twelfth century gradually developed into a more and more complicated pattern until, under the Mongols, it became almost baroque in character. A number of monuments, most of them from the province of Azerbaijan, show this style in all its richness. Mongol stucco ornament is preserved in the Masjid-i-Haidaria, in Kazvin, which is assigned to the second half of the thirteenth century. Here heavy arabesques in high relief and elaborate lacelike surface patterns of star motives, lozenge diapers, and interlacings are placed on a background of palmette scrolls cut in low relief. Probably contemporary with the Haidaria is another early Mongol monument, the mausoleum Gumbadh-i-'Alawiyyan in Hamadan, in which the peculiar Mongol stucco technique reached its height. A particularly fine example of fourteenth-century Mongol stucco decoration is the mihrab in the Great Mosque of Isfahan, erected in 1310 by one of the grand viziers of Uljaitu. The design shows many Saljuk features, Naskhi writing and arabesques forming a highly decorative pattern in the best tradition of Islamic art.

Mongol sculpture of the fourteenth century is represented in the

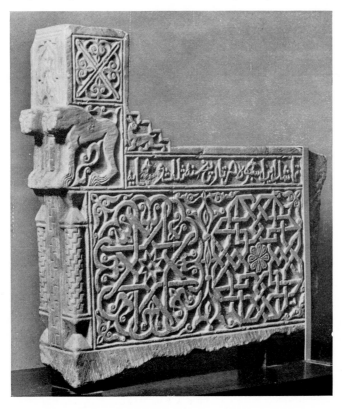

Fig. 58. Stone Relief Dated 1303/4, Iranian, Mongol

Museum by three interesting stone reliefs. Two of them are probably the end pieces of a balustrade (see fig. 58) and are said to have come from Hamadan. The pieces show a variety of patterns cut in low relief. The stones are inscribed with the name of the owner, Hajji Hasan; the name of the sculptor, Sharaf (?) ibn Mahmud; and the date A.H. 703 (1303/4). One side of the stone in figure 58 is decorated with two units of geometrical interlacings and arabesques, while the opposite side has a representation of a lion attack-

99

ing a stag. The other piece is carved with patterns of interlacings and arabesque devices, well known from fourteenth-century Mongol decoration, particularly of Korans (see p. 71). There are several similar stones in European and American collections that have been assigned to the twelfth and thirteenth centuries. Most of them, however, are not earlier than the thirteenth century.

Another interesting example of Mongol sculpture in our collection is a fourteenth-century marble tombstone, carved in the form of a prayer niche. In the center is the actual niche, with a stalactite conch supported by two columns; above is a panel of rectangular Kufic writing. The niche is framed by three receding bands of inscriptions written in three forms of Arabic script. Two bands are in Kufic, one with square letters which became popular in the Mongol period. The middle band is in Naskhi and contains the name of the deceased, Shaikh Mahmud ibn Muhammad of Yazd, and the date A.H. 753 (1352). On the threshold of the arch appears the name of the sculptor, Nizami ibn Shahab. The tombstone is an excellent miniature replica of a Mongol mihrab of the middle of the fourteenth century.

6. Fatimid Sculpture in Egypt (X-XII Century)

The monuments of Cairo dating from the second half of the tenth, eleventh, and twelfth centuries show a rich stucco and stone decoration with many features peculiar to the Fatimid period. The earliest Fatimid stucco ornament appears in the mosque of al Azhar in Cairo, which was begun in 970 and completed in 972. The sanctuary (maksura) and the kibla wall are decorated with a dense pattern of palmette scrolls in which the background, like those in the Tulunid period, is reduced to the space essential for separating the motives. This decoration of al Azhar is derived from ninth-century Abbasid and Tulunid ornament but shows a definite change of style. The most important innovation is the greater prominence of the connecting scrolls, which frequently have two stripes.

The development of new decorative forms, particularly the arabesque, is evident in the stucco and stone decoration of the mosque of al Hakim (990-1012) in Cairo. Here, in both stucco and stone, we find perfect examples of foliated Kufic. In the windows, niches, and bands of the mosque and the minarets appear arabesques of the developed type. The traditional patterns have been replaced by a graceful and rhythmic play of scrolls, which run in various directions and often cross each other. It is very probable that both the arabesque and the foliated Kufic are of East Iranian origin.

Fatimid stucco decoration of the late eleventh century is known to us from several prayer niches in Cairo. The ornament of the mihrab in the tomb mosque of al Juyushi (1085) shows a great stylistic difference from that of the mosque of al Hakim. The whole surface of the mihrab is covered with a bold arabesque design, the palmettes of which are patterned with various geometrical designs and crowded with detail, a characteristic already observed in tenth-century Iranian stucco decoration from Nishapur and Nayin (see p. 90). As there are no Egyptian prototypes for this ornament, the style must have come from Iran, spreading with the Saljuks over the whole Near East. The Saljuk style was also popular in Egypt in the twelfth century, as may be seen in the stucco decoration of the entrance cupola in the mosque of al Azhar and the triple mihrab of the mausoleum of the brothers of Yusuf (1100). The two stucco mihrabs of the mausoleum of Sayyida Rukayya (1133) show a new decorative feature, two or three rows of the shallow stalactites which were so popular in Egypt. The windows of the mosque of as Salih Talaye (1160), a monument of the end of the Fatimid period, show beautiful examples of openwork in stucco. In all these monuments the stucco decoration was rendered in flat relief. The high relief characteristic of many Saljuk monuments in Iran was not adopted by Fatimid sculptors.

7. Ayyubid and Mamluk Sculpture in Egypt and Syria (Late XII-XV Century)

Under the Ayyubid dynasty, which the great Saladin established in 1169 in Egypt and in 1176 in Syria, sculpture and other arts at first continued in the Fatimid style. No architecture of Saladin's time remains in Cairo, with the exception of the walls of the old city of Fustat and the citadel. Of the later Ayyubid period only a few buildings have been preserved, among them the mausoleum of the imam ash Shafi'i (1211), the tomb of the amir Abu Mansur Isma'il (1216), the madrasa (1242/3) and tomb (1249/50) of as Salih Najm ad Din Ayyub, and the tomb of the Abbasids (about 1242). In all these buildings we find differences of style resulting from differences in material. The stone doorway of the tomb of Abu Mansur, for example, has Naskhi inscriptions and a broken frieze alternately patterned with geometrical interlacings and ara-' besques, in which the carving is of beautiful quality, resembling some of the contemporary Ayyubid woodwork.

In Syria and Palestine, particularly in Aleppo, a number of Ayyubid monuments exist, but these are not well known as only a very few have been published. Among the more important Aleppo buildings are the madrasa of al Ma'ruf (1193), the Great Mosque in the Citadel (1213/4), and the madrasa of as Sultaniya (1223). In Damascus, where Saladin resided after 1182, little Ayyubid architecture remains, although in 1184 the city had twenty colleges, two hospitals, and many monasteries. The stucco decoration of an anonymous mausoleum in Damascus shows an interesting relation to the Saljuk arabesques with "button" motives, which are seen chiefly in the monuments of Mosul and Konia.

In 1250, with the rise of the Mamluk dynasty, a new and glorious period of Muhammadan art began in Egypt and Syria. Cairo, one of the most important centers of Mamluk art, was adorned with numerous magnificent mosques, colleges, and mausoleums. The decoration of the exteriors and interiors of buildings was very rich, depending chiefly for effect on the wonderful Mamluk masonry, in which stones of different colors, reddish and white or gray and white, were often used. Other structural features which became ornamental were the stalactite niches and the joining of stonework with joggles. Marble slabs and mosaics and carved stucco and stone were used for the interior decoration of the mosques and other buildings. The ornament was carved in low relief and was mostly confined to bands and plaques, which were subordinated to the architectural scheme.

Among the early Mamluk mosques in which stone and stucco decoration played an important part was the mosque of Baibars I, built between 1266 and 1269. Part of the interior stucco decoration is still preserved and consists of grilled windows with bands of Kufic inscriptions and arabesques, some of the grilles having geometrical interlacings or arabesque scrolls arranged in two planes. Other important buildings in which rich stucco decoration may be found are the mausoleum of Kalaun (1285) and the madrasa of his son an Nasir Muhammad (1295-1303). In these buildings the Mamluk arabesque appears fully developed; its characteristic features are the surface decoration of the palmettes and connecting bands which show either a series of ribs or linear scrolls. The arabesque scrolls are frequently arranged in several planes, leading to such elaborate patterns as are seen in the niche of the mihrab in the madrasa of an Nasir. That Mamluk stone carving of the early fourteenth century was not inferior to the stuccowork is evident from magnificent marble screens in the madrasa of Salar and Sangar al Gauli (1303), which are decorated with arabesque patterns in openwork.

The most important monument of the period of Sultan Hasan is his madrasa, built between 1356 and 1362. With its magnificent portal sixty-six feet high, which has stone carvings in panels and vertical bands, it is one of the greatest masterpieces of Islamic architecture.

The Burji, or Circassian Mamluks (1382-1516), were responsible for the tomb mosques of sultans and court officials, with beautiful domes and minarets, known as the Tombs of the Caliphs, in the cemetery of Karafa. Stone sculpture was more frequently used under this dynasty than before, although stucco was not entirely abandoned. During the fifteenth century the ornament became gradually more elaborate.

A number of stone sculptures and stone vessels of the Mamluk period are preserved in Cairo mosques and in museums. They are mostly of marble and consist of prayer pulpits, fountain plaques, basins, water jars, and stands. A magnificent example of Mamluk stone carving is a marble basin in the Victoria and Albert Museum in London, decorated with bold arabesques in high relief placed on a background of dense scrollwork and inscribed with the name of Mansur Muhammad, the Ayyubid sultan of Hama, and the date A.H. 676 (1278). The Arab Museum of Cairo possesses several important fourteenth- and fifteenth-century ovoid jars and reliefs from various mosques. A fluted jar with Arabic inscriptions of Mamluk titles on the shoulder is in the Metropolitan Museum (fig. 59). Such jars were usually set into low stands with a small basin, one of which is in the Museum's collection. In many cases the basins are earlier than the jars, some of them being of the Ayyubid or even of the Fatimid period. Several fine marble reliefs are also in the

Arab Museum. An important example of Mamluk stone carving is the prayer pulpit in the mausoleum of Barkuk, which was made in 1483 in the time of Sultan Kait-Bey.

Fig. 59. *Alabaster Water Jar, Egypto-Arabic, Mamluk, XIV Century*

8. Moorish Sculpture in Spain and North Africa

With the conquest of Spain in 710 the Muhammadan civilization obtained a strong foothold in western Europe. Cordova, chosen the capital and residence of the Spanish Umayyads, became an oriental city. In 786 Abd ar Rahman began the construction of the Great Mosque, which was gradually enlarged and embellished by his successors. The most important period of Umayyad art in Spain began in the tenth century with Abd ar Rahman III (912-961), who erected a magnificent palace at Madinat az Zahra, near Cordova. The decoration of the stone reliefs of the palace consists chiefly of floral scrolls, which differ radically from contemporary Abbasid work of the Islamic East. The disintegrated acanthus of Syrian variety is mixed with geometrical palmette scrolls in which Byzantine and local Visigothic traditions are evident. We have to go back to Syrian art of the seventh and eighth centuries, known to us from stone and wood carvings (see p. 85), to find prototypes for the decoration of Madinat az Zahra. This ornament did not come directly from Syria, however, but via North Africa, where interesting parallels are found in the ninth-century sculptures of the mosque at Kairwan in Tunisia. That direct Byzantine connections existed is evident from Muhammadan sources, which tell us that Byzantine emperors helped Abd ar Rahman to decorate the palace. The Umayyad style of the tenth century is represented in several museums by marble capitals and bases, some of which belonged to the old palace. The Metropolitan Museum has the base of a column and four capitals (see ng. 60). They are derived from composite capitals, in which the acanthus leaves are transformed into thin scrolls with leaves. The ornament is often deeply undercut so as to form a pattern of light and dark, a feature very popular in Hispano-Moresque decoration.

Al Hakam (961-76) made additions to the mosque of Cordova, giving both the interior and the exterior some of their finest decoration. The beautiful marble plaques at each side of the mihrab, decorated with palmette scrolls and trees of life, are masterpieces of Hispano-Moresque sculpture. A characteristic feature of these marble reliefs is the absence of solid surfaces; all the motives are dissected into small thin scrolls which together form a lacelike pattern. Cordovan sculpture of the late tenth century is known also from two important rectangular marble ablution basins, one in the Archaeological Museum in Madrid, bearing the name of al Mansur and dated A.H. 377 (987/8), the other in the madrasa of Ben Yusuf in Marrakesh, Morocco.

In the eleventh century Muhammadan Spain was ruled by a number of petty Berber dynasties, known as Reyes de Taifas, "Party Kings." Although Cordova remained the chief art center, some of the provincial cities had a prominent part in the development of Hispano-Moresque art. An important monument of the eleventh century is the palace of Aljafería at Saragossa, erected by the ruler Abu Ja'far Muktadir (1046-81). The remains of the palace, now partly in Spanish museums, have a rich stone and stucco decoration which, although based on the tenth-century Cordovan style, shows features associated with the new style developed in Muhammadan Spain. Palmettes, used to some extent in the tenth century, have entirely replaced acanthus motives but are stylized in a fashion peculiar to Hispano-Moresque art. Derived from the Arabic half palmettes, they are often considerably curved and show a dense ribbed veining which occasionally suggests natural leaves. The carving is more deeply undercut than in the tenth century and the decorative effect of light and dark therefore more pronounced.

With the Berber Almoravides, who in 1090 combined Muhammadan Spain and Morocco into one empire, began a new chapter in Hispano-Moresque art. In the twelfth century the civilization and arts of Andalusia invaded the Maghrib, where, in such cities as Marrakesh, the capital of the empire, Fez, and Tlemcen, richly decorated monuments were erected. In the stucco decoration of the mosque in Tlemcen we find a floral ornament which must be the work of an Andalusian sculptor. In the second half of the twelfth century, the Almohades favored a comparatively simple style of

Fig. 60. *Stone Capital, Hispano-Moresque, X Century*

architecture and preferred a decoration of East Islamic arabesques to the exuberant floral scrollwork of Spain.

The political decline of Western Islam began about 1235 with the gradual reconquest of Spain by the Christians. The only great dynasty able to hold out against the Christians was that of the Nasrids of Granada, who revived the old splendor of Muhammadan Spain. The most magnificent example of fourteenth-century Moorish art in Spain is the Alhambra at Granada. Here a rich and elaborate stucco decoration covers the walls and arches of the rooms and courts. The principal ornament consists of geometrical interlacings and arabesques, of both the Spanish and the Moorish type. The intricacy of the ornament is further enhanced by the polychromy, chiefly in white, blue, red, and gold, peculiar to Hispano-Moresque art. This type of painted stucco decoration spread to other parts of Spain and is to be found in the so-called Mudejar art. It appears in the Alcázar of Seville, the Mudejar chapel of the Cordova mosque, and various buildings in Toledo. Hispano-Moresque sculpture of that period is represented in the Museum by a marble capital of the Alhambra type which is quite different from the earlier ones based on antique prototypes.

Chapter 7

WOOD CARVING

1. Umayyad and Abbasid Wood Carving (VII-X Century)

Hellenistic and Sasanian traditions continued to be followed in wood carving of the early Islamic period, and from them an entirely new style was gradually evolved. This development may be followed in numerous examples found in Egypt, particularly in Fustat and 'Ain as Sira, in the vicinity of Cairo. Hellenistic influence is still strong in the decoration of the wooden consoles in the mosque of al Aksa in Jerusalem. Here Syrian acanthus motives and vine scrolls are combined into rich patterns not unlike those found in the mosaics of the Dome of the Rock in Jerusalem (691) and the Great Mosque in Damascus (about 715). The new Islamic style, best known from the façade of the Mshatta palace (see p. 85), appears in a number of wood carvings from Egypt and Mesopotamia. Some of them, like the fine door in the Benaki collection in Athens, may be Umayyad, that is, of the first half of the eighth century, while others are of the early Abbasid era, that is, the second half of the eighth or the beginning of the ninth century.

The best-known wood carving of the early Abbasid era is the famous prayer pulpit, or mimbar, in the mosque of Kairwan in North Africa, which according to literary sources was imported from Baghdad in the early ninth century, together with lustered tiles (see p. 169), by one of the amirs of the Aghlabid dynasty. The pulpit consists of rows of panels divided into rectangular fields decorated with either geometrical interlacings or an abstract plant ornament and vine scrolls. The denaturalizing tendencies already apparent in Umayyad work, as, for instance, on the Mshatta façade, are carried further here. In one of the fields a palmette tree, derived from the oriental tree of life, ends in a pair of horns surmounted by a pine cone and a globular motive, the latter flanked by Sasanian wing palmettes stylized in Abbasid fashion. The abstract style of the Abbasid art is apparent in the rendering of the vine scrolls, which

Fig. 61. Carved Wooden Panel, Mesopotamian, Abbasid, about 800

bear highly stylized leaves and pine cones instead of bunches of grapes. Some of the pine cones preserve a natural appearance; others end in half palmettes, and their surface shows a series of leaves instead of scales. Other fields are filled with purely abstract designs composed of several superimposed motives, which appear to be the artistic forerunners of certain elements of the second and third styles of Samarra stucco decoration. The Kairwan pulpit, which probably dates from the time of Harun ar Rashid (786-809), is one of the great masterpieces of wood carving of the Baghdad school. As in the Samarra stuccoes, the decoration shows a skillful rendering of details and variation in the planes of relief.

Fig. 62. Carved Wooden Door from Samarra, Mesopotamian, Abbasid, IX Century

Several other important wood carvings of the period of Harun ar Rashid —some of them found at Takrit, north of Baghdad, some in Egypt—are in the Metropolitan Museum. The finest piece is a long panel (fig. 61) from Takrit, probably part of a pulpit, decorated with vine scrolls, which, with their circular offshoots and attached motives, form a highly decorative pattern. The unnaturalistic style is apparent in the treatment of the vine scrolls in the two rectangles and squares. Here vine leaves are replaced by palmettes derived from Sasanian art, and, as in the Mshatta façade and the Kairwan pulpit, numerous pine cones grow out from vine branches. The pine cone became popular in the Umayyad period and continued to play a prominent role in early Islamic ornament. We find it in mosaics at Jerusalem, the reliefs of Mshatta and Kasr at Tuba, the Kairwan pulpit, and the ninth-century stuccoes of Samarra.

Another Takrit panel in the Museum's collection has a dense pattern of vine scrolls with compartments formed by interlaced bands describing a large central circle and several smaller ones. The vine leaves are mostly trefoil with a schematic rendering of the veins. A third panel from Takrit is divided into three rectangular compartments. In the central one are highly stylized wing motives with wavy ribbons, a survival of the Sasanian era; in the two narrower ones are niches containing vines. Related to the latter is a larger panel in the Arab Museum in Cairo, found in the cemetery of 'Ain as Sira, which should also be assigned to the Baghdad school.

In the chapter on stone and stucco sculpture (p. 89), it was stated that at the end of the eighth century Muhammadan artists developed a new style of ornament suited to a new method of carving— the slant, or beveled, method—which most probably originated in wood. This Abbasid style is represented in the Metropolitan Museum by a complete door (fig. 62) and two panels which may have been used for doorjambs or ceiling decoration. Found in Takrit, they undoubtedly came from near-by Samarra and are the largest and most complete examples of wood carvings from that site. The ornament of the doors has the traditional division into rectangular and square panels within a plain framework. The combination of arabesquelike scrolls with various superimposed "vase" motives in purely abstract compositions is quite apparent in both doors and panels. The Abbasid style of decoration was also introduced into Egypt where in the Tulunid period (868-904) it became very popular. The Arab Museum in Cairo possesses a rich collection of Tulunid wood carvings, which consists of parts of doors, ceilings, decorative friezes, and furniture, often painted in vivid colors. Several good examples are also in the Metropolitan Museum.

In the early tenth century the Abbasid technique was modified to some extent by Egyptian craftsmen. The motives were more deeply undercut, and there was a tendency toward roundness. This local style is represented in the Museum's collection by two pieces.

2. Fatimid Wood Carving in Egypt and Syria (X-XII Century)

The new tendencies which changed the style of stone and stucco sculpture decoration also influenced the development of wood carving under the Fatimids. Traditional Tulunid ornament and slant carving survived longer, however, in wood carving, as may be seen on the wooden tie beams of the mosque of al Hakim and the door from the mosque of al Azhar (970) now in the Arab Museum in Cairo. According to the inscription this door was made at the order of al Hakim, who restored the mosque of al Azhar in 1010. It is decorated with rectangular panels carved with Abbasid arabesque scrolls forming symmetrical patterns. In the rendering of tradi-

111

tional patterns, the Fatimid artist followed the artistic principles apparent in the stucco ornament of the mosque of al Azhar. In al Hakim's door, however, the connecting stems of the ornament are given greater prominence than heretofore and the motives are separated from each other.

In al Hakim's time traditional Tulunid designs and methods of wood carving had begun to be replaced by the true Fatimid style, which is best illustrated in the Metropolitan Museum's collection by a splendid rectangular door panel (fig. 63). The deeply undercut ornament shows a highly decorative combination of horses' heads and arabesque scrolls bearing half and full pal-

Fig. 63. Carved Wooden Door Panel, Egypto-Arabic, Fatimid, XI Century

mettes. Another feature of this panel, and of related ones in the Arab Museum, is the fine rendering of details in the palmettes, the beaded bands, and the horses' bridles. One of the best examples of early Fatimid wood carving in existence is the wooden iconostasis, or partition, from the church of Sitt Barbara in Old Cairo, exhibited in the Coptic Museum. Although it is undoubtedly the work of Coptic artists, the rectangular panels with which it is decorated show all the richness and variety of ornament characteristic of Fatimid art. The panels of the partition are decorated with arabesque scrolls, some of which issue from bases and combine with birds, animals, and figure subjects. We find here magnificently carved hunting scenes, court scenes, and symmetrical compositions of single birds and animals or groups of animals. The figures and scrolls form a complete decorative unit, which is typical of Fatimid ornament. Although partly influenced by Coptic tradition, the Fatimid animal decoration of the partition is rendered in a style based on the tendencies current in other provinces of the Islamic world.

The popularity of animal decoration and figure subjects in Fatimid wood carving continued throughout the eleventh century. The most remarkable examples are the numerous richly carved boards and doors discovered in the hospital (maristan) and tomb mosque of Kalaun and his son an Nasir Muhammad. Originally they formed part of the decoration of the Western Palace of the Fatimids, begun by the caliph al 'Aziz (975-96) and completed by the caliph Mustansir between 1058 and 1065. This palace, which was partly destroyed by Saladin, stood on the site of the Kalaun buildings mentioned above. Some of the Fatimid panels were recarved on the reverse by Mamluk artists and used as a wall frieze in the hospital of Kalaun. They are decorated with figure subjects—hunters, dancers, revelers, musicians, merchants with camels, animals, and birds—within compartments formed by interlacings and placed on a background of floral scrolls carved in a lower relief than the figures. The genre scenes give us an interesting insight into the life and customs of the Fatimid period. The carving is less formal and elaborate than that of earlier Fatimid wood carvings, and a certain realism, due perhaps to Coptic influence, is apparent in the rendering of figures and animals. Fine details are lacking, as the panels were originally painted. Several panels with animal decoration in the Metropolitan Museum, one illustrated in figure 64, for example, may be assigned to the second half of the eleventh century.

The Fatimid style of wood carving continued in the twelfth century, the technique becoming more elaborate and full of detail. The finest work of the twelfth century is exemplified by a mihrab from the mosque of Sayyida Nafisa made between 1138 and 1145. The decoration of the niche, which is now in the Arab Museum, consists of beautiful arabesques and vine scrolls interlacing with geo-

Fig. 64. Carved Wooden Panel (Detail), Egypto-Arabic, Fatimid, XI Century

metrical bands forming polygons. The rectangular framework is divided by geometrical bands into various compartments enclosing panels carved with arabesques and vine scrolls. This new method of decorating larger surfaces gradually became more popular in Islamic wood carving, reaching its height in the Mamluk period. The decoration does not form a continuous pattern but is split into small units such as hexagons and stars, each containing a separate design. An elaborate example is the beautifully carved mihrab from the mosque of Sayyida Rukayya made between 1154 and 1160. The whole front of this mihrab, which is also in the Arab Museum, has a polygonal pattern with arabesque scrolls. The sides and back are richly carved with interesting arabesque patterns and vine scrolls issuing from vases. Although the arabesque remains the chief orna ment of Fatimid decoration, vine leaves and grapes appear occa sionally among the palmettes, as on the mimbar in the Amri mosque at Kus dated A.H. 550 (1155/6).

The animal decoration so popular in eleventh-century wood carv ings continued to be used in the twelfth century. But the work manship became less careful, the animals and birds being often treated as silhouettes, with little surface detail. Several such panels are in the Metropolitan Museum. One of the best examples of the twelfth-century style is the partition screen of the church of Abu as Saifain at Cairo, which may be dated between 1094 and 1121. It is decorated with rectangular panels containing figures of animals and of saints and arabesques with crosses.

Syrian wood carvers of the Fatimid era were not behind those of Egypt in craftsmanship and ability in design. Several important monuments have survived in Syria and Palestine, among them the intact pulpit in the Great Mosque at Hebron in Palestine, made for the mosque of al Husain at Ascalon in 1091/2 and magnificently carved with intricate arabesques. There are a number of fine Syrian wood carvings in Damascus, including the maksura screen from the mosque of Bab al Musalla (1103), which is now in the Arab Mu seum there.

3. Ayyubid and Mamluk Wood Carving in Syria and Egypt (XII-XV Century)

In the wood carving of the Ayyubid period, which began in 1168, Fatimid traditions continued but the arabesques became even more

Fig. 65. Carved Wooden Panel, Egypto-Arabic, Mamluk, XIII-XIV Century

elaborate and Naskhi replaced Kufic in the inscriptions. A magnificent example of Ayyubid wood carving is the cenotaph of Princess al Adeliya in the mausoleum of the imam ash Shafi'i (1211/2). There are a number of fine examples in the Arab Museum in Cairo, including fragments of a cenotaph from the tomb of the imam ash Shafi'i, dated A.H. 574 (1178), and four sides of a cenotaph from a tomb of the amir Thalab, dated A.H. 613 (1216), of which one side is in the Victoria and Albert Museum, London. In some of the early Ayyubid wood carvings, particularly those from Syria, we notice the influence of Saljuk ornament. This is exemplified in the Metropolitan Museum by a rectangular door panel from Damascus.

In the second half of the thirteenth century, under the Mamluks, carving became even more elaborate than in the Ayyubid period. The Mamluk artists created new varieties of palmettes and combinations of arabesques in which richness of fine detail played an important role. Geometrical patterns composed of small panels now became exceedingly popular, usually consisting of hexagons arranged around central stars, all carved with arabesques forming intricate patterns (see fig. 65). Woods of different colors, including ebony, were frequently used, and sometimes ivory and bone were added. Complete Mamluk mimbars of the thirteenth, fourteenth, and fifteenth centuries may still be seen in Cairo mosques—

for instance in those of as Salih Talaye and Ibn Tulun. Panels from the pulpit of the latter mosque, erected in 1296 by Sultan Lagin, are now in the Victoria and Albert Museum, which also possesses other fine specimens of Mamluk wood carving, including a number of panels from a pulpit in the mosque of al Maridani. The arabesques of these panels are carved in two planes, like those in the Lagin pulpit, but are more delicate in workmanship. In the same collection are panels which probably come from a pulpit in the mosque of Kusun, built about 1347.

The art of carving began to deteriorate in the fifteenth century. Some good wood carving was done, but even the best work was inferior to that of the earlier period. A complete pulpit from the mosque of Kait-Bey (1468-1496) in Cairo is in the Victoria and Albert Museum in London. A type of woodwork popular in Egypt, probably from Coptic times, was turned latticework, or mushra-biyya, which reached perfection in the fourteenth and fifteenth centuries. Screens of latticework were used to separate the sanctuary from the rest of the mosque and, even more extensively, in the windows of private houses to ensure privacy for the women of the harems. They were often provided with projecting niches to hold porous water jars to cool the drinking water. By varying the arrangement of the turned balls and connecting links, the makers of latticework were enabled to produce a great variety of designs. Examples dating from the eighteenth and nineteenth centuries may still be seen in houses in Cairo and in various museums, including the Victoria and Albert Museum in London and the Metropolitan Museum.

4. Early Islamic Wood Carving in Iran and Turkestan (X-XI Century)

Islamic wood carving which antedates the Saljuk invasion is known to us from very few examples. Several Iranian wooden panels with tenth-century Kufic inscriptions are in museums and private collections. Interesting tenth- and eleventh-century examples from western Turkestan are preserved in the museums of Tashkent and Samarkand. Others are still in situ, as for instance a number of columns in the Juma mosque at Khiva. In the earliest of these wood carvings we find an ornament and method of carving not unlike that of the early Fatimid period in Egypt.

Of importance in the history of Islamic wood carving is the door from the tomb of Mahmud of Ghazna (998-1030), now in the Agra Museum. The door consists of four vertical panels separated by pilasters and decorated with seven rows of applied stars, all richly carved with geometrical arabesque scrolls. The scrolls are usually of the two-striped variety and interlace with each other or with beaded bands as in some Fatimid wood carvings (see fig. 63). The deep undercutting of the ornament is arranged in several planes, a feature which seems to be of Iranian origin. A relation between this door and Fatimid wood carving is evident from the rows of square panels on the back. Here we find an arabesque ornament combining the traditional Abbasid motives with new artistic tendencies known from the al Hakim wood carvings. Historical and artistic evidence seems to support the opinion that these innovations were introduced from Central Asia and Iran, becoming gradually stronger as a result of the migration of Turks and their conquest of the Muhammadan East.

5. Saljuk Wood Carving in Iran and Asia Minor (XI-XIII Century)

Not many Saljuk wood carvings are known to have survived in Iran, but there may be some still hidden in unknown mosques. The Metropolitan Museum is fortunate in possessing two pieces from a twelfth-century pulpit. One is a large panel which has Kufic inscriptions in several rows in the niche and an arabesque design typical of Saljuk art in the spandrels. The other piece is part of the framework of the pulpit, showing an openwork decoration of hexagonal panels with a palmette design which appears on several contemporary Iranian tombstones. The inscription is of great interest, as it gives the name of the donor and the name of the ruling prince, 'Ala ad Dawla Abu Kalijar Garshasp of Yazd, who was in the service of the Saljuks. The date is also given, A.H. 546 (1151).

The wood carving produced in Asia Minor during the twelfth and thirteenth centuries was of unusually high quality and in beauty of design equaled the finest work of Egypt and Syria. A number of doors, pulpits, sarcophagi, and Koran stands, richly decorated with geometrical patterns and arabesques, have been preserved in museums in Konia and Istanbul. The arabesques in these Saljuk wood carvings have peculiar characteristics which reveal their Asia Minor origin. One of the finest and also the earliest of the objects is the magnificent pulpit dated A.H. 550 (1155) in the mosque of 'Ala ad Din in Konia; it is decorated with arabesques whose circular leaves and palmettes end in "button" motives which can be traced back to the eighth-century wood carvings of the Turkish Uighurs in Central Asia. Such leaves and palmettes are especially prominent in a thirteenth-century Koran stand dated A.H. 678 (1279/80) in the museum at Konia and in another one in the Chinili Kiosk at Istanbul. Of great beauty are three doors in the museum in Istanbul, decorated not only with the usual arabesques but also with stylized lions, griffins, peacocks, and human figures which recall the contemporary ornament of Mosul and Baghdad. Other examples of thirteenth-century Saljuk wood carvings are the sarcophagi in the tomb of Sayyid Mahmud Hairani at Akshehir and several doors in museums at Istanbul and in the Islamic collection of the Berlin Museum, all richly decorated with inscriptions and arabesques.

6. Mongol and Timurid Wood Carving in Iran and Turkestan (XIV-XV Century)

Wood carvings of the early Mongol period, that is, of the second half of the thirteenth century and the beginning of the fourteenth, are relatively rare. In the sanctuary of the mosque of Bayazid at Bistam are fine doors of about 1307-1309, carved with arabesques, Kufic inscriptions, and geometrical interlacings similar to those in contemporary Iranian stone and stucco decoration. Next in date is the pulpit dated A.H. 711 (1311) in the mosque of Nayin, with rectangular panels decorated with geometrical scrolls bearing circular leaves. The carving is somewhat mechanical and the ornament, derived from Saljuk prototypes, is inferior.

In the second half of the fourteenth century the Iranian school of wood carving, particularly in western Turkestan, reached a high artistic and technical level. The Metropolitan Museum possesses a richly carved Koran stand (fig. 66), which is generally regarded as a masterpiece of Iranian wood carving of the Mongol period. The elaborate decoration consists of arabesques, inscriptions, floral

*Fig. 66. Carved Wooden Koran Stand with the
Date 1360, Iranian, Mongol*

scrolls, and seminaturalistic plants bearing blossoms and palmettes
derived from Chinese art. The inscriptions give, besides the names
of the Twelve Imams, the name of the artist, Hasan ibn Sulaiman

119

Fig. 67. Carved Wooden Door from Kokand, Western Turkestan, XV Century

of Isfahan, and the date A.H. Dhu'l Hijja 761 (October-November, 1360). The origin of the carver indicates that the stand may have been made in Iran proper, but stylistic similarities to late fourteenth-century woodwork of western Turkestan make this region the more likely place of origin. The carver has introduced all the elements of Mongol decoration, placing them effectively in compartments and niches, sometimes using openwork and sometimes superimposing two or three different patterns one over the other.

To the period of Timur are attributed several doors of Turkestan workmanship. Two of them are in the mosque of Khoja Adhad Yasawi in the city of Turkestan. The main one is dated A.H. 799 (1397), the inner one A.H. 797 (1394/5). The rich arabesque and floral decoration of the central panels of the latter door recall that of our Koran stand of 1360. Common to both is the elaborate carving of ornament, showing several planes of relief. Others are the doors of the tomb of Gur-i-Mir at Samarkand (about 1405), now in the Hermitage, and the door of the mosque of Shah Zinda in Samarkand.

Under the Timurids wood carving followed the traditions of the Mongol period. Dating from the early fifteenth century is a door in the theological seminary of Ulugh Beg (1417) in Samarkand. Of the second half of the fifteenth century is a pair of doors in the Metropolitan Museum. They are composed of squares divided into small compartments simulating separate panels. The decoration consists of geometrical scrolls, arabesques, and delicate leaf ornament of the type frequently seen in Timurid illumination. The carving is in low relief and much less elaborate than that of western Turkestan. The four panels with inscriptions give us the name of the donor, Dawud ibn 'Ali, the name of the maker, Muhammad ibn Husain, and the date 20 Ramadan 870 (May 7, 1466). Similar in style of decoration is a cenotaph in the Rhode Island School of Design in Providence, made, according to Wiet, at the order of Prince Gustahm in Ramadan 877 (February, 1473), probably in the province of Mazandaran. The style of wood carving as practiced in western Turkestan is exemplified in our collection by a magnificent door which comes from Kokand (fig. 67). The central panel is carved in high relief with a beautiful pattern of arabesques interlaced with floral scrolls bearing large palmettes and bordered by delicate floral scrolls and arabesques in low relief. The door was originally painted, as was usual in western Turkestan. Traces of colors are still apparent: the background was blue, the pattern done in red, green, brown, and gold. Comparison with works of the fifteenth century, for example, the window frames and doors of the tomb of Timur at Samarkand, permits us to assign the door to the end of the fifteenth century. It anticipates many of the features of sixteenth-century Safavid ornament.

7. Safavid Wood Carving in Iran (XVI-XVIII Century)

Safavid wood carving of the sixteenth century is known to us mostly from doors preserved in mosques in Iran and western Turkestan and in various museums, such as the Gulistan Museum in Teheran and the Islamic collection in the Berlin Museum. The decoration consists either of arabesques or of floral patterns, sometimes combined with animals. Fine specimens of Safavid work are a pair of doors in Teheran made by 'Ali ibn Sufi in 1509 and a door in Berlin made by Habib Allah in 1590.

In the seventeenth and eighteenth centuries the art of wood carving declined, the doors of this period being often painted and

*Fig. 68. Lacquered Doors from the Chihil Sutun at
Isfahan, Iranian, XVII Century*

lacquered instead of carved. A pair of such doors in the Metropolitan Museum (fig. 68) and another in the Victoria and Albert Museum in London come from the palace of Chihil Sutun at Isfahan

and may be assigned to the first half of the seventeenth century. They are decorated with garden scenes bordered by floral scrolls.

8. Moorish Wood Carving in Spain and North Africa

Early Hispano-Moresque wood carving is very little known today, as most of it, including such noted examples as the sanctuary screen and pulpit of al Hakam in the Cordova mosque, has disappeared entirely. But several important eleventh- and twelfth-century pulpits have been preserved in North Africa. The earliest mimbar is in the Great Mosque of Algiers, built by the Almoravides in 1082. Its decoration consists of square panels carved with geometrical interlacings, palmette trees, and arabesque scrolls in the Hispano-Moresque style introduced into North Africa by artists from Andalusia. Typical Hispano-Moresque arabesque decoration in wood is still preserved in the screen and the ceiling of the mosque of Tlemcen, which is carved with a rich floral arabesque known from contemporary stuccowork. The twelfth-century pulpit of the mosque at Karawiyin is another example of Almoravid wood carving.

Hispano-Moresque wood carving of the Almohad period is known from two magnificent pulpits, one in the mosque of Kutubiya in Marrakesh, Morocco, made between 1150 and 1160, the other in the mosque of the Kasba. The sides of these mimbars have polygonal interlacings with inserted panels forming a geometrical pattern adapted to the structure of the furniture. The panels contain rich floral arabesque scrolls carved with great precision and fine detail, recalling some of the Hispano-Moresque ivory carvings of the tenth and eleventh centuries. The pulpit is further enhanced by the use of marquetry in bone and precious wood. The mihrab of the Kasba mosque is particularly rich in marquetry mosaics, which form geometrical patterns based on early Egypto-Arabic prototypes.

Hispano-Moresque wood carvings of later periods, particularly the fourteenth century, either follow earlier Moorish prototypes or are decorated in the Mamluk style of Egypt. To the former group belongs the mimbar in the mosque of Bu Ainaniya at Fez, to the latter the doors in the Hall of the Sisters in the Alhambra at Granada and the doors in the Alcázar at Seville.

$C\!\!\!\!\int ap\mathit{ter}$ 8

IVORY AND BONE CARVING

1. Umayyad and Abbasid Ivory and Bone Carving (VII-X Century)

Early Islamic bone carvings have been found at various sites in Egypt, among them Fustat. As in wood carvings, Coptic traditions are evident in many of these bone carvings, particularly those with a vine decoration. Until recently all plaques with vine scrolls were indiscriminately attributed to the pre-Islamic era. That some of them date from the early Islamic period, however, is evident, not only from the low relief of the design, but also from the schematic rendering of the leaves. They may be regarded as the work of Copts, who continued to be employed as skilled craftsmen under Islamic rule. A round Copto-Arabic plaque with vine decoration and eight triangular plaques are used as inlays in a panel from a wooden coffin decorated with marquetry mosaics (fig. 69) in the Metropolitan Museum. It may be assigned to the second half of the eighth century, that is, to the early Abbasid period. Under the Tulunids the style of bone carvings followed that of wood carvings, as may be seen in a fragment from Fustat now in the Arab Museum in Cairo.

2. Fatimid Ivory and Bone Carving in Egypt (X-XII Century)

A number of bone plaques of various shapes, decorated with figure subjects, have been found in Fustat. The scenes and the style of carving recall the eleventh-century Fatimid wood carvings from the hospital of Kalaun (see p. 113). A fragmentary plaque in the Metropolitan Museum (fig. 70) depicts a hunter and a gazelle against a background of arabesque scrolls.

Because of similarities to Fatimid wood carvings, a number of ivory plaques from boxes have been rightly regarded as Fatimid. Six of them are in the Bargello Museum in Florence, two are in the Louvre, and others were formerly in the Figdor collection in

Fig. 69. Panel with Marquetry Decoration, Egypto-Arabic, VIII Century

Vienna. The figures of musicians, dancers, hunters, and griffins, amid fine scrolls, are elaborately carved in openwork, with a great deal of detail, particularly in the costumes. These plaques, which represent the height of Fatimid ivory carving, may be assigned to the period of the caliph Mustansir (1036-1094).

3. Ayyubid and Mamluk Ivory and Bone Carving in Egypt (XIII-XIV Century)

In the Ayyubid and Mamluk periods Fatimid traditions in ivory and bone carving continued to be followed, but the ornament consists entirely of arabesques and geometrical patterns. In the thirteenth, fourteenth, and fifteenth centuries bone plaques were used in combination with wood for the decoration of doors and pulpits. Specimens of Mamluk ivories are in most of the large museums in Europe as well as in Cairo. In addition to many single panels, the Metropolitan Museum possesses a complete and very fine pair of doors (fig. 71), probably from a pulpit, which may be assigned to the late thirteenth or early fourteenth century. The ivory plaques of this door are elaborately carved in two planes of relief in an intricate arabesque pattern typical of the Mamluk style.

4. Moorish Ivory Carving in Spain

Under the Umayyad rulers of Spain, ivory boxes, both round and rectangular, became exceedingly popular, and a great number were dated and inscribed with the names of sultans or court officials. The earliest ones, which date from the tenth century, when the Umayyad style of ivory carving had become fully developed, are inscribed with the name of 'Abd ar Rahman III (912-961) and are in the Victoria and Albert Museum. An important tenth-century box from the cathedral of Zamora is now in the National Museum in Madrid. It is dated A.H. 353 (964) and bears the name of Caliph al Hakam II. Two rectangular boxes in Spanish collections, both dated A.H. 355 (966), were made at Madinat az Zahra, near Cordova, famous for its palace (see p. 104). The main decoration of these boxes consists of palmette scrolls into which are occasionally

introduced animals and birds. The exuberant palmettes, with finely carved veins, give the illusion of naturalism which is characteristic of Hispano-Moresque art. Two round boxes, one, dated A.H. 357 (968), in the Louvre, the other, dated A.H. 359 (970), in the Victoria and Albert Museum, are of great interest because of the fact that their decoration, consisting of court scenes with entertainers and hunters, is derived from the contemporary Islamic art of Egypt and Mesopotamia. In the eleventh century the Umayyad style became even more elaborate, the palmette scrolls more formal, and the compositions frequently overcrowded. Famous eleventh-century pieces include a jewel casket in the cathedral of Pamplona dated A.H. 395 (1004/5), a box at Burgos dated A.H. 417 (1026), and a box in

Fig. 71. Door with Ivory Panels (Detail), Egypto-Arabic,
Mamluk, XIII-XIV Century

Madrid dated A.H. 441 (1049) and made at Cuenca, another great
center of ivory carving.

In the Metropolitan Museum's collection there are two interesting ivories, one a round box (fig. 72) with palmette scrolls and birds, dating from the end of the tenth century, the other a panel from a rectangular eleventh-century box elaborately carved with a dense pattern of scrolls and lobed compartments containing groups of birds, animals, and dancers.

5. Ivory Oliphants and Caskets from Southern Italy

Fig. 72. *Ivory Box, Hispano-Moresque, End of the X Century*

Carved ivory oliphants and oblong caskets constitute a class of ivories that have been variously described as Fatimid, Mesopotamian, Hispano-Moresque, Sicilian, and South Italian. In the Museum there are six pieces of this class. Four of them are oliphants decorated with birds and animals, often in combat, placed in circular compartments formed by interlaced scrolls. The other two, a writing case and a casket (fig. 73), are in the same style but also show hunting scenes and pairs of bearded figures in oriental costume. These ivories may be divided into two groups: one attributed to southern Italy, which, like Sicily, was under Muhammadan influence in the time of the Norman kings; the other, with strongly pronounced oriental features, assigned by some to Fatimid Egypt. Although related to Hispano-Moresque as well as to Fatimid ivories, both groups show features which point to southern Italy as the place of manufacture. The fact that Christian subjects are included in the decoration of a few of the oliphants, for example, the oliphant in the Cluny Museum in Paris, strengthens the theory of a South Italian origin.

6. Sicilian Ivories with Painted Decoration

Preserved in various European and American collections are a number of ivory caskets and boxes with painted decoration which is

Islamic in style but includes many Western features. The motives consist of arabesques, human figures, animals, and birds in yellow or brown, with dark brown outlines and touches of red, blue, and gold. Among the finest pieces are the rectangular box in the Institute of Valencia de Don Juan, Madrid, and the caskets in the Würzburg cathedral and in the Islamic collection of the Berlin Museum. The Metropolitan Museum has two round boxes—the larger decorated with Westernized arabesques, floral scrolls, and lions (fig. 74); the smaller with a dragon, a centaur, and lions amid scrollwork.

For some time these ivories were attributed to Syria or Mesopotamia, but a Near Eastern origin must be entirely rejected because of the naturalistic Western forms in the decoration. Kühnel has advanced excellent reasons for attributing the group to Sicily, where the ornament and figure subjects of the wall paintings of the Cappella Palatina in Palermo, executed in the middle of the twelfth century, furnish direct parallels. Most of the ivories may also be assigned to the second half of the twelfth century. The smaller box in the Museum's collection, in which Western influence is especially strong, probably dates from the thirteenth century.

Fig. 73. Ivory Casket, South Italian, XI-XII Century

7. Intarsia and Marquetry

An art which is associated with the Near East is the decoration of furniture, chests, boxes, and other objects with geometrical patterns composed of many pieces of wood, ivory or bone, and mother-of-pearl. This art is of ancient oriental origin and was adopted by the Greeks and Romans. Two methods were known in antiquity, intarsia and marquetry. In the former, pieces of bone and wood were inserted into a wooden surface; in the latter, a more elaborate and tedious process, small tesserae were assembled into geometrical patterns and glued to a wooden base. As in the case of many other arts and crafts, the Muhammadan artists of Egypt inherited these methods from the Copts. Several panels with wood and bone mosaic work, probably from a wooden coffin, were found in 'Ain as Sira, near Cairo, and other sites of the early Islamic era. Most of them are in the Arab Museum in Cairo; others are in Berlin. One of the finest panels of this type is in the Metropolitan Museum's collection (fig. 69). The pattern is divided into three sections. The middle one shows a large square with a central medallion of carved bone (see p. 124). On each side is a series of five niches, separated by columns with pomegranate capitals surmounted by pairs of wing palmettes enclosing a simplified pomegranate. The pomegranate motives and winged palmettes are survivals from Sasanian art which are frequently found in early Islamic ornament. The niches and all the intervening spaces of the panel are filled with minute tesserae of ebony, rosewood, and bone, arranged in elaborate patterns—lozenge diapers, checkerboards, squares with stars, and other geometrical designs resembling mosaics in stone or glass.

Fig. 74. Ivory Box, Sicilian, XII Century

Intarsia and marquetry were popular in the eastern and western Islamic world in all periods. During the thirteenth and fourteenth centuries, under the Mamluks of Egypt and Syria, these methods of decoration became highly developed, being applied to doors, boxes, and tables. One of the finest examples is the fourteenth-century table (kursi) in marquetry from the mosque of Sultan Sha'ban II (1369) now in the Arab Museum in Cairo.

Not many early examples of intarsia and marquetry from Turkey, Iran, and Syria are known. An important Turkish box with wood and ivory mosaics, in the collection of Baron Edmond de Rothschild, was made for Sultan Bayazid II in 1483. Of Iranian and Indian origin only late examples of marquetry are known, that is, pieces of the eighteenth and nineteenth centuries. In Damascus, which also became a well-known center of inlay work at this period, bone was combined with or replaced by mother-of-pearl. In Spain and Sicily the arts of intarsia and marquetry were also practiced. One of the finest examples preserved is a thirteenth-century wooden box in the Cappella Palatina in Palermo, which has a rich decoration of ivory inlay.

Chapter 9

METALWORK

1. Early Islamic Metalwork of Iran (VII-IX Century)

The continuation of the Sasanian style of decoration is strongly apparent in early Islamic metalwork, particularly in silver vessels, some of which are often wrongly assigned to the Sasanian era. To the early Islamic period belong several silver dishes with hunting scenes and other purely Sasanian figure subjects. Some of them bear the names of their owners in Pahlavi, which permits an accurate dating. A dish in the Hermitage was made, according to Herzfeld, to the order of Sharwin of the Masmughan dynasty of Demavend, which ended in 758/9. Another well-known post-Sasanian dish in the Hermitage, once the property of the Sasanian prince Datburz-mihr, who ruled from 728 to 738 in Tabaristan (the province of Mazandaran), has a representation of a goddess, probably Anahit, seated on the back of a griffin and playing a flute. The relief is flat and the animal is strongly stylized, a feature seen so often in early Islamic metalwork. Two post-Sasanian silver dishes in the Hermitage, illustrating the well-known legend of Bahram Gur and Azada, also bear Pahlavi inscriptions with the names of their owners, Mihrbojet and Perozan. The decoration of these two dishes is rendered in a conventional style in low relief with the heavy outlines characteristic of a number of post-Sasanian silver vessels.

Silver vessels with representations of animals and birds form an important group of Sasanian and post-Sasanian metalwork. Among the most popular animals of Sasanian art was the fantastic winged monster, *senmurv* or hippocampus, part bird, part lion and dog. A silver dish in the British Museum decorated with a *senmurv* is generally assigned to the eighth or ninth century. As in so many post-Sasanian silver vessels, the engraving plays a much more important role than the relief. This dish shows artistic values which were newly created in the Islamic era.

Other post-Sasanian silver dishes are even later in date. One of the most interesting pieces is a dish in the Hermitage showing the ancient oriental scene of combat between a lion and a deer. The stylization of the bodies, the schematic rendering of the muscles of the face and mane, and the strong emphasis on the contours indicate that this dish is not only post-Sasanian but as late as the tenth century. The style is definitely Islamic and may be regarded as a forerunner of the Saljuk style. The plant ornament filling out the intervening spaces of the composition, although based on Sasanian prototypes, has many features, such as circular leaves and heart-shaped full palmettes, which indicate that this dish and related pieces were most probably products of Central Asia.

Two post-Sasanian silver jugs in the Hermitage, decorated with birds and griffins within interlaced medallions, are definitely of the Islamic era, since they bear Kufic inscriptions which could not be much later than the tenth century. They might be examples of the little-known metalwork of the Samanids, who ruled in Khurasan and Transoxiana. Both pieces give us a clue to the dating of some other silver vessels, for instance, the octagonal tray in Berlin decorated with monsters within compartments of angular interlacings.

Early Islamic bronzes consist of trays, ewers, and aquaemanalae in the shape of animals and birds. In some of the trays the Sasanian tradition is so strong that the pieces are frequently assigned to the pre-Islamic era. An example is a plate in Berlin, which has in the center an engraved representation of a building, probably the Takht-i-Takdis, the throne of Khusrau. Around it is an arcade with horseshoe arches, containing vine and palmette scrolls, some of which are combined with pairs of Sasanian wings. The character of the ornament shows many similarities to that of works of the eighth and early ninth centuries, for instance, the wooden mimbar of Kairwan, which may be dated to the period of the Abbasid caliph Harun ar Rashid (786-809).

Post-Sasanian bronze ewers are sometimes plain and sometimes decorated with ornament engraved or in relief. Most of them are of the well-known Sasanian type; others show new forms developed by Iranian metalworkers of the eighth century. One type has a globular body and a long tubular neck, with a spout in the shape of birds. About six ewers of this type are known, one in the Metropolitan Museum (fig. 75), three in the Hermitage, one in the Harari collection, and one in the Arab Museum, Cairo. The latter, which

Fig. 75. *Bronze Ewer, Iranian, Umayyad, VIII Century*

is particularly fine, was found in Egypt near the tomb of the last
Umayyad caliph, Marwan II (744-49). The richly engraved decoration of animal groups in arcades and the relief decoration of palmette
scrolls are in the Islamic style which developed in the eighth cen-

tury. The crowing rooster of the spout is skillfully modeled in the best tradition of Sasanian art.

A companion piece to the Cairo ewer, but without its elaborate surface engraving, is now in the Metropolitan Museum (fig. 75). The upper part of the neck has a decoration of palmette trees in openwork; on the handle is a floral scroll and beneath it a device of Sasanian motives of pomegranates and half palmettes, in relief.

Of great importance is a small group of early Islamic bronze ewers from Iran in which the decoration, engraved and in relief, is enhanced by inlay of red copper. Most of these ewers are in the Hermitage; one, with a decoration of pomegranate trees and palmettes in low relief sparingly inlaid with copper, is in the Walters Gallery in Baltimore. This group, which can be dated in the eighth century, represents the work of the earliest Islamic school of inlay technique, which was probably situated in eastern Iran.

2. Saljuk Metalwork of Iran (XI-XIII Century)

With the arrival of Saljuks in eastern Iran in 1037 began a brilliant era of Islamic metalwork. The vessels of bronze, gold, and silver reveal new ornament and schemes of decoration developed by artists of the Saljuk period. The majority of Saljuk silver vessels, which date from the eleventh to the thirteenth century, are in Russian collections and were published in 1909 by Smirnow. Most of them were found in Central Asia or the Caucasus. The group consists of bowls, vases, and bottles, with figure subjects, birds, animals, arabesques, interlacings, and Kufic inscriptions on a background of fine scrollwork. The ornament is usually engraved, sometimes in relief, and occasionally enriched with niello inlay, like a bowl in Berlin decorated with a central medallion framing the figure of a musician.

Fig. 76. Gold Earring, Iranian, Saljuk, XI Century

Enamelwork also was known to the Saljuks. The most magnifi-

cent example of Muhammadan enamelwork in existence is a bronze
plate in the Innsbruck Museum decorated in polychrome enamel
with figure subjects, birds, and animals within medallions separated
by palm trees and dancers. The inscription contains the name of the
Ortukid sultan Rukn ad Dawla Dawud (1108-45), who ruled in
Kaifa and Amida in northern Mesopotamia.

*Fig. 77. Gold Pendant, Iranian,
Saljuk, XII Century*

Gold jewelry of the period of the
Saljuks was also of high standard,
although not many pieces have
been preserved. The majority of
those in existence come from Iran.
From time to time forgeries appear
on the market, but these can be
easily recognized. Most of the Saljuk jewelry consists of earrings and
pendants, some of them in the
shape of animals and birds. The
Metropolitan Museum has several
examples of Saljuk gold jewelry. A crescent-shaped earring (fig. 76)
has an openwork decoration of birds separated by a palmette tree.
It is similar in style to a gold pendant or buckle with openwork
decoration in Berlin, which together with the Museum's piece
should be assigned to the first half of the eleventh century. Of
the twelfth or thirteenth century are an earring in the shape of a
bird in rich filigree and a pendant in the form of a lion (fig. 77).
The fur and the details of the face of this strongly stylized lion are
in filigree of braided gold wire. The pendant was further enhanced
by stone inlay, as is indicated by two cavities. It has openwork motives, among them a rosette of seven circles of the type seen in
Saljuk bronzes of the twelfth to thirteenth century (see page 141)
made in Iran.

A. BRONZES WITH RELIEF DECORATION AND ENGRAVING

The art of casting bronze objects with relief decoration, such as
mirrors, plaques, and animal figures, was practiced under the Saljuks in both Iran and Mesopotamia. Typical examples are small
mirrors (see fig. 78) with addorsed sphinxes and Kufic inscriptions
which date from about the twelfth century and are most probably
of Iranian origin.

Two dated mirrors, one of the year A.H. 548 (1153), the other of A.H. 675 (1276), are in the Harari collection in Cairo. They are decorated with signs of the zodiac and a frieze of running animals, which likewise appear on mirrors in the Louvre and the Metropolitan Museum. There are also Saljuk mirrors with hunting scenes, represented by a mirror in the Victoria and Albert Museum. An example of Ortukid metalwork is a mirror in the collection of Count Wallerstein, decorated with the signs of the zodiac, a frieze of animals, arabesques, and inscriptions with the name of the Ortuk shah who ruled in Kharput about 1260.

Saljuk bronzes with engraved decoration include a great variety of objects for daily use, such as ewers, kettles, mortars, candlesticks, lamps, incense burners, and boxes. Most of the known pieces are of Iranian origin, although their exact provenance is not always certain. Some of them come from northeastern and eastern Iran, others from Hamadan and Rayy. Through its expedition to Nishapur, the Metropolitan Museum acquired a Saljuk bronze ewer of about the twelfth century which shows an engraved decoration of hunting scenes and animals. The shape of the ewer, with a pomegranate on top of the handle, is derived from the post-Sasanian type represented in the Museum by a ewer identical in shape with the Nishapur one but dating from about the tenth century. The Nishapur ewer is most probably of local origin. There is literary evidence that Nishapur and other cities in the province of Khurasan had a developed metal industry in the Middle Ages.

A fine Saljuk bronze of the twelfth century is a mortar (fig. 79) with a frieze of well-drawn animals —a lion, a gazelle, and a dog separated by circular medallions — against a background of arabesques

Fig. 78. Bronze Mirror, Iranian, Saljuk, XII Century

between bands of Kufic inscriptions. The similarity of style between the animals of this mortar and those on the Nishapur ewer suggests that the mortar was also made in Khurasan. An important piece of the same period is a large bronze vase with an engraved design in

Fig. 79. *Bronze Mortar, Iranian, Saljuk, XII Century*

this Museum. It is said to have come from Hamadan, and it bears the usual Saljuk decorative scheme of running animals, pairs of dragons with knotted bodies, and Kufic inscriptions with knotted letters.

Openwork was skillfully employed by Iranian metalworkers for the decoration of candlesticks and incense burners, often in the shape of birds and animals. A fine incense burner, in the shape of a lion, is in the Museum (fig. 80). The lion is stylized in a manner characteristic of Saljuk art and decorated with interlacings in openwork on the shoulders, the collar, and the thighs. There are two other important incense burners in the shape of a lion, a large one in the Hermitage and another in the Louvre. All can be assigned to the twelfth century.

B. BRONZES WITH SILVER AND COPPER INLAY

Saljuk metalworkers developed and perfected the technique of

Fig. 80. *Incense Burner, Iranian, Saljuk, XII Century*

inlaying objects of bronze and brass with other metals such as copper and silver. There is conclusive evidence that its beginnings were in eastern Iran, particularly the province of Khurasan, whence it spread westward to the rest of Iran and to Mesopotamia. It was in eastern Iran, too, that inlay first achieved artistic prominence, and the style created in Herat, Nishapur, Sistan, and Merv, the centers of Iranian metalwork, was eventually adopted by the whole Near East. By the thirteenth century Mosul, in northern Mesopotamia, had become a great center of Islamic inlay work. In fact, its fame was so firmly established that for some time all bronze and brass work with copper and silver inlay was indiscriminately attributed to the Mosul shops. Now, however, with the help of a few pieces definitely known to be of Iranian origin we are able to reclassify other inlaid bronze and brass vessels as Iranian.

As in the pre-Saljuk era, Iranian metalwork of the eleventh and twelfth centuries and the early thirteenth was made of bronze (alloy of copper and tin), and not of brass (alloy of copper and zinc) as was usual in Mosul work and in later Iranian work. Some of the vessels were inlaid in the traditional Iranian manner, that is, with copper; others were inlaid with copper and silver in combination or with silver alone. Although engraving still predominated in the decoration, inlay had become an essential part. A bronze vessel which is of the greatest importance in establishing the priority of Iran in the development of inlay technique is a kettle in the Hermitage which gives us not only the names of the makers but also the place of manufacture. According to inscriptions the kettle was made in Herat by Muhammad ibn al Wahid

Fig. 81. Brass Ewer with Silver Inlay, Iranian, Early XIII Century

and inlaid by Hajib Mas'ud ibn Ahmad in A.H. 559 (1163). The decoration consists of five horizontal bands, two with representations of warriors, hunters, and scenes depicting Saljuk festivities, with men drinking and playing games, dancing girls, and musicians.

Three bands have Kufic and Naskhi inscriptions of different types. Of particular interest are the animated inscriptions, whose letters end in bodies or heads of humans or beasts. This type of writing was probably developed in the province of Khurasan and appears almost exclusively in Saljuk metalwork from Iran (see fig. 84). The kettle is engraved and inlaid with both copper and silver, the effective coloring thus produced being typical of many Iranian bronzes of the twelfth century. With the help of this Herat kettle we are able to distinguish a separate school of Saljuk inlaid bronze and brass vessels of Iranian origin.

Also of Iranian origin is a group of candlesticks and related ewers with fluted or duodecagonal bodies and straight necks (see fig. 81). A characteristic feature of these bronzes is the decoration of birds

Fig. 82. Bronze Box with Silver and Copper Inlay, Iranian, Herat, XII Century

and animals, mostly lions, in relief and in the round. There are two candlesticks, one in the Harari collection in Cairo, the other in the Hermitage, and a ewer in the Sarre collection in Berlin with bodies crowned by rows of birds embossed in the round. The figures are all conventionalized in the Saljuk manner but still show their relation to post-Sasanian style. Ewers of this type are in the Hermitage, the British Museum, the Louvre, the Berlin Museum, and the Gulistan Museum at Teheran. Some of them, related to the Herat kettle, are of the twelfth century. Other ewers belong to the beginning and the first half of the thirteenth century (see fig. 81); and still another group should be assigned to the fourteenth century.

Typical of the early thirteenth-century group is a ewer (fig. 81) formerly in the collection of the late J. P. Morgan. The body has an all-over pattern of interlacings, which end in heads of various animals and form twelve compartments containing signs of the zodiac and symbols of the planets. Kufic and Naskhi inscriptions ending in human heads decorate the neck and other parts of the ewer.

Although the engraving is still conspicuous, the silver inlay is richer than in that of twelfth-century pieces.

These ewers and candlesticks have usually been attributed to northern Iran or Armenia. However, a comparison of their style of decoration with that of the Herat kettle of 1163 points to Khurasan as the province of origin. An important document which strongly supports such an attribution is a ewer in the Tiflis Museum, inlaid with copper and silver, dated A.H. 577 (1181) and bearing the signature of the artist Mahmud ibn Muhammad of Herat. The inlaid bronzes made in Herat and other centers of Khurasan show certain decorative features which are peculiar to this province. Among the most characteristic is a rosette of seven disks (see fig. 82) which may be regarded almost as a trade-mark of Khurasan metalworkers. Rosettes of this type appear on the Herat kettle, on several ewers (including the Morgan piece), and on two candlesticks, one in the Hermitage and the other in the Harari collection, on which they form the main decoration.

Also to Khurasan may be attributed a group of round boxes, probably inkwells, inlaid with silver and copper, some of them decorated with figure subjects similar in style and technique to those on the Herat kettle. A box in the Museum is a fine example of this group (fig. 82). It is decorated with inscriptions and three compartments containing arabesque scrolls separated by vase motives, which occur in a number of early Saljuk bronzes, and the circular rosettes of seven disks, mentioned above.

A small group of ewers, with engraved and inlaid decoration, have spouts shaped like an oil lamp. The one in the Louvre is dated A.H. 586 (1190) and was made for 'Uthman ibn Sulaiman of Nakhchivan in northern Iran. Two other ewers, one in the Peytel collection, Paris, the other in the Metropolitan Museum (fig. 83), should be attributed to the province of Khurasan. The Peytel piece, inlaid with silver and copper, is signed by 'Ali of Isfarayin, a town in Khurasan. The ewer in the Museum, perhaps the earliest of the group, is decorated with bands of inscriptions, arabesques, vase motives, and running animals. It was made for 'Ali ibn Abd ar Rahman ibn Tahir al Adib of Sistan. The silver inlay of this ewer is sparingly applied, being confined to narrow lines. Of particular beauty is the handle in the shape of a lion, gracefully stylized in Saljuk manner.

Fig. 83. Bronze Ewer with Silver Inlay, Iranian, Saljuk, XII Century

An important piece for the dating of Iranian metalwork of the thirteenth century is a pen case in the Freer Gallery in Washington, made by the chiseler Shahi in the year A.H. 607 (1210) for Majd al Mulk al Muzaffar, the grand vizier of Khurasan, who resided in Merv. It was probably made in Merv, which was a great artistic center in eastern Iran. The style of the decoration and the type of writing, both Naskhi and Kufic, are typical of Iranian pieces, the letters of the main Naskhi inscription ending in human and animal heads. This box permits us to date a number of Iranian bronzes definitely to the beginning of the thirteenth century. In the Metropolitan Museum there are four pieces, a mortar, a container in the shape of a bird, a vase, and a bowl (fig. 84), which should be assigned to that period. The exterior of the bronze bowl is decorated with interlaced medallions containing the signs of the zodiac and symbols of the planets. Each medallion has a border of "lotus" petals similar to those on the Herat kettle of 1163. Around the rim

Fig. 84. Bronze Bowl with Silver Inlay, Iranian,
Early XIII Century

is a Naskhi inscription with letters ending in human heads. Peculiar to Iran are the lilylike palmettes, in which end the scrolls of the arabesques between the medallions and in the background of the inscription; also Iranian are the crescent-shaped "vase" motives from which the main scrolls issue.

Iranian bronzes of the first half of the thirteenth century, contemporary with brass objects of the Mosul school (see p. 144), are often profusely inlaid with silver. To this group may be assigned a ewer and a candlestick in the Gulistan Museum at Teheran and a ewer in the Homberg collection in Paris. Another ewer in the Victoria and Albert Museum in London, probably of the middle of the thirteenth century, shows the influence of the Mosul school.

3. Saljuk Metalwork of Mesopotamia and the School of Mosul (XIII Century)

In Arghana Ma'adin and Ma'adin Khapur there are rich copper mines which supplied Mesopotamia and Syria with the necessary ore for the manufacture of brass and bronze objects. The most important center of silver-inlaid metalwork during the thirteenth century in Mesopotamia was Mosul, which from 1127 to 1262 was in the hands of the Saljuk atabegs of the Zangid dynasty, great patrons of arts and crafts. An early example of Mosul work is a

Fig. 85. Brass Ewer with Silver Inlay Dated 1226,
Mesopotamian, Mosul

Fig. 86. Brass Ewer with Silver Inlay, Egypto-Arabic, Mamluk,
First Half of the XIV Century

silver-inlaid brass ewer in the Metropolitan Museum (fig. 85), the
shape of which was developed in Mosul and adopted in Syria and
Egypt (see fig. 86). The surface is elaborately decorated with figure
subjects, geometrical patterns, and inscriptions within bands and
compartments. The scenes of revelry and hunting show a style which
follows Iranian prototypes but has features characteristic of Mosul
work. It was made by Ibn Hajji Jaldak, disciple of Ahmad ad Daki,

the engraver of Mosul, in the year A.H. 623 (1226/7).

From a technical point of view the Mosul school shows a definite advancement in inlay technique. The engraved outlines so prominent in Iranian metalwork are gradually becoming subordinated to the inlay. The great progress made by the Mosul artists is evident in a later work of Ahmad ad Daki, the engraver of the Museum's ewer. His basin in the Louvre, which was made for Abu

Fig. 87. Base of a Brass Candlestick with Silver Inlay, Mesopotamian, Mosul, XIII Century

Bakr II, the Ayyubid sultan of Egypt and Damascus (1238-40), is richly inlaid with silver.

An outstanding piece of the Mosul school is a brass ewer in the British Museum, the work of Shuja ibn Man'a of Mosul, made there in the month of Rajab, 629 (March, 1232). Here the Mosul style is fully developed. Every inch of the surface is inlaid with silver, and the whole background is covered by a meander pattern, which was greatly favored by Mosul metalworkers.

Several brass objects with silver inlay are known which bear the name of Sultan Badr ad Din Lulu (1233-59) of Mosul. The outstanding piece of this group is the basin in the State Library of Munich. A fine candlestick base of the Mosul school in the Metropolitan Museum (fig. 87) may also be attributed to the period of this ruler. The decoration consists of four large medallions with scenes from the life of a sultan and of twelve smaller medallions containing the signs of the zodiac and the symbols of the planets. Two bands depict scenes of festivity; there are groups of animated men and women drinking wine from cups or beakers while others are playing cymbals, lutes, and harps, to the strains of which girls are dancing. Several faces, notably those of old bearded men, are excellent studies of character. The two narrow bands at the top and bottom between the moldings are also of interest. Here the artist has represented all kinds of animals, waterfowl, and fantastic birds and griffins ingeniously combined with scrolls. There is no inscription to indicate the ownership or the place of manufacture. However, there are sixteen small circular medallions containing a personification of the moon—a seated man holding a moon crescent around his face—which apparently was the badge of some of the Zangids, since it appears on late coins of Sultan Badr ad Din Lulu and on the Bab Sinjar gate at Mosul. It is therefore probable that our candlestick was made for one of the Zangids, possibly Badr ad Din Lulu, whose name means "full moon of religion." In many other pieces, particularly those made in Syria, Iran, and Egypt, these seated figures simply represent the moon.

4. Fatimid Metalwork of Egypt (X-XII Century)

Egyptian metalwork made during the Fatimid period (X-XII century) consists of jewelry and a small group of bronze animals. Fatimid jewelry is relatively rare. Outstanding examples are in the Harari collection, the Arab Museum, Cairo, and the Benaki Museum, Athens. Three fine pieces, a pair of earrings and a crescent-shaped pendant (fig. 88) of about the middle of the eleventh century, are in the Metropolitan Museum. Their decoration is in filigree technique in which gold wires, straight and braided, form a geometrical design in openwork. The pendant is enriched with a turquoise stone and polychrome decoration of two birds in cloisonné

enamel, a technique popular in Egypt during the Fatimid era.

The finest of the Fatimid bronzes is a large griffin in the Campo Santo at Pisa, which has an elaborate engraved design. In the Metropolitan Museum there is a bronze ornament which represents an eagle attacking a deer. The graceful outline of the animals is characteristic of Fatimid animal decoration, known from cut-crystal vessels and wood carvings.

Fig. 88. *Gold Pendant with Enamel Inlay, Egypto-Arabic, Fatimid, XI Century*

5. Ayyubid Metalwork of Syria and Egypt (XIII Century)

During the thirteenth century, Mosul metalworkers frequently migrated to Syria and Egypt, working for the Ayyubid princes in Damascus, Aleppo, and Cairo. The style they took with them is that of the Mosul school, and, unless inscriptions indicate, it is often difficult to say where a piece was made. A brass ewer with the name of the Ayyubid sultan Malik Nasir Yusuf of Aleppo and Damascus (1236-60), dated A.H. 657 (1259), in the Louvre, was made at Damascus by an artist from Mosul. The name of the same sultan appears on the so-called Barberini vase in the Louvre.

Of great interest to students of Islamic metalwork are vessels with Christian subjects, some of them inscribed with the names of the Ayyubid sultans. Some of the Ayyubids, particularly those of Damascus, were tolerant toward Christians and at times were even allied with the kingdom of Jerusalem. A famous piece of this group is a basin in Brussels belonging to the Duke of Arenberg; it is inscribed with the name of the Ayyubid sultan Salih Ayyub of Egypt and Damascus (1240-9). Another noteworthy piece with Christian scenes is the candlestick in the Musée des Arts Décoratifs in Paris that bears the name of the maker, Dawud, son of Salama of Mosul, and the date A.H. 646 (1248). A magnificent bronze canteen now in the Freer Gallery in Washington is richly decorated with scenes from the life of Christ, figures of saints, and fighting warriors, combined with the usual decoration found on other Islamic vessels of the period. Among the scenes appear Crusaders, which indicates that the piece was made for a Christian prince, probably in Damascus about the middle of the thirteenth century.

6. Mamluk Metalwork of Syria and Egypt (Second Half of the XIII to the XV Century)

Under the rule of the Mamluk sultans of Syria and Egypt, fine metalwork was produced in Damascus, Aleppo, and Cairo, where the work was carried on by artists imported from Mosul and later by native craftsmen. The height of Mamluk metalwork was reached under the sultan Nasir ad Din Muhammad ibn Kalaun (1293-4, 1308, and 1309-40). A number of fine pieces are known which bear the name of this Mamluk ruler or his courtiers. A magnificent piece of this period is the *kursi*, or table, in the Arab Museum at Cairo, dated A.H. 728 (1327). It is richly decorated with silver and gold inlay of high quality.

Mamluk metalwork shows distinctive features which permit us to identify it as such. New decorative motives have been added to the traditional arabesques. Most frequent among these are pairs of birds in compartments, which occasionally are arranged in a lozenge diaper, as on one of the ewers in the Metropolitan Museum inscribed with the name of Nasir Muhammad. Other elements gradually invading the ornament are naturalistic motives, such as leaves and peonies, derived from Chinese art, which came into the Near East with the Mongol conquest. Floral motives of this kind and flying ducks often surround official blazons and medallions with the titles and the names of the early Mamluks and their courtiers, as in the ewer shown in figure 86 made for Muhammad the treasurer. Another distinctive feature is a medallion with a Z-meander, regarded by Lane-Poole as one of the characteristics of the Damascus school of inlay under the Mamluks (see fig. 89). Of the Damascus group, with its inlay technique of unusually high perfection, the Museum possesses four pieces—a writing case, two incense burners, and a dish, all the gift of J. Pierpont Morgan. Each of them is richly inlaid, not only with silver but also with gold. Their style indicates that they should be dated at the end of the thirteenth century and the beginning of the fourteenth. The writing box (fig.

Fig. 89. Writing Case with Gold and Silver Inlay, Syrian, Damascus,
XIII-XIV Century

89), one of the finest known, is a masterpiece of Mamluk craftsmanship. Exquisitely inlaid with gold and silver, an intricate design covers every inch of the exterior and interior of the case with medallions, lozenge diapers, key patterns, arabesques, interlacings, and other familiar motives.

Several brass bowls and basins decorated with large figure compositions, such as hunting scenes and combats, should be assigned to the Mamluk period. The most famous piece of this group is the so-called Baptistery of Saint Louis in the Louvre, made by Muhammad ibn az Zain. The rich silver inlay of this basin and other pieces of the group shows a great deal of fine detail work in the rendering of the human figures and animals. These brass vessels with large figures, related to some enameled glass of Aleppo and Damascus manufacture, may also be attributed to Syrian craftsmen of the end of the thirteenth century and the beginning of the fourteenth.

All through the fourteenth century the Mamluk metalwork made in Cairo and Syria was still of good quality. The style evolved in Nasir Muhammad's time was further developed. The naturalistic floral motives became more evident in later work, as may be seen in some pieces in the Metropolitan Museum and on a pen box in the Arab Museum in Cairo, which is inscribed with the name of the sultan Mansur Salah ad Din Muhammad (1360-2). Some good work was still done in the fifteenth century. Makrizi, writing about 1420, makes the following comment: "The demand for . . . inlaid copper [brass] work has fallen off in our time [in Cairo], and since many years the people have turned away from purchasing, . . . so that but a small remnant of the workers of inlay survive in this market." There are several objects known which bear the name of the Mamluk sultan Kait-Bey (1468-96). A remarkable piece is a basin in Constantinople, which is decorated with geometrical inter-

lacings, arabesques, and foliated scrolls. The Metropolitan Museum
possesses a large, flat, circular bowl inscribed with the name of the
same sultan.

7. Metalwork with the Names of the Rasulid Sultans of Yemen (XIII-XIV Century)

Many silver-inlaid objects, such as trays, braziers, and candlesticks,
were made in Cairo for the Rasulid sultans of Yemen, who were on
friendly terms with the Mamluk sultans. A ewer in the Musée
des Arts Décoratifs in Paris, inscribed with the name of al Muzaffar
Yusuf (1250-95), was made in Cairo by 'Ali ibn Husain ibn
Muhammad of Mosul, in the year A.H. 674 (1275). A rare and
exceptionally fine brazier (fig. 90) in the Metropolitan Museum's
collection bears the name of the same Rasulid sultan. It is richly
decorated in Mamluk style with arabesques, Arabic writing, and a

Fig. 90. Brass Brazier with Silver Inlay, Made for the
Rasulid Sultan Muzaffar Yusuf (1250-1295)

frieze of animals, and shows a five-petaled rosette, which is a badge
of the Rasulids, since it occurs on all the work made for these sultans. Two large trays in the Museum's collection bear the name of
Sultan Muayyad Dawud ibn Yusuf (1296-1321); one of them was

Fig. 91. *Brass Basin with Silver Inlay, Iranian, Mongol, XIV Century*

made in Cairo by Husain ibn Ahmad ibn Husain of Mosul. Also of importance is a deep basin decorated with a seminaturalistic floral pattern and bearing the name of the Rasulid sultan 'Ali ibn Dawud (1321-63).

8. *Mongol Metalwork of Iran (Mid-XIII—XV Century)*

Iranian metalwork of the Mongol period shows a decoration often similar to that of the Mosul school and of the Mamluk work of Syria and Egypt. There are, however, certain features of style which may be recognized as peculiar to Iran. Some of the pieces bear inscriptions with the titles or, more rarely, the names of the Mongol rulers of Iran. Definitely Mongol are three bronze balls inlaid with silver and gold, in the Harari collection in Cairo, bearing the name of the sultan Uljaitu Khudabanda Muhammad (1304-16) and showing a mixture of Syrian and Iranian motives.

To the beginning of the fourteenth century may be attributed an important large brass basin with an elaborate silver inlay (fig. 91) in the Metropolitan Museum's collection. The inside of the bowl is decorated with concentric rows of compartments framing standing figures holding wine cups, bows, and swords; seated musicians and revelers; hunting scenes and enthroned princes; pairs of aureoled sphinxes and griffins. For a long time this basin was regarded as Mamluk. Some of the compartments, however, are decorated with meanders, others with naturalistic plants, designed in a style more Iranian than Mamluk. The numerous sphinxes and griffins, seen less frequently in Mamluk work, also indicate an Iranian origin.

In the second half of the fourteenth century the distinctive Iranian features of Mongol metalwork are more strongly pronounced. Several dated pieces give us a basis for the classification of this material. A dated candlestick in the Harari collection is decorated with naturalistic plants and arabesques. According to the inscription it was the work of Muhammad ibn Raf [i] ad Din, of Shiraz, and is dated A.H. 761 (1360).

In the Moore Collection of the Museum there are several caskets and candlesticks dating from the second half of the fourteenth century. Some of them, showing a marked decline of technique and design, are as late as the end of the century, that is, of the period of Timur.

Fig. 92. Bowl with Silver Inlay, Iranian, Mongol, XIV Century

An important group of Mongol metalwork of the second half of the fourteenth century consists of bowls inlaid with silver and gold, which vary in quality. They are decorated with figure subjects depicting court life, garden parties, and polo games. Some of the finest pieces are in the Harari collection in Cairo and the Walters Art Gallery in Baltimore. The Metropolitan Museum has two examples. The figures are conventionalized, often elongated (see fig. 92), as in certain late Mongol miniature paintings. Most of the figures wear the "sugar loaf" caps which appear in the miniature paintings of Khwaju Kirmani's *Diwan* of 1396 in the British Museum.

Jewelry of the Mongol period is relatively rare. A fine specimen is a signet ring (fig. 93) of about 1400 in the Metropolitan Museum. It is decorated with Chinese dragon heads in openwork, inscriptions, arabesques, and plant motives typical of the late Mongol and and early Timurid periods.

9. Safavid Metalwork of Iran (XVI-XVIII Century)

The inlaying of brass objects with silver, which declined considerably during the fifteenth century, continued to be practiced under the Safavids. Copper vessels were often tinned to simulate silver, and iron and steel became popular. The decoration reflected the

changing fashions of the time. A typical example of the sixteenth century is a copper bowl with relief decoration of arabesques in the Moore Collection of the Metropolitan Museum. It is inscribed with the name of the maker, al Imami from Aleppo, the guild master, and the year A.H. 942 (1535/6). Another bowl in the Museum's collection is decorated with a Safavid pattern of animals, floral scrolls, and arabesques and bears the date A.H. 1010 (1601/2) and the name of the owner, Mahmud Khan.

Safavid brass candlesticks with engraved and relief decoration are pillar-shaped. One in the Museum's collection (fig. 94) is dated A.H. 986 (1578/9). The inscriptions on such candlesticks are usually taken from the Iranian poem, "The Moth and the Candle." The decoration consists of arabesques and floral scrolls, usually covering the whole surface but occasionally being confined in compartments.

The Safavid metalworkers achieved great skill in the handling of iron and steel, producing some excellent pieces which technically are not inferior to earlier work. Steel plaques, belts, and other objects show an openwork decoration with or without gold inlay. In each case the design of arabesque and floral scrolls is of high quality. One of the belts in the Topkapu Saray Museum bears the name of Shah Isma'il I and the date A.H. 913 (1507).

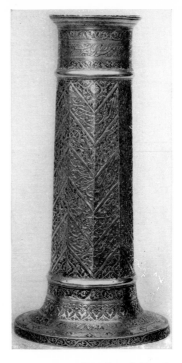

Fig. 94. Brass Candlestick Dated 1578/9, Iranian, Safavid

The more luxurious type of Safavid metalwork is known to us from representations in sixteenth-century miniature paintings. Only a few pieces have survived and these are now in the Topkapu Saray Museum at Istanbul. Bottles of silver alloy have both an applied and an inlaid gold decoration. They are enriched with precious stones, such as rubies, turquoises, and emeralds. According to tradition the treasure at Istanbul was a part of the booty of Sultan Salim in the war against the Iranians under Shah Isma'il in 1514.

Iranian metalwork of the late seventeenth and eighteenth centuries retained the conventional decorative schemes of the Safavid style.

10. Venetian Metalwork (XV-XVI Century)

Metalwork in the style of the Near East, particularly that of Syria, was produced in Italy in the fifteenth and sixteenth centuries. Venice was the principal center for work of this kind, which was carried on first by craftsmen from Syria and other oriental countries and subsequently by native artists who called themselves "Azzimini." However, Venetian metalwork, which consists of bowls, jugs, and trays, has a distinctive character that is easily recognized. There is a tendency toward overcrowding and roundness of forms in the arabesques and interlacings that does not occur in true oriental work. The design is usually in relief, the inlay being used more sparingly than in the East. Several trays and bowls in existence bear the name of Mahmud al Kurdi. Coats of arms occur occasionally as well as European decorative motives. Of this Venetian metalwork in the oriental style, the Metropolitan Museum possesses several good examples in the Moore Collection.

11. Moorish Metalwork of Spain and North Africa

Moorish metalwork of Spain follows in general the style of Islamic art, with the addition of characteristic features of this country. Hispano-Moresque gold jewelry, made mostly in Granada, is frequently in filigree work and sometimes combined with enamel inlay, as in a group of fourteenth-century necklaces and bracelets in the Morgan Collection of the Museum.

The treasuries of Spanish churches contain several silver boxes with relief decoration and filigree work. Most famous among them is a gilded silver box in the cathedral of Gerona, which has an ornament of palmette scrolls. According to an inscription, it was made at the order of Caliph al Hakam II (961-76) for his successor, Hisham II.

Noteworthy among the bronzes is a lamp from the Alhambra mosque, now in the Archaeological Museum of Madrid. It was made to order for Muhammad III in the year A.H. 705 (1305) and has an openwork decoration of arabesques and Arabic inscriptions. There are several bronze doors of Moorish workmanship, including one in the Cordova cathedral bearing the date 1415 of the era of Caesar (1377), and one in Seville cathedral which is similar in style.

In North Africa the art of metalwork never achieved a high standard. Inlay, if not entirely unknown, was at least very rare. Such metalwork as we know is mostly of later date and decorated in the usual Moorish style.

12. Indian Metalwork

During the Mughal supremacy the use of brass and other alloys for domestic and ritual vessels was continued by Indian craftsmen, who frequently encrusted the vessels with silver. Jewelry, which was extensively worn in India, was made of gold and silver, often with stone inlay and enameled enrichment. There is a notable collection of such jewelry in the Metropolitan Museum.

13. Arms and Armor

In the Moore Collection of the Museum are several specimens of Near Eastern arms. Of special importance are a seventeenth-century Iranian helmet and a cuirass of steel damascened in the Safavid style with gold. Other fine pieces are in the Bequest of George C. Stone and are shown in the galleries of the Department of Arms and Armor. Among the exhibits may be seen helmets, shields, cuirasses, swords, and daggers of Iran, India, Turkey, and the Caucasus.

Chapter 10

CERAMICS

1. The Ceramic Art of the Umayyad and Abbasid Periods in Iran and Mesopotamia (VIII-X Century)

The conquest of the Near East by the Arabs inaugurated a new era in the history of ceramic art. At first the Muhammadan potters of Egypt, Syria, Mesopotamia, and Iran followed local traditions, adopting the ceramic techniques of the conquered countries. Gradually, however, these artists developed new methods of ceramic decoration, and by the ninth century they had evolved a great variety of patterns, color schemes, and techniques which became characteristic of the ceramic art of the Islamic world. The influence of Chinese ceramic art was of great importance in the formation of many types of Islamic pottery. It is often difficult to say which Muhammadan country deserves credit for a particular technique or design, as the same varieties of pottery are found in several provinces of the empire. There are other types, however, which are peculiar to certain provinces.

Systematic excavations of various sites, such as Fustat, Samarra, Ctesiphon, Susa, Rayy, Nishapur, and Afrasiyab, have furnished us with material important for the history of early Muhammadan ceramics. Since Samarra was founded in 836 and abandoned in 883, the ceramics excavated on that site are dated exactly in the ninth century, helping thus to date similar pottery from other localities. The excavations of The Metropolitan Museum of Art at Nishapur in eastern Iran established the importance of this city as a great ceramic center of the Islamic world. Among the objects excavated there are many hitherto unknown types of early Islamic pottery, the earliest of which according to coins and other archaeological evidence can be dated at the end of the eighth and the beginning of the ninth century. These finds also help to classify material from sites which have not produced sufficient evidence for dating.

Early Muhammadan pottery varies a great deal in quality of

design and technique. Pottery of high artistic craftsmanship was made for wealthy persons and members of the court. Other pieces must be classified as peasant ware, although even these show the great decorative qualities which are so characteristic of Islamic art. Luster and enamel painting were reserved for the high-grade ware only, and pieces in these techniques must have been manufactured chiefly in places where the court resided. Other techniques, such as incising and underglaze painting in monochrome and polychrome, were employed by Near Eastern potters for both types of pottery.

Iranian potters of the eighth to tenth century knew various methods of decorating their pottery, and the great quantities of ceramics found all over Iran reveal an astounding richness of pattern and color scheme. The effectiveness of some of the pieces depends entirely on design, while others derive added charm from the skillful use of color. Frequently pieces of the greatest decorative beauty show extremely simple patterns, which Iranian potters knew how to use to good advantage. Sometimes a single Kufic inscription in monochrome, running around or across a bowl, forms the sole decoration. The decoration may be incised, or painted in monochrome or polychrome, under the glaze or over the glaze, and often it is painted in luster technique.

The classification and dating of Iranian pottery of the early Islamic period has been difficult because of lack of systematic excavations. Furthermore, in most cases the provenance has been uncertain, often being supplied by dealers who were not eager to disclose the true source of supply. In 1920 Pézard attempted the first systematic classification of Iranian ceramics from various sites, some of them excavated at Susa by a French expedition. Pézard's dating, however, was occasionally erroneous. The presence of traditional Sasanian motives induced him to regard some of the ceramics as pre-Islamic, that is, of the seventh century. Other pottery he dated in the eighth century, although it shows motives and patterns of later periods.

A. POTTERY WITH RELIEF DECORATION AND MONOCHROME GLAZES

Abbasid pottery with monochrome glazes can be divided into two groups. One group consists of large jars covered with blue or green glazes similar to those of the Sasanian era. The relief decoration of bands and scrolls is applied in the so-called barbotine technique, so often used in unglazed pottery (see p. 171). Much finer ware, consisting of small dishes, cups, and other vessels, including pilgrim bottles, has a molded relief decoration covered with a green glaze.

The patterns of this ware, found in Samarra and Susa, show geometrical designs, arabesques, and stylized leaf motives which often recall patterns on similar ware of the Parthian and Sasanian periods. Related to the above group are small vessels, mostly dishes, covered with a yellow alkali-lead glaze, often showing on the surface a golden luster which by some authorities is regarded as true luster, by others as iridescence. Some of the brilliant fragments found at Samarra, Ctesiphon, Susa, Rayy, and Fustat indicate that it may be true luster obtained by coloring the glazes with iron and antimony. It is probable that this ware was made in imitation of gold vessels.

Fig. 95. *Bowl from Nishapur, Iranian, IX Century*

B. POTTERY WITH INCISED DECORATION AND COLORED GLAZES

One of the largest groups of early Islamic pottery from Iran has a decoration incised through a white slip and covered with a transparent lead glaze. The pottery thus decorated is called sgraffito ware and is known commercially as "Gabry" (fire worshiper). The glaze is either entirely green or creamy yellow splashed with other colors, such as green and brown, or with yellow, green, and purple manganese. The method of incising the decoration, one of the simplest ceramic processes known, was used during many periods and in many countries. Iranian *sgraffito* ware may be classified into several groups according to period, the earliest possibly belonging to the Umayyad era.

A distinctive group of Iranian pottery consists mostly of bowls, made of red earthenware, with incised decoration of stylized birds and animals, palmette scrolls, and Kufic writing, often within compartments formed by interlacings. The background usually shows hatching of parallel lines and sometimes scroll patterns. The glaze is creamy, occasionally with a green band around the rim. Sometimes, as in a bowl in the Metropolitan Museum, the highly decorative design of a bird, probably a peacock, occupies the whole center of the bowl. Most of this pottery is supposed to have come from Rayy and was wrongly regarded by Pézard as Sasanian because of a certain similarity of the animal and bird designs to those of late Sasanian metal-

Fig. 96. Bowl, Iranian, Amul, X-XI Century

work. That this ware was inspired by metalwork is quite evident, but the style is related rather to the post-Sasanian metalwork of the eighth and ninth centuries than to that of the Sasanian era. The palmettes, although derived from Sasanian art, also show characteristic features of the early Abbasid period, that is, the end of the eighth and beginning of the ninth century. The shapes and the bases with flat surfaces, sometimes with circular rings, indicate that the ware cannot be much later than the tenth century.

This type of pottery, with incised decoration, was made at Nishapur and other localities in eastern Iran during the ninth century and continued during the tenth. Several fine bowls with incised decoration under a creamy yellow or green glaze are in the Museum. The patterns consist of palmette designs, scrollwork, and writing. An unusually fine bowl shows compartments alternating with large leaves, and the word "Allah." As in the later Saljuk ware from Garus (see p. 176) the design is both incised and carved.

Incised decoration was often applied to pottery streaked or splashed with yellow-brown, green, and touches of purple manganese in imitation of Chinese T'ang ware, which was imported by the Abbasids and found in various places, including Samarra, Ctesiphon, and Nishapur. Great quantities of Iranian pottery of this type, ranging in date from the end of the eighth century to the tenth, came to light in many sites all over the Muhammadan East, for instance, Samarra, Ctesiphon, Susa, Rayy, Nishapur, and Samarkand. Some of the pieces are carefully potted; others are inferior in color and design. Our excavations at Nishapur have yielded interesting examples, together with evidence that the ware was being made in the early part of the ninth century. The Iranian potters imitating Chinese ware were not satisfied with mere copying. As the finds indicate, the engraved design and colors were often combined into bold patterns, producing new decorative effects not seen in Chinese ware. The Iranian potters also varied the Chinese color scheme, lightening the yellows and greens and adding more purple manganese. Very often they arranged the color splashes and streaks, with the help of incised designs, into regular geometrical patterns such as circular segments, concentric rings, lozenge diapers, and cross patterns. The compartments thus formed are filled with irregular linear scrollwork and conventionalized palmettes, some of which suggest lotus rosettes. One of the finest incised patterns appears on a bowl from Nishapur (fig. 95), which is decorated alternately with large palmettes and split palmette scrolls within tuliplike compartments. The pattern is characteristic of early Abbasid ornament and indicates a date which could not be later than the ninth century. An interesting large dish in the Museum from an unknown site in Iran has an incised design of circles containing conventionalized Chinese lotus flowers. This was presented to the Museum by Henry Walters.

Fig. 97. Bowl from Nishapur, Iranian, X Century

Another type of developed sgraffito ware, in which the incised decoration is enhanced by spots and green lines and lozenge diapers, comes from North Iran, mostly from Amul, in the province of Mazandaran. It is represented in the Museum by three pieces. There are two types of this pottery: one shows geometrical patterns and a spotted decoration, the other has birds and animals often grotesquely stylized. The dating of this ware varies considerably. At first Pézard assigned it to the eighth century and the end of the seventh, and other authorities dated it as late as the eleventh and twelfth centuries. Some of the motives, for instance, the birds in the bowl of figure 96, continue the late Sasanian tradition, while others appear in the *graffiato* and other Abbasid ware of the eighth to ninth century. Many of the vessels of the Amul ware show advanced shapes and more developed bases and should therefore be assigned to a later period—to the tenth century and in some cases, where the design suggests the Saljuk period, even to the eleventh or twelfth century.

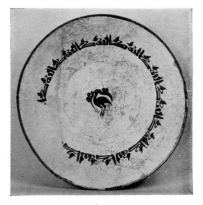

Fig. 98. Bowl from Nishapur, Iranian, IX Century

C. POTTERY WITH PAINTED DECORATION

The Muhammadan potters developed the art of decorating vessels by painting designs under a transparent glaze or over an opaque one. In the former case the painting was usually applied over a white slip, although dark slips are not uncommon, as we shall see in the discussion of Nishapur and Samarkand pottery. In another group of early Islamic ware the decoration is painted over an opaque tin glaze with cobalt blue or with luster of various colors. In all these ceramic techniques the Muhammadan potters, chiefly of Mesopotamia and Iran, created types of pottery which may be regarded as prototypes of the later magnificent ware of the Saljuk period.

Pottery with underglaze painting is known through pieces found in northern Iran and through the rich finds at Samarkand in Turkestan. The Museum's excavations at Nishapur in Khurasan also

Fig. 99. *Bowl, Iranian, Amul, X Century*

brought to light a great wealth of painted pottery. From the many examples from Nishapur and Samarkand we may conclude that pottery with painted decoration was particularly in favor in the eastern part of the Muhammadan world. On the other hand, it seems that luster painting was not practiced in Khurasan and Turkestan. The few examples found in Nishapur and Samarkand are doubtless importations from western Iran, probably from Rayy and Susa. The theory that lusterware was not made in the province of Khurasan in the early Islamic period is strengthened by the finding of imitations at Nishapur.

D. POTTERY WITH UNDERGLAZE PAINTING

Excavations at Nishapur have furnished us with numerous varieties of Iranian pottery with painted decoration, covering a period from the end of the eighth until the beginning of the tenth century. Certain types are similar to those from Samarkand; others are peculiar to Nishapur and probably to the whole province of Khurasan. The patterns of the Nishapur ware, painted in monochrome or polychrome, are quite varied. We find single geometrical designs, bands of Kufic writing, palmettes and arabesque scrolls, rosettes, birds, and human figures, often combined into elaborate all-over patterns.

Fig. 100. *Bowl from Nishapur, Iranian, Samanid, X Century*

A type of pottery which comes from the deepest stratum of wells and cellars at Nishapur, and thus dates from the end of the eighth century to the beginning of the ninth, consists of deep bowls of buff earthenware. The heavy outlines of the design are drawn in black or purple manganese and filled with yellow

164

and green colors. Interlaced bands with arabesque scrolls on a background of crosshatching are popular patterns. An attractive example of this ware is the bowl with groups of half palmettes, arabesque scrolls, rosettes, and disks, in purple manganese, yellow, and green owned by this Museum.

An interesting type of pottery peculiar to Nishapur shows a decoration of animals and birds, human figures, and Kufic writing painted in bl. ck only or in black combined with

Fig. 101. *Bowl from Samarkand, Western Turkestan, Samanid, X Century*

yellow, green, and other colors. In a number of pieces, several of these motives are used at random to cover the interior surface of a bowl, recalling some of the lustered pottery from Rayy. Several examples of this group are in the Museum. One is a ewer ending in an animal's head. The body of this vessel, which dates from the ninth century, is decorated with fantastic birds and rosettes in black, brick red, and green on a yellow ground. To this group also belongs a bowl which must be regarded as one of the most important pieces of early Islamic pottery brought to light in recent years (fig. 97). The interior of the bowl shows a standing figure of a warrior holding a scimitar, surrounded by birds with crests (typical of Nishapur), rosettes, and Kufic writing, painted in black and green on a yellow

ground. The figure itself and the peculiar costume with the lapelled coat and the skirt suggest some of the Central Asiatic figures in the wall paintings from Chinese Turkestan.

An attractive group of Nishapur pottery is decorated with inscriptions in brownish or purplish black on a white ground. The inscriptions are placed either in the center of the bowl or across it or along the rim. This group of pottery is

Fig. 102. *Lustered Bowl, Iranian, Abbasid, IX Century*

usually well made and of great decorative beauty. The Museum possesses several such bowls which date from the ninth century and early tenth. The bowl shown in figure 98 is decorated with Kufic inscriptions and with a bird which has one palmette in its beak and another attached to its head. The bird motive appears on several pieces and seems to have been popular in Nishapur. Other bowls with inscriptions show slender letters similar to those which appear in a number of Samanid bowls found in Afrasiyab, a suburb of Samarkand. The great number of fragments of this black and white ware with inscriptions indicates that it must have been very popular in Nishapur and in the whole province of Khurasan. Occasionally the potters added a few strokes of red to the black writing or painted the letters entirely in red slip, outlining them in black, as on a very fine fragmentary bowl in the Museum.

Fig. 103. Lustered Bowl, Iranian or Mesopotamian, Abbasid, IX Century

Black with red or red alone was used very effectively in the decoration of other Nishapur pottery, of which interesting examples are both in this Museum and in Teheran. A noteworthy piece of the ninth century or early tenth is a bowl in Teheran decorated with concentric rows of heart-shaped motives in black and red on a white ground. In our collection there is a fragment of a large Samanid platter with a black design of interlacings ending in graceful palmettes. Pottery with painted decoration, related to the Samanid ware, was found in western Iran, chiefly at Amul, in the province of Mazandaran. The polychrome decoration consists of birds, leaves, Kufic inscriptions, and circular medallions (see fig. 99) in purple manganese, brick red, and olive green.

It would be impossible in the limited space of this handbook to enumerate all the Nishapur types of painted pottery, the study of which is not yet completed. The Metropolitan Museum and the Teheran Museum have now representative collections, containing many hitherto unknown types of Iranian ceramic art.

Some of the types of painted pottery from Nishapur were known

166

also in Samarkand. In 901 the province Khurasan, with its capital Nishapur, was annexed by the Samanid rulers to Transoxiana. We have already mentioned black and white pottery with inscriptions, which was made in both provinces. Other ware which was common to both Nishapur and Samarkand has a decoration painted in purple manganese, olive green, and brick red on a white ground. The decoration consists of Arabic inscriptions and arabesque patterns. The Museum has two unusually fine bowls of this type, one from Nishapur (fig. 100) and one from Samarkand (fig. 101). The decoration of the latter, a pattern of arabesques and a vase motive in triangular compartments, is reminiscent of the Abbasid style, known to us from Samarra.

Other types of Nishapur pottery known also in Samarkand have a decoration painted in colored slips on backgrounds of various colors, such as purple or brown manganese, or brick red. Several fine examples of this pottery are in this Museum and in Teheran. Among the patterns we find rosettes with rows of pearls, survivals of Sasanian art, often combined with lilylike palmettes, as in two small bowls in the Museum. The background of these pieces is purple manganese, upon which the design is painted in white, yellow, and brick-red slips. In other pieces abstract scrollwork, palmettes, or clusters of dots form the usual pattern. Of great decorative beauty are bowls with inscriptions, of which the Museum has one of the finest pieces known. It shows an elegant Kufic inscription repeating the word *baraka* (blessing) in white over a black-brown slip and may be dated at

Fig. 104. Drawing of a Lustered Bowl (with Reconstructed Pattern), Mesopotamian, Abbasid, IX Century

the end of the ninth or the beginning of the tenth century.

E. POTTERY WITH PAINTED LUSTER DECORATION

Abbasid pottery has been found in Mesopotamian sites such as Samarra and Ctesiphon; in Iran, chiefly in Susa and Rayy; and in the rubbish heaps of Fustat (Old Cairo) in Egypt. Abbasid pottery with luster decoration is justly regarded as among the finest products of Muhammadan ceramic art. The luster technique was a great invention of Muhammadan potters of the eighth or ninth century. Although efforts have been made to trace the luster technique to the pre-Islamic era of Egypt, none of the existing examples with true luster can be dated earlier than the eighth or ninth century. This ware is usually made of fine yellowish clay covered with an opaque tin enamel upon which, after the first firing, the decoration was painted with metallic oxides. The objects were fired a second time slowly, at a lower temperature (about 500°-800° Fahrenheit), and through contact with smoke the metallic oxides were reduced to a thin layer of metal. The color of the luster thus produced was either gold or one of various shades of brown or red. By the ninth century the potters had become masters of this ceramic process, which is so characteristic of the Near East. The excavations at Samarra by Sarre and Herzfeld brought to light some of the most magnificent examples of lusterware (see p. 169), which soon led to the theory that the technique originated in Mesopotamia. Another theory on the origin of luster, favored by the French school, particularly Koechlin, is that Rayy was the cradle and artistic center of the technique and that from there it spread to other parts of Iran and Mesopotamia. There is still a third theory which attributes its invention to Egypt. To decide which of these theories is correct is not possible at present; future excavations may throw some new light on the matter of origin. The belief that all lusterware found in Iran was an importation from Mesopotamia cannot be upheld today.

The lusterware found in Iran may be divided into two classes, one showing a style typical of Iran, the other elements common to Iran and Mesopotamia. To the Iranian group belong vessels with a decoration of animals, birds, human figures, and arabesques, with the addition of Kufic inscriptions painted in gold luster. This lusterware, represented in the Museum by two bowls, one with running hares (fig. 102), the other with a gazelle and Kufic writing, found at Rayy, shows characteristic features of the Iranian animal style discussed previously in connection with Nishapur pottery. As no lustered pottery with animal decoration was found in Samarra or other Mesopotamian sites, we may regard this type as peculiar to Iran. Another type of lusterware which seems to be characteristic of Iran has bold arabesque scrolls with half palmettes and Kufic writing forming an all-over pattern. Examples have been found chiefly in Rayy and Susa, which were probably the manufacturing centers of this ware and that with animal decoration.

Pottery with polychrome luster decoration has been found at Susa and Rayy in Iran and also in Egypt, but it is best known from excavations at Samarra, where the most beautiful pieces came to light. Whether this Abbasid lusterware with polychrome decoration, found in Iran and elsewhere, was of Mesopotamian origin, as Sarre and Herzfeld believe, or of local manufacture is still a matter of controversy.

The Mesopotamian lusterware of the Abbasid period is best known to us from the excavations of Samarra, although other sites, such as Ctesiphon near Baghdad, have yielded many fine examples. The lusterware made for the use of the Abbasid caliphs between the years 836 and 883 and found at Samarra surpasses in the beauty and brilliancy of its colors all Islamic lusterware made in later periods. The decoration of the Samarra ware is painted over a tin enamel either in monochrome or polychrome luster. The monochrome luster is yellow- or green-gold and brown.

The most beautiful pieces among the Samarra lusterware are those with polychrome decoration. In one group the colors of the luster are gold, olive green, light green, and red-brown. The decoration, characteristic of the Abbasid period, consists of scrolls with cone-shaped motives, highly stylized floral devices, arabesques, trefoiled palmettes, and Sasanian wing palmettes (see fig. 103). The motives and intervening spaces are filled with a mosaic-like pattern of hatchings, lozenge diapers, scrolls, and circles with dots.

Samarra lusterware is very similar to the magnificent tiles with lustered decoration in monochrome and polychrome (gold, ocher, red-brown) of the mihrab in the mosque of Sidi 'Okba at Kairwan in Tunisia. There are 139 square tiles so arranged as to form a frame for this mihrab, and according to Arabic literary sources, they were mostly imported from Baghdad, together with the famous wooden mimbar also in the mosque (see p. 108), at the beginning of the ninth century by one of the amirs of the Aghlabid dynasty, probably the amir Ziyadat Allah I (817-38). The excavations of Samarra furnished us with actual proof for the support of these literary sources, which had been doubted by some authorities. The Kairwan tiles, which are earlier than the Samarra ceramics, must have been chiefly the work of Baghdad potters. Samarra, which was a temporary residence of the caliphs, was a branch of the great Mesopotamian school of ceramics, of which Baghdad was the center. The richness of decoration and the great variety of ornamental compositions of the Kairwan tiles indicate how highly developed the luster technique was in Mesopotamia by the first half of the ninth century.

Fig. 105. Jar with Overglaze Decoration, Iranian, Abbasid, IX Century

The high quality of the lusterware just described is even surpassed by a group of Samarra ceramics painted with ruby luster, often combined with yellow, green, gold, and purple. This combination of rich colors was used not only for the decoration of vessels but also on tiles for wall decoration of the Samarra palace. Several examples of great beauty were found and are now in the Berlin Museum. Some of these tiles were decorated with a cock within a wreath on a yellow marbled background. Other tiles, of which the Metropolitan Museum possesses examples, were painted with splashes of red, yellow, green, and brown luster in imitation of marbleized stones. The brilliancy of the ruby luster and the blending of various colors are best exemplified by a rare bowl in the Museum (fig. 104). The decoration of the interior consists of a large stylized cone motive with long narrow "leaves," surrounded by arched compartments, painted in several shades of red and gold luster on a ground of deep ruby-red luster. The whole exterior, including the base, is also covered with ruby luster. Although the provenance of this piece is uncertain, we may presume that it was made in Mesopotamia, where some of the finest pottery with ruby luster was found.

As has been stated, Abbasid polychrome lusterware was also

found in Iran and Egypt. A comparison of the pieces from Iran, for instance the bowl in the Museum (fig. 102), with those from Mesopotamia shows clearly that the former are inferior in design and were most probably local imitations. Mesopotamia, chiefly Baghdad, was the great artistic center for the production of this luxurious ninth-century pottery. In Iran polychrome lusterware of the Mesopotamian type was limited to western ceramic centers. In Khurasan, as excavations at Nishapur indicate, it was imitated by local potters in underglaze painting. The polychrome lusterware found in Egypt, chiefly in Fustat, Bahnasa, and other places, was most probably imported from Mesopotamia.

Fig. 106. Ewer, Iranian, XI Century

F. POTTERY WITH OVERGLAZE DECORATION

Interesting examples of Abbasid pottery with overglaze painting in cobalt blue and green were found in Samarra, Susa, and Rayy. Like the Abbasid lusterware, this pottery, made of fine yellowish earthenware and covered with a tin enamel, has been also attributed to Samarra kilns. The decoration of this ware consists of Kufic inscriptions in blue with splashes of green, as may be seen on a bowl in the Museum, or of leaf patterns (fig. 105) or floral stems with palmettes rendered in a summary fashion in blue or blue and green. The many fragments found in Iran indicate that this ware was not confined to Mesopotamia, as has been generally believed, but was made also in western Iran, probably at Rayy and other places. The excavations at Nishapur brought to light East Iranian imitations in which the decoration, mostly inscriptions, is painted in black over a white slip, under the glaze and not over the glaze as in the West Iranian group.

G. UNGLAZED POTTERY

Unglazed pottery of the early Islamic era continued the shapes and decoration known in the Sasanian period and consists of large water and storage jars, smaller jugs, pilgrim bottles, and ewers, found in various sites of Mesopotamia, Syria, and Iran. The decoration of this unglazed pottery was done in various ways. The simplest method was the engraving of horizontal or wavy lines, simple plant motives, and arabesques. Pieces with this type of decoration have come from Ctesiphon and Samarra and from Nishapur in Iran, where fine examples of the eighth and ninth centuries were uncovered by the Museum's expedition. The engraved decoration is sometimes combined with relief decoration in barbotine technique, which was produced by forcing moist clay, probably through a funnel. The relief decoration is rather crude and consists of various plant motives, animals, and human figures. A large jar in the Museum, found near Ctesiphon in Mesopotamia, is decorated with stylized trees and large rosettes in relief, with the addition of incised linear ornament. An interesting type of unglazed ewer with decoration in barbotine technique, partly incised, comes from various sites in Iran. The decoration on a ewer in the Museum, said to have been found at Sava, shows a pair of gazelles separated by a stylized tree against a background of plants, on two of which birds are resting. The Sasanian tradition is still alive in this group of Iranian pottery, which may be assigned to about the ninth century.

In another group of unglazed pottery the decoration was produced by means of stamps, mostly round but sometimes of other shape, a method known in the Sasanian era. The motives of this stamped decoration consist of animals, birds, human figures, rosettes, and Kufic inscriptions. Examples of this ware were found all over Mesopotamia and belong both to the end of the Sasanian era and to the early Islamic. Interesting ninth-century examples, many with animal decoration, were found in Samarra.

In the manufacture of great quantities of unglazed vessels with relief decoration, such as jugs and ewers, the potters of the Near East used earthenware molds. The round body of the vessels was usually made of two separate molds, to which the neck, handle, and foot were added later. As the examples from Samarra indicate, the decoration of this type of unglazed vessel of the ninth century was less elaborate than that of the eleventh or twelfth century and consisted of single lozenge diapers and leaf patterns.

2. Saljuk Pottery of Iran (XI-XIII Century)

Of great importance for the development of Islamic art was the conquest of Iran by the Turkish Saljuks. The Saljuk rulers of the eleventh and twelfth centuries were great patrons of art and gathered artists and craftsmen at their courts at Merv, Nishapur, Herat, Rayy, and Isfahan. Under the Saljuks and their successors, the shahs of Khwarizm, Iranian potters created magnificent ceramic ware which must be classified among the most beautiful ever produced. Many patterns and ceramic techniques known in the pre-Saljuk era were perfected by the potters of the twelfth and thirteenth centuries. Techniques like luster decoration, overglaze and underglaze painting in monochrome and polychrome, engraving, and carving were discriminately employed in various ceramic centers. New methods of decoration, such as openwork, were used with great effect. Rayy, a flourishing Saljuk city near Teheran, was a ceramic center of great importance. The ruins of Rayy, exploited by dealers for years, yielded great quantities of fine pottery which today fill museums and private collections. Another important ceramic center of the thirteenth and fourteenth centuries was Kashan, where several prominent Iranian potters whose names are known (see p. 185) had their workshops. Other Iranian sites, such as the region of Sultanabad, Sava, and Nishapur, which yielded pottery and wasters, must also be regarded as ceramic centers. As many types of ware were made all over Iran, it is sometimes difficult to attribute a piece to a particular locality. The great variety of Saljuk pottery of Iran may be divided into several groups according to their techniques.

A. POTTERY WITH INCISED, CARVED, AND PAINTED DECORATION

There are various types of Iranian pottery of the Saljuk era with incised and carved decoration. Some of them were made in Saljuk court manufactories; others must be classified as peasant ware. The Iranian potters of this period, like their Abbasid predecessors, attempted to imitate Chinese porcelain. The creamy-white bowls, cups, and ewers found in various sites of Iran, especially in Rayy, often have a translucent body like porcelain. The white body is much harder and thinner than in the ninth- and tenth-century specimens, showing a great advance in ceramic technique. The decoration of this ware, represented in the Museum by several fine pieces, is incised and carved in low relief, to which openwork is frequently added. An early example of this type is a ewer (fig. 106) in the Havemeyer Collection of the Museum. It is decorated in relief with a frieze of birds separated by scrolls and has a band of

Fig. 107. *Bowl, Iranian, Saljuk, XI Century*

leaves with a simple openwork decoration, representing an early attempt at a technique which gradually became more elaborate. Openwork was not confined to white ware, however, for it occurs on pieces with turquoise-blue and even green glazes dating from the eleventh to the thirteenth century. They were found in Rayy and Nishapur and most probably were made all over Iran. An important piece of the early eleventh century is a blue bowl with an incised design of fishes (see fig. 107) and pierced dots.

Fig. 108. *Bowl, Iranian, Saljuk, XI-XII Century*

Related to the Saljuk pottery just described is a group of luxurious eleventh- and twelfth-century white plates with a carved and incised decoration in low relief, painted with colored glazes in cobalt blue, turquoise blue, yellow, and purple manganese. Most of this type of Saljuk ware of Iran, known sometimes as Lakabi ware, was found in Rayy and may be regarded as of local manufacture. It is exemplified in the Museum by eight pieces presented by Horace Havemeyer. The decoration of this ware consists of birds and animals with arabesque scrolls and occasionally of human figures, and to a certain extent it shows a relation to early Saljuk metalwork and textiles of the eleventh and twelfth centuries. The highly decorative style is best seen in the Havemeyer bowl with a stag (fig. 108), the well-known eagle dish in Berlin, and a large dish with a bird group, formerly in the Macy collection, now in the Cleveland Museum.

A large group of Saljuk pottery of the twelfth century consists of plates, bowls, and ewers covered with a monochrome glaze of cobalt blue, turquoise blue, green, or purple manganese. This ware was once generally believed to be of Sultanabad origin and was frequently labeled as such. This attribution, however, can no longer be sustained, since other sites, such as Rayy, Kashan, and Sava, have produced numerous pieces, which probably were made locally. The decoration of this twelfth-century ware is more broadly treated than that of thirteenth-century pottery. It is in the developed Saljuk style and displays a great variety and richness of design, which, like the shapes of the pieces, was frequently borrowed from metalwork. Birds and animals are the favored motives, and some of the ewers end in heads of birds. The decoration is either incised or carved in relief. Among the pieces with engraved design are thin bowls covered with a cobalt-blue glaze; a bowl in the Metropolitan Museum, decorated with a frieze of running animals on a background of arabesque scrolls, is a typical example. In other pieces the design appears in slight relief, as may be seen on several plates and ewers in the Museum.

Fig. 109. *Bowl, Iranian, Saljuk, XI Century*

Among the *graffiato* pottery of the Saljuk period there are several interesting groups which come from various sites and are often called "Gabry" ware. Although the design is often highly decorative, this ware is of peasant manufacture. An interesting group from North Iran, attributed to the Amul or Zanjan region, has an incised decoration of animals and birds against a background of debased floral scrollwork. The glaze is colorless but the pattern is colored yellow-brown, green, and purple manganese, following the tradition of splashed Chinese ware of the T'ang period. The decoration shows many characteristic features of the Saljuk period and should be also dated in the twelfth century.

The best-known type of "Gabry" has been often attributed to the Hamadan and Zanjan region, although lately the Garus region, particularly Yasukand, has come to be regarded as the place of origin. This pottery, which consists of ewers, tiles, and bowls of various sizes, is decorated with boldly drawn animals, birds, human figures, and Kufic inscriptions combined with arabesque scrolls. The decoration is either incised or is formed by cutting away the slip around the pattern, which then stands out in relief. The glaze is either yellowish (often with green, sometimes with purple, splashes) or green, the scraped-away portion appearing darker. Although some of the pieces, such as the bowl shown in figure 109, are very striking in design, generally the decoration is somewhat crudely drawn, which is

Fig. 110. Ewer, Iranian, XIII Century

characteristic of provincial or peasant ware. This pottery has been dated in various periods. Some have regarded it as of the eighth or ninth century, others as later, chiefly because of the style of the Kufic characters, which suggest the eleventh or twelfth century. New material now confirms the later date, and the majority of this "Gabry" ware should be assigned to the twelfth century, although some of it may be as early as the eleventh century.

The various types of twelfth-century Saljuk pottery described above continued to be made in the thirteenth century. In general, however, the decoration became more elaborate in the thirteenth century, and in the case of ewers was often molded instead of carved.

A cobalt-blue ewer (fig. 110) is decorated with a frieze of huntsmen on foot or horseback against a background of linear arabesques in low relief. Other favored subjects of ewers in cobalt- or turquoise-

Fig. 111. Vase, Iranian, XIII Century

blue are dancing dervishes, animals, arabesque patterns, and Kufic inscriptions. To this group of pottery also belong large storage jars, one of which, with a turquoise-blue glaze, is in the Metropolitan Museum (fig. 111) and may be dated at the beginning of the thirteenth century. The ornament of the neck consists of a Kufic inscription and a band of arabesque scrolls in low relief. The shoulder of the jar has a frieze of marching griffins on a background of arabesques, a design well known in Saljuk ornament. Below this frieze are two other bands, one with a trefoil diaper, the other with a scale pattern. Only about six such jars are in existence. These were once attributed to the kilns of Sultanabad, but lately to Kashan.

The Saljuk potters of the late twelfth century were familiar with the technique of underglaze painting, which they often combined with other techniques. In an interesting group of pottery, fragments of which were found at Rayy, the decoration in relief is cut from a black slip covered with a blue glaze. The decoration consists of palmette scrolls, sphinxes, griffins, birds, and figure subjects rendered in an effective silhouette style. Two pieces of this ware are in the Museum. One of them represents a seated figure in the style of the Rayy lusterware of the late twelfth century or beginning of the thirteenth. The other, a cup, has an incised inscription and vertical bands. One of the finest examples of this type, decorated with a horseman on a rich arabesque background, is in the Horace Havemeyer collection in New York. In another variety of this ware the silhouette design in dark brown or black is painted under a cream-colored glaze.

In a group of pottery with underglaze painting in black under a colorless or blue glaze the highly effective decoration consists of foliated scrolls, wreaths, plants, rosettes, birds, and fishes rendered in a sketchy, impressionistic manner which reflects the Abbasid style of the ninth century. Bands with incised inscriptions often accompany this ornament on both the exterior and interior. This type of pottery can be assigned with certainty to the beginning of the thirteenth century, as several dated pieces are known. The earliest piece is of the year 1204 and is in the Gamsaragan Bey collection in Alexandria; pieces dated 1211 and 1214 are in the National Museum at Stockholm and in the Sir Ernest Debenham collection in London. This ware has been usually assigned to Sultanabad and, recently, to Kashan. Finds of complete pieces and fragments at Rayy and Sava indicate, however, that it was made in several ceramic centers. The foliated scrolls of this ware appear also in a number of pieces with figure subjects, for instance, the jug in the Brangwyn collection in London and a bowl with two seated figures in the

Pillsbury collection in Minneapolis. A foliated scroll decorates the interior of an important bowl (fig. 112) in the Metropolitan Museum. Around the rim we see arabesque scrolls cut through the wall of the vessel and covered with a colorless glaze.

One of the great masterpieces of thirteenth-century Iranian ceramic art is the blue jug (fig. 113) in the Museum. Various ceramic processes, such as molding, openwork, engraving, and underglaze painting, are combined in the manufacture of this piece and similar ones, of which very few are in existence. Over an inner wall of the neck and body is an openwork decoration of animals, harpies, and sphinxes against a background of arabesque pattern. Among the animals on the neck we recognize deer grazing or turning their heads, and on the main body there are hares in full flight pursued by hounds. The details of the decoration, as well as the leafy scrolls and plants, are painted black and the arabesques cobalt-blue. The incised inscriptions contain verses from poems and the date A.H. 612 (1215/6). The piece was said to have been found at Sultanabad and it was generally attributed to the kilns of this region. Similarities

Fig. 112. *Bowl with Openwork Decoration, Iranian, XIII Century*

with other ware from Rayy, Sava, and Kashan now make this attribution doubtful. Lately Kashan, because of the resemblance of certain details of its lusterware (see page 185), has been suggested as a possible place of manufacture. There are, however, just as many if not more analogies with various types of Rayy pottery, so that attributions to a certain locality must be given with caution. Systematic excavations of Kashan sites may throw more light on this question.

B. POTTERY AND TILES WITH PAINTED LUSTER DECORATION

The Saljuk potters of the twelfth century were responsible for the revival of the luster technique which was so popular in the ninth century under the Abbasids. The color of Iranian lusterware of the Saljuk period varies from a pale greenish gold to a dark reddish brown painted over a white glaze, sometimes entirely or partially tinted cobalt- or turquoise-blue, as may be seen in several plates and a ewer in the Museum. The vessels and tiles for wall decoration and prayer niches are richly embellished with various decorative

Fig. 113. Jug with Openwork Decoration, Dated 1215/6, Iranian

motives, among which are animals and birds, arabesques, and large inscriptions, the latter used especially on tiles for prayer niches. Figure subjects were also popular and consisted of hunting scenes or seated figures, singly or in groups, frequently a prince with entertainers. In a type which is perhaps the earliest of these twelfth-century ceramics, the motives are reserved in a solid luster background.

That the luster technique was flourishing during the twelfth century is evident from several dated pieces, the earliest of which is a fragmentary bottle in the British Museum dated A.H. 575 (1179). It is decorated with bands of seated figures, running animals, and arabesques rendered in a bold style, which also characterizes a bowl in the Art Institute of Chicago dated A.H. 587 (1191). In both pieces the designs are either painted in luster or reserved in a solid luster ground. The style of these twelfth-century pieces is quite different from that of lustered vessels and tiles bearing dates of the first half of the thirteenth century.

The Museum possesses several bowls and a tile which are similar in style to the British Museum bottle of 1179. One of the finest pieces of this group is a bowl with a representation of a pegasus (fig. 114) against a background of bold arabesques, rendered in the highly decorative style characteristic of Saljuk art. Other important pieces of this group are a bowl with a bird and a seated figure and a star-shaped tile with a design of a hare. As many of the pieces, including numerous fragments and wasters in the Saljuk style of the twelfth century, were found at Rayy, we may regard them as products of that important ceramic center. To the end of the twelfth century may be attributed the lustered ware from Rayy which is decorated with horsemen or seated figures in a conventional landscape of checkered trees similar to that on the bowl of 1191.

In the bottle of 1179, the bowl of 1191, and related pieces dots, arabesques, and comma-shaped palmettes, on the figures and in the background, play an important role in the formation of the design. In a number of Rayy pieces these arabesques form a dense pattern which is combined with figure subjects. This design is best exemplified by a large dish (fig. 115) in the Museum, formerly in the V. Everit Macy collection. This is not only one of the finest products of Rayy but a masterpiece of Iranian ceramic art. The dish is decorated with two figures, a prince and a court entertainer playing cymbals, which, with the exception of a narrow band, occupy the whole interior. The figures are heavily outlined and are reserved in a dense background of arabesque scrolls. The costumes of the two figures show a design of either arabesque scrolls or dots. Another interesting feature of this dish, which is also seen in Rakka pottery (see p. 189), is the clear separation of the figures from the background by a double outline, one in luster, the other in white. The unusually fine drawing and the elaborate luster technique indicate that the piece must have been made in one of the court manufactories.

The lusterware of the second half of the twelfth century represents the height of the Saljuk style. In 1193 Rayy fell into the

Fig. 114. Lustered Bowl, Iranian, Rayy, XII Century

hands of the shahs of Khwarizm, who kept up the artistic tradition of the Saljuks. The thirteenth-century style of Iranian lusterware is known to us from a great number of dated vessels and tiles, the earliest one being a star-shaped tile in the Arab Museum in Cairo dated A.H. 600 (1203). The patterns of the thirteenth-century pieces show firm outlines and an abundance of ornament on a small scale, with the addition of birds and animals covering the whole field. Typical examples are the tiles of 1208 and 1210 in the Boston Museum, the bowl dated A.H. 607 (1210) in the Havemeyer Collection of the Museum, and a tile in the Gayer Anderson collection, Cairo, of the year 1211. The background and costumes are patterned with minute spirals painted in luster or etched in the luster ground. Such minute spirals are the comma-shaped palmettes of the twelfth century detached and degenerated.

The thirteenth-century style is well illustrated by the bowl in

Fig. 115. Lustered Dish, Iranian, Rayy, about 1200

figure 116, which is decorated with seated figures, two in the center surrounded by four couples, possibly representing lovers. Such groups appear, particularly in the center, on a number of dated tiles and bowls, for instance, a bowl in the University Museum in Philadelphia dated A.H. 608 (1211). The male and female figures on this bowl and related ones represent the conventional Turkish type. In only a few cases, as on a bowl and a star tile in the Havemeyer Collection, is the prince bearded. Another fine example of thirteenth-century style is the large dish from the Macy collection, in the decoration of which Kufic and Naskhi play an important role. The broad band of Kufic inscriptions has interlaced letters and arabesque scrolls with large half palmettes which suggest actual leaves. Such palmettes occur in almost all the pottery and tiles discussed above and are often combined with flying ducks, motives possibly of Chinese origin, that became very popular during the fourteenth

Fig. 116. Lustered Bowl, Iranian, Kashan, XIII Century

century. The flying-bird motive may be seen on a bowl in the Museum in which luster is combined with painted polychrome decoration and also on a large star tile dated A.H. 608 (1211/2) (fig. 117), the gift of Horace Havemeyer, which pictures a prince surrounded by his courtiers.

The lusterware of the first half of the thirteenth century described above was formerly attributed to Rayy but lately to Kashan because of analogies with work definitely of Kashan origin. That Kashan was an important ceramic center in the thirteenth and fourteenth centuries is now generally recognized, thanks to the discovery and publication of a treatise on Iranian faïence technique in Kashan written in 1301 by Abu'l Kasim 'Abd Allah ibn 'Ali ibn Abi Tahir of Kashan. The author of this treatise was a member of a famous family of Kashan potters, who made some of the most

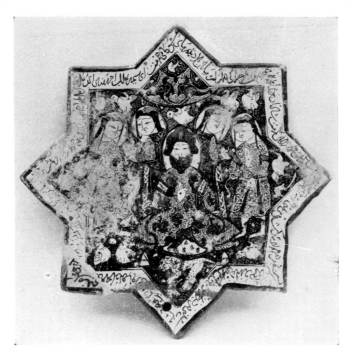

Fig. 117. *Lustered Tile Dated 1211/2, Iranian, Kashan*

beautiful mihrabs known. The earliest works of this family are the three mihrabs of A.H. 612 (1215/6) in the sanctuary of the imam Riza at Mashhad, which were made by Muhammad ibn Abi Tahir. The fame of Kashan was so great that all tiles were often called "Kashi" or "Kashani." A masterpiece of Kashan potters is the mihrab from the Maidan mosque of that city, now in the Islamic collections of the Berlin Museum. According to the inscription, it was made by Hasan ibn 'Arabshah in the year A.H. 623 (1226). Although Kashan is not mentioned in the inscription, there is little doubt that it was made locally. It is very similar to a mihrab from the Imam-Zada Yahya at Varamin, made forty-one years later by 'Ali ibn Muhammad ibn Abi Tahir, who also made the mihrab from Kum dated A.H. 663 (1264) now in Berlin. 'Ali was the father of the man who wrote the treatise on Kashan faïence technique. The elaborate decoration of this mihrab shows Iranian ceramic art at its height. The pattern consists of several varieties of arabesques, some on a smaller, others on a larger scale, which form the background for inscriptions in relief painted in cobalt blue. Through the combination of writing and ornament in luster, turquoise blue, and cobalt blue, partly painted flat and partly in relief, Iranian artists, probably of Kashan, created a new decorative scheme for tilework, which was followed all through the thirteenth and fourteenth centuries. Examples may be seen in the Museum in a number of single tiles (see fig. 132) and central portions of mihrabs. This style is a further development of the one which occurs on vessels and tiles of the beginning of the thirteenth century and which Ettinghausen also attributes to Kashan potters. In the beginning of the thirteenth century, until its destruction by the Mongols in 1220, Rayy played an important role in the making of ceramics, and much of the polychrome ware (see p. 187) is of that period. The finds and recent excavations show that the so-called Kashan style was also known in Rayy and in other parts of Iran. We find in pieces from Rayy not only minute scrollwork but also the trefoiled leaves which are so typical of later Kashan work. It is probable, therefore, that the style attributed to Kashan originated in Rayy and after its destruction was continued in other centers, of which Kashan was the most important one.

C. POTTERY WITH POLYCHROME OVERGLAZE DECORATION

To the technical skill of the Iranian potters of the twelfth century we owe the invention of a technique of painting with pigments of various colors over white, turquoise-blue (fig. 118), or cobalt-blue glaze. There are several varieties of pottery with overglaze decoration, all of which are represented in the Museum. The treatise of 1301 on Kashan faïence technique mentions two types of overglaze decoration: one decorated with gold leaf and painted with white, red, black, and yellow enamels; the other painted with seven colors, although this method was no longer practiced in 1301. Pottery of both types, after being painted, was placed in earthenware containers and fired a second time for half a day. The process of decorating the ware with seven colors is the real "Minai" technique, closely related to miniature painting, as has been already stated (see p. 28). The magnificent decoration of this pottery, made probably for princes and nobles, consists mostly of figure subjects, such as horsemen, seated and standing figures, sphinxes, court scenes, hunting

Fig. 118. Bowl with Polychrome Decoration,
Iranian, Rayy, XIII Century

scenes, and legendary episodes from the *Shah-nama*. The popular story of Bahram Gur and his sweetheart Azada is represented on two bowls in the John Schiff collection in New York. The figures are usually on a small scale; occasionally a single figure or two large ones are used, as in the bowl shown in figure 119, which is decorated with a horseman on a background of arabesques. Among the motives of this ware are geometrical patterns, including arabesques, interlacings, and rosettes. The richest of the polychrome ware, as seen in the jug shown in plate II, is painted in white, pink, cobalt blue, green, brown, purple manganese, and black, to which gold is frequently added. Not all the pottery with overglaze decoration is as rich in color as this jug. There are pieces in which cobalt blue, turquoise blue, and black, with the addition of red and gold, are used. In another group the decoration of figures or arabesques in relief is rendered in gold and outlined in red. Several pieces of the gilded variety are in the Metropolitan Museum. Among the best are a bowl with two horsemen separated by a tree and a ewer with an arabesque pattern and a frieze of animals on cobalt- or turquoise-blue ground.

Fig. 119. Bowl with Polychrome Decoration, Iranian, Rayy,
XIII Century

In another variety of pottery the decoration is applied directly to the biscuit. One of the finest examples known is a jug in the Museum decorated with vertical bands alternately containing arabesques and parallel zigzag lines painted in cobalt-blue glaze, partly gilded.

Most of the pottery with overglaze decoration came from Rayy, although some pieces were found in other sites. Until recently Rayy was regarded as the chief center of this ware, particularly of the poly-

188

chrome "Minai" ware. Today, however, it is certain that some of it was of Kashan manufacture. To this group probably belong bowls with large figures, as the one in figure 119, and vessels with gilded relief decoration. The Kashan style of the thirteenth century is evident in pieces in which luster is combined with polychrome decoration. To Rayy should be attributed all the pieces (see pl. II and fig. 119) which are similar in style to the lusterware of the end of the twelfth century and the beginning of the thirteenth.

3. Saljuk Pottery of Rakka and Rusafa (XII-XIII Century)

A well-known type of Islamic pottery has been long associated with Rakka on the Euphrates. Quantities of this pottery passed through the hands of Syrian dealers, who supplied the market with many fine pieces, seen today in museums and private collections. Although no systematic excavations were ever made in Rakka, investigations of the site by Sarre and Herzfeld and wasters found there indicate that it was an important ceramic center. Rakka ware has often been erroneously attributed to the period of Harun ar Rashid (786-809), who resided there for some time. The ornament and style of the figure compositions, however, point to a later date. Although some of the Rakka ware may belong to the eleventh century, the majority dates from the twelfth or thirteenth, showing decorative elements which are characteristic of the era of the Saljuk atabegs of Syria and Mesopotamia.

There are several varieties of Rakka ware with both painted and lustered decoration. The lusterware consists of small and large vases, jugs, bowls, and tazzas. The color of the luster is usually dark brown, which seldom appears in other ceramic centers. The decoration, painted in luster over a transparent greenish glaze, frequently enhanced by the addition of cobalt blue, consists of arabesques, Kufic or Naskhi inscriptions, and occasionally highly stylized birds. Some of the pieces have great elegance and beauty of design; the finest ones are doubtless of the twelfth century. The arabesques and writing either are reserved in white or are rendered in brown luster. The design is placed against a background of a spiral pattern, as may be seen in a vase in the Museum (fig. 120). In large jars (fig. 121) the luster decoration is combined with relief ornament.

Another well-known type of Rakka pottery has a decoration

painted in black under a turquoise-blue glaze. The principal ornament of this group consists of arabesques (fig. 122), interlacings,
Kufic letters, and birds, supplemented by dots, commas, and spirals
within compartments. This Rakka ware is often confused with simi-

Fig. 120. Lustered Vase, Mesopotamian, Rakka, XII-XIII Century

lar Iranian pottery with black and blue decoration. However, the
body of these two types of ceramics is different; the Iranian is
harder, less sandy, and grayish white instead of buff. Some of the
Rakka pottery in black and blue is classified among the masterpieces
of Muhammadan ceramic art. One of them is a bowl in the Horace

190

Havemeyer collection in New York, with a design of two peacocks, in which the curving contours of the bodies and the flowing lines of the tails form an effective composition within a circle. Another famous piece, probably of the twelfth century, is in the Metropolitan Museum (fig. 124). Here the decoration, reserved in the black background, shows two interlaced dragons with knotted serpent bodies and arabesques. The dragon motive plays an important role in Saljuk art, probably being used as a symbol of evil. In a number of large jars the decoration not only is painted in black but also is in relief. The Museum possesses several vases of this type, two of which are a gift of John D. Rockefeller, Jr. Their bold patterns show mostly arabesques combined with Kufic characters.

Fig. 121. Lustered Jar, Mesopotamian, Rakka, XII-XIII Century

Besides Rakka ware in black and blue, there is also a group with polychrome decoration, which recalls some of the Iranian ceramics of the thirteenth century. The decoration, painted in black, blue, green, and brown manganese, under a transparent, slightly greenish glaze, consists of sphinxes, warriors, hunters, animals, and arabesques. The style, similar to that of lustered Rakka ware, is typical of Saljuk art. Several fine complete pieces are in the Museum. A bowl (fig. 123) is decorated with a sphinx and plants, while an albarello shows large camels, realistically drawn. An interesting small bowl shows a horse in a conventional landscape.

Related to Rakka ware is the pottery which was found in Rusafa (the Christian Sergiopolis) in the Syrian desert not far from Rakka. The decoration is mostly identical with that of Rakka pottery. There are two varieties of Rusafa ware, one with lustered decoration, the other with painted decoration. In the case of the former the luster is not brown, as in Rakka ware, but dark reddish brown or purple. The painted Rusafa pottery is also similar to that of

Fig. 122. Bowl, Mesopotamian,
Rakka, XII-XIII Century

Rakka; in addition to the colors mentioned above, a thick red-brown pigment is used. Three specimens of Rusafa ware are in the Museum, a vase (fig. 125), a bowl with arabesques, and a small bowl with a design of a bird encircled by a foliated wreath.

4. Unglazed Pottery of the Saljuk Period (XI-XIII Century)

The unglazed pottery of the Near East in the time of the Saljuks and their immediate successors reflects the richness of decoration so characteristic of glazed ceramics and other arts and crafts of that period. The decoration of jars and jugs was produced mostly with the help of molds, which by this time had almost entirely replaced the earlier method of stamping. The Museum possesses a large and representative collection of such vessels, mostly from Mesopotamia, which has lately been enriched by pieces found in Nishapur by the Museum's Iranian expedition. The decoration of this unglazed ware consists of birds, animals, arabesques, inscriptions, and geometrical motives and patterns such as lozenge diapers (see fig. 126).

Fig. 123. Bowl, Mesopotamian, Rakka,
XII-XIII Century

Sometimes the design is of high artistic quality, as may be seen on a jar cover found in Syria and decorated in Saljuk style with two birds on a background of arabesques (fig. 127).

The other technique which was greatly favored for unglazed pottery in the Near East in the Saljuk period, chiefly in Mesopotamia, was the barbotine technique. An interesting group of large ovoid jars, used for storage of water or wine, shows a rich relief decoration in this technique. Not many complete pieces are known; generally, only the upper part of the vases is preserved. A piece in the Museum shows the ornament characteristic of this type of ware. The decoration consists of arched compartments with an animal design in openwork against a background of arabesques, the arches being separated by female busts. Several techniques are here combined; bar-

Fig. 124. Bowl, Mesopotamian, Rakka, XII-XIII Century

botine, free modeling, and stamping. Most of the known vessels came from Mesopotamia, where similar patterns may be found in the building decoration of the second half of the twelfth century and the beginning of the thirteenth. Some of them were supposed to have been found in Mosul, which might have been one of the production centers of this ware.

5. Ceramic Art of the Mongol Period in Iran (XIII-XIV Century)

The conquest of Iran by the Mongols and the establishing of a royal dynasty in 1256 at first brought little change in the decoration of pottery and wall tiles. The techniques and patterns of Iranian

Fig. 125. Vase, Syrian, Rusafa, XIII Century

ceramics of the first half of the thirteenth century continued to be used under the Mongols in the second half of the thirteenth century and in the fourteenth. Among the techniques of the Mongol period we find underglaze painting in black and blue, relief decoration, and overglaze painting with luster or with pigments and gold. The numerous dated tiles and vessels of the second half of the thirteenth century reveal clearly that the Mongols were patrons of Islamic arts and crafts. The old ceramic centers, with the exception of Rayy, produced magnificent pottery and tiles, which are seldom inferior to those of the Saljuk era. Kashan, the region of Sultanabad, Sultaniya, Nishapur, Samarkand, Sava, and Mashhad were some of the ceramic centers of the Mongol period. The dated pieces permit us to follow the evolution of style caused by the Mongol invasion; Chinese naturalism in the rendering of animals, birds, and landscapes gradually penetrated all branches of Islamic art, including ceramics.

Fig. 126. Unglazed Jug, Mesopotamian, XI-XII Century

Mongol ceramics with underglaze painting are covered with either a creamy or a turquoise-blue glaze. The decoration consists of arabesques, scrolls, and trefoils (known from lusterware), and plants, often with the addition of animals and birds. The pattern either covers the entire interior of vessels or is placed in compartments, as may be seen in several bowls in the Metropolitan Museum. An interesting type of Iranian pottery of the second half of the thirteenth century is represented in the Museum by a bowl (fig. 128). The interior shows a landscape of tall grass with running hares painted in cobalt blue, turquoise blue, and dark olive green with touches of purple manganese under a creamy yellow glaze. On the exterior, around the rim, is a band of inscription in relief, in white on a blue ground. The plant decoration is related to that of the beginning of the thirteenth century (see p. 178), showing the same sketchy rendering but more naturalistic forms. A piece which dates this group is a bowl in the Kelekian collection of the Victoria and Albert Museum with an inscription containing the year A.H. 672 (1274). It shows two birds in a landscape identical with the one on our bowl. Other pieces are almost direct copies of lusterware and range in date from the end of the thirteenth century to the beginning of the fourteenth. Some of this ware comes from Sava, some from Rayy, Sultaniya, and the region of Sultanabad.

The Mongol ceramic style was fully developed by the beginning of the fourteenth century. The influence of Chinese art is evident not only in the borrowing of motives, such as plants with peony and lotus blossoms, clouds, and phoenixes, but also in the naturalistic rendering of the design. This Mongol style is best exemplified by a group of pottery with painted decoration which is generally attributed to the Sultanabad region. Naturalistic plants and a mosaic-like pattern of small leaves either form the sole decoration of bowls, vases, and tiles or are combined with flying birds, phoenixes, hares, deer (fig.

Fig. 127. *Cover of Unglazed Jar, Mesopotamian, XI-XII Century*

129), and human figures in Mongol costumes in black, cobalt blue, and turquoise blue. The background is either cobalt blue or white with spiral motives in black. In some pieces the decoration is also in relief, as may be seen on several bowls and star-shaped and rectangular tiles in the Museum. The design of this Sultanabad pottery is identical with that of the lusterware of Kashan dating from the first half of the fourteenth century, so that they may be regarded as contemporaneous. The Mongol style of pottery continued in the second half of the fourteenth century, but the execution is inferior to that of the earlier pieces.

An important group of Mongol pottery has a relief decoration under a cobalt-blue (sometimes turquoise-blue) glaze. This ware, consisting of large vases and tiles, can be dated at the end of the thirteenth century and the beginning of the fourteenth. Two cobalt-blue vases are in American collections: one, in the Horace Have-meyer collection on loan in the Metropolitan Museum, is dated A.H. 681 (1282/3); the other, in the Freer Gallery in Washington, is dated A.H. 683 (1284/5). Both have a relief decoration of animals and flying geese in a seminaturalistic landscape. The Chinese influ-

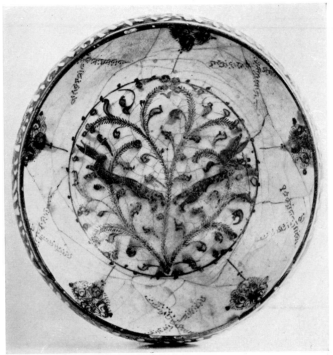

Fig. 128. Bowl, Iranian, Mongol, Second Half of the XIII Century

ence is here evident in the motives, such as the geese and the clouds, and also in the partly naturalistic treatment of the landscape. To the end of the thirteenth century may be assigned another large cobalt-blue vase in the Freer Gallery, decorated with bands of figure subjects and animals. Pottery with relief decoration and mono-chrome glazes continued to be made in the fourteenth century. The Chinese motives and naturalistic style on vases and tiles of this period are more conspicuous and are similar to those on contemporary lusterware (see p. 199). This ware has been usually attributed to Sultanabad, but it is probable that some of the finest pieces, with cobalt-blue glaze, were made in Kashan, since great quantities of cobalt are found in the village of Kamsar, in the mountains near Kashan.

The lusterware of the Mongol period followed in the brilliant tradition of the Rayy and Kashan schools of the first half of the

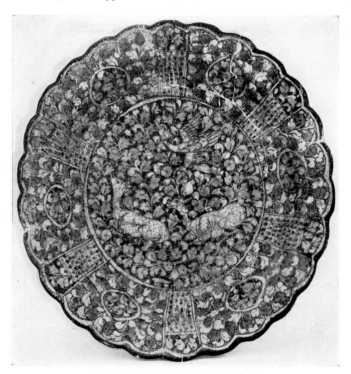

Fig. 129. Plate, Iranian, Sultanabad, XIV Century

thirteenth century. Numerous dated tiles, mihrabs, and vessels, scattered in various museums and private collections, give us a complete picture of the stylistic development from the second half of the thirteenth century to the end of the fourteenth. The use of lustered tiles for the decoration of dwellings, public buildings, mosques, and tombs was considerable. Some are star- or cross-shaped, others are rectangular, being used for mihrabs or decorative friezes.

Several types of tiles can be recognized. One group is related to star- and cross-shaped tiles which come from the Imam-Zada Yahya at Varamin and usually bear the date A.H. 661 (1262/3) but occasionally 662 and 663 (1263/4, 1264/5). The tiles are decorated with arabesques and palmette scrolls reserved on a luster ground with etched minute spirals. There is a great richness and variety of pattern, exemplified in the Museum by three tiles (see fig. 130). These tiles are of the same group as the Kevorkian mihrab of 1264, which also comes from the Imam-Zada at Varamin and was made by the famous Kashan potter 'Ali ibn Muhammad ibn Abi Tahir. As this mihrab was made in Kashan, it is reasonable to assume that the star- and cross-shaped tiles from Varamin, sometimes regarded as of local origin, were also made at Kashan. Potters of the Rayy school ceased to play any role in Iranian ceramic art after the destruction of Rayy in 1222. They were replaced by potters of the Kashan school, whose fame became so great that tiles for mihrabs were exported to other cities, such as Kum, and even as far as Mashhad. The potter who made the Varamin mihrab was also responsible for the Kum mihrab of 1264, now in Berlin.

Fig. 130. Lustered Tile Dated 1263, Iranian, Kashan

Another group of tiles centers around star- and cross-shaped tiles which supposedly came from Damghan and bear the date A.H. 665 (1266/7). Tiles of this type are decorated with groups of animals, birds, and figure subjects in conventionalized landscapes of trees and plants, painted in a rich gold luster, occasionally with touches of cobalt and turquoise blue. Other tiles show an arabesque pattern or abstract plants without any trace of naturalistic design, which appears in tiles and pottery dated about twenty years later. In their precision of drawing and highly decorative quality the tiles of the Damghan type are among the finest of lustered wares, and most probably they are products of Kashan. In later thirteenth-century Kashan lusterware the color, cobalt blue or turquoise blue, began to play a more important part in the design, covering large surfaces. The style reached its height in the beginning of the fourteenth century and is exemplified in the Metropolitan Museum by a number of fine tiles and bowls.

Toward the end of the thirteenth century the naturalistic element started to invade the pattern of lusterware. Abstract motives such as scrolls and palmettes began to be treated as growing plants, to which artists added here and there naturalistic leaves, as seen in several mihrab tiles in the Museum which may be dated about 1300. Here among the scrolls are birds, either resting or flying, motives

Fig. 131. Bahram Gur and Azada, Lustered Tile, Iranian,
Kashan, about 1300

which appear in thirteenth-century tiles of the Kashan type. A large and deep bowl in the Museum, of the beginning of the fourteenth century, shows the same motives, with naturalistic leaves more conspicuous than in the tiles. Figure subjects depicting scenes from daily life or legendary episodes continued to be popular on tiles and vessels. An important tazza of about 1300 in the Museum shows seated figures in costumes which are partly Mongol surrounded by naturalistic leaves and plants. Several tiles dating from the end of the thirteenth century and the beginning of the fourteenth, decorated with figure subjects, are in the Museum. A characteristic feature of these tiles is the combination of relief and luster painting, which in the earlier periods was confined to inscriptions only. The most beautiful tile of this type represents the famous episode from the *Shah-nama* showing Bahram Gur (fig. 131) seated on a camel with his lute player Azada, hunting gazelles. The decoration, partly in relief, is painted in cobalt and turquoise and brown-gold luster. Chinese influence is apparent in a number of dated fourteenth-

Fig. 132. Lustered Tile, Iranian, Kashan, Early
XIV Century

century tiles, one of which, in a private collection in New York, is inscribed with the name of the potter Yusuf ibn 'Ali ibn Muhammad ibn Abi Tahir and is similar to several other tiles dated 1310 and 1311. Yusuf is also the maker of the mihrab of 1305 in the Hermitage at Leningrad and of another one in the Museum at Teheran, dated A.H. 734 (1333/4), which comes from a mosque at Kum. He was the son of the Kashan master who made the Varamin mihrab of 1264 and a brother of the author of the treatise of 1301 on the faïence technique. The tiles of 1310 and 1311 show in the main field the traditional arabesque pattern; in the top border, however, the design is purely naturalistic, consisting of Chinese peonies and leaves. Similar naturalistic plants combined with birds may be seen in the border of a tile in the Metropolitan Museum dated A.H. 707 (1308). This mixture of traditional and new motives may be

Fig. 133. Tile with Overglaze Decoration, Iranian, Kashan, XIV Century

seen on two small mihrabs in the Museum, one of which is signed by Hasan ibn 'Ali ibn Ahmad Babuya, "the builder." In another, later group of star-shaped tiles the naturalistic style is used almost exclusively. A tile of this type in the British Museum bears the date A.H. 729 (1328/9) and is decorated with naturalistic plants in relief and gold luster, the inscription in the border being reserved in a cobalt-blue ground.

Birds and animals appear frequently in combination with the plant forms. The Chinese phoenix becomes a favorite motive, as seen on a beautiful square tile (fig. 132) in the Museum, painted in brown luster, cobalt blue, and turquoise blue. Here all the motives are borrowed from Chinese art, as was characteristic of Iranian art during the fourteenth century and even later. Together with this change of design, we observe a gradual decline in the luster technique and in the design, which is noticeable in a group of tiles dated 1337 and 1338. That many of these tiles were made at Kashan is directly stated in the inscriptions, for instance, on star tiles in the British Museum, in the Museum at Kum, and in private collections. Some of these tiles show figures dressed in purely Mongol costumes and familiar to us from a number of fourteenth-century manuscripts of the Shah-nama.

The overglaze painting of vessels and tiles continued in the Mongol period, but the colors were limited to white, red, and gold over a cobalt- or turquoise-blue glaze. Polychrome "Minai" ware with figure subjects became less popular in the second half of the thirteenth century, being gradually replaced by lusterware. "Minai" ware is represented in the Museum by several interesting vessels and tiles dating from the second half of the thirteenth century and the beginning of the fourteenth. A bowl and a jug with scrollwork and disks on cobalt-blue ground may be assigned to the thirteenth century. To the beginning of the fourteenth century belong a star-shaped tile and a square cobalt-blue tile, probably from a mihrab, in the Moore Collection (fig. 133). The inscription in relief is placed against the background of white arabesque scrolls; in the top border appear naturalistic leaves and peonies similar to those of luster tiles of the beginning of the fourteenth century. The star-shaped tiles are decorated with similar naturalistic plants, to which occasionally a flying bird is added. Birds appear in a number of tiles and vessels. The gilded portions of the patterns are not painted in liquid gold but consist of applied gold leaf, a technique which was practiced in Kashan. It is described in the 1301 treatise on faïence technique, which states that the gold leaf was cut into pieces with scissors, glued to the background, and then burnished with cotton.

A. FAÏENCE MOSAIC

In the Mongol period another ceramic technique, the faïence mosaic, became popular in Iran. In this technique the design is composed in mosaic fashion of small units of various shapes and sizes cut from large slabs of earthenware glazed in solid colors. The pieces, which follow the contours of the design, are held together with plaster, poured from the rear, which penetrates all the crevices. Faïence mosaic is related to the glazed-brick decoration of ancient Mesopotamia and Iran. Its development, which was gradual, was the result of a desire for more elaborate and colorful patterns. The art of faïence mosaic began to be practiced under the Saljuks and is best known to us from thirteenth-century buildings of Konia in Asia Minor. Here the interior decoration of several mosques, such as the Laranda, Bey Hakim, and Sirchali, some with mihrabs, was executed by Iranian ceramists in faïence mosaic. In the fourteenth century this technique was fully developed, and the Iranian ceramists not only perfected the process but evolved new color schemes which were used for centuries. Among the examples of the early Mongol period are the mausoleum of Uljaitu (1310) at Sultaniya

Fig. 134. Mihrab of Faïence Mosaic from the Madrasa Imami at Isfahan, Dated 1354, Iranian, Mongol

and buildings at Natanz, Yazd, and Varamin, in which the faïence mosaic has begun to cover larger surfaces of the exterior and interior.

The great development of faïence mosaic seems to have taken place in Isfahan, as a number of monuments indicate. An important monument is the tomb mosque of Baba Kasim, erected in

1340/1 by a certain Sulaiman Abu'l Hasan Talut ad Damghani, which contains a mihrab made entirely of faïence mosaics, with a bold pattern of arabesques in white, dark blue, and light blue. Not far from the tomb of Baba Kasim stands the madrasa Imami, dated A.H. 755 (1354), which is richly decorated with geometrical patterns and bands of inscription in faïence mosaic. The magnificent mihrab of this madrasa is now in the Metropolitan Museum (fig. 134). The decoration of this mihrab, which is representative of the art of faïence mosaic under the Mongols, consists of bands of Koranic inscription in Kufic or large round cursive writing, arabesques, and geometrical interlacings. The latter form elaborate patterns in the central niche and spandrels. The colors of the design are white, turquoise blue, cobalt blue, golden yellow, and dark green. The background is mostly cobalt blue; this sets off effectively the bold pattern, which is characteristic of the Mongol period. A further feature of the Mongol style is the introduction of naturalistic plants and lotus blossoms, but these motives are used only sparingly here. The further development of the fourteenth-century faïence mosaic may be seen in the mosque Masjid-i-Jami at Isfahan and the mosque of Yazd, which contains a magnificent mihrab of the year 1375.

6. Ceramic Art of the Timurid Period in Iran (XV Century)

There is relatively little Iranian pottery of the Timurid period in existence. In the known pieces, however, some of the techniques and decorative patterns of the Mongol era which were continued under the Timurids reveal a noticeable decline in quality. Judging from representations of pottery in fifteenth-century miniatures, the Chinese influence was predominant in the Timurid period. Some of the ceramics shown there were most probably true porcelain imported from China, while other pieces were Iranian copies, of which very few exist. A bowl in the Metropolitan Museum may be assigned to the end of the fifteenth century. Its thin body is made of white sandy earthenware and is decorated with a Chinese dragon with an elongated body painted in black and a landscape with cloud bands in blue, rendered in a sketchy manner.

To the fifteenth century belongs a group of plates and bowls with a black decoration of plant motives and scrollwork under a turquoise-blue or green glaze, which came from Kubatcha in the province of Daghestan (see p. 211). Several of such pieces, in the Kelekian collection in the Victoria and Albert Museum, London, decorated with plants and geometric scrolls, bear the dates A.H. 873, 878, 885, and 900 (1468, 1473, 1480, and 1495). Several bowls of this type are in the Metropolitan Museum (see fig. 135). This fifteenth-century pottery and later examples of the sixteenth and seventeenth century were regarded by some as products of Daghestan. It is, however, much more probable that they were imported from Iran proper and that they were made in the province of Azerbaijan in northwestern Iran.

In the fifteenth century Iranian potters not only continued the art of faïence mosaic, but used it more frequently and over larger

surfaces than in the fourteenth century. Magnificent mosaics covered the interior and exterior walls of mosques and tombs, a number of which are still preserved. The decorative motives of such mosaics consist of arabesques and floral scrolls bearing leaves, rosettes, and peonies, often within lobed medallions. The background is

Fig. 135. Bowl, Iranian, XV Century

a brilliant cobalt blue, and the pattern is in white, yellow, turquoise blue, or green, with the addition of purple manganese and black. A well-known fifteenth-century monument with splendid faïence mosaics is the Blue Mosque in Tabriz, built under Jahan Shah (1437-1467) of the Black Sheep Turkomans. Isfahan is particularly rich in monuments with fifteenth-century faïence mosaics; one of the most important and beautiful is the portal of the tomb Darb-i-Imam in Isfahan, which was completed in 1453 under Jahan Shah. Other fine Timurid mosaics are in Samarkand in the mausoleum of Timur, built in 1434 by Muhammad of Isfahan, in Mashhad, and Shahr-i-Sabz (Kash), the palace of Timur which was partly built in 1395/6. The art of mosaic faïence was thus known all over Iran and was not limited to any particular center, although Isfahan was one of the most prolific.

7. Ceramic Art of the Safavid Period in Iran (XVI-XVIII Century)

A. SEMIPORCELAINS

The ceramic art of the Safavid period may be divided into two groups. One group has purely Safavid decoration, which is known to us from manuscript illuminations, rugs, and textiles. The other group imitates Ming porcelain, for the Iranian potters of the sixteenth century continued attempts to produce true porcelain in imitation of Chinese ware, which was greatly admired by the Safavid rulers. Shah 'Abbas (1587-1628) imported great quantities of Chinese porcelains, and even Chinese potters. As in the Timurid period, in the first half of the sixteenth century only the decoration was Chinese, the body consisting of soft brown earthenware similar to other Iranian pottery of the "Kubatcha" type. Two plates of this early variety, in which the Chinese design is adapted to Iranian style, are in the Museum. Toward the end of the sixteenth century, probably under Shah 'Abbas, the potters achieved a semiporcelain, which, although not so hard as true porcelain, often closely approached the true porcelain. Sometimes the imitation was so well done that many Iranian pieces have been mistaken for Chinese. Often even fake Chinese characters are placed on the bottom of the vessels. These Safavid semiporcelains vary in quality of design and style. The best pieces date from the late sixteenth and seventeenth centuries, a gradual decline having begun in the eighteenth century. The Chinese design is often combined with Iranian motives, as in three splendid bottles in the Museum, two of which (see fig. 136) are decorated with carefully drawn storks and arabesque medallions in blue with the addition of brown. The usual decoration consists of Chinese landscapes with birds and animals, Chinese symbols, and cloud bands familiar from Ming porcelains. Several dated vessels of the seventeenth and eighteenth centuries are known. The British Museum has several such pieces, among them a ewer dated A.H. 1025 (1616) which according to an inscription was made at Yazd. According to Chardin, who traveled in Iran in the seventeenth century, the best pottery was made in Shiraz, Mashhad, Yazd, and Kirman. This Iranian pottery, states Chardin, was as pure and had as fine grain and transparency as Chinese porcelain. In many pieces,

Fig. 136. Bottle, Iranian, Safavid, XVI-XVII Century

particularly those of the eighteenth century, the blue is not so pure as in Chinese ware; it becomes a dull blue or even black and the design is heavily outlined, a technique unknown in Chinese porcelains.

The Iranian imitations of Chinese ware were not confined to white porcelains. We also find copies of celadons in the form of bottles and dishes, which frequently show a white slip decoration of floral sprays and arabesques.

A group of white semiporcelains, mostly of the eighteenth century and the beginning of the nineteenth, is often associated with Gombrun, a port on the Persian Gulf, which, however, must be regarded as a shipping center and not the manufacturing place for this type of ware. The "Gombrun" type consists usually of deep bowls with a low or high foot, the pierced decoration filled with glaze, which was popular in Iran in earlier periods (see p. 174). The pierced decoration is supplemented in many pieces by floral design painted in blue or black.

B. POTTERY WITH LUSTER DECORATION

Among the Safavid ceramics, those with luster decoration occupy a distinguished place. The art of luster painting, which declined in the fifteenth century, was revived in the time of Shah 'Abbas by the potters of Isfahan and other places. Pear-shaped bottles with slender necks, bowls, vases, and small drinking cups were richly decorated in luster of various colors, such as gold, brown, and copper red on a white, dark blue, light blue, or yellow ground. Sometimes the bottles are fluted, with alternation of colors and also of the decoration of flutings, as in figure 137. The decoration is purely Iranian and is characteristic of the Safavid style. The most common motives are naturalistic landscapes with birds, animals, and plants painted in a sketchy, almost impressionistic manner. In several pieces, as in a bottle and a dish in the Moore Collection of the Museum, underglaze painting in grayish blue and luster painting are effectively combined.

C. CERAMICS WITH PAINTED DECORATION

As we have stated above, the Iranian semiporcelains in blue and white and the celadons are often decorated with purely Iranian motives as well as Chinese ones. Among the monochromes we find not only blue but other colors, including dark brown. Sometimes the blue of the decoration is supplemented by other colors, such as olive green and red-brown, the latter applied as a slip. The design of this ware, attributed to Kirman, Shiraz, and Isfahan, is usually floral in character, as may be seen in two plates in the Moore Collection.

The Safavid style of Iranian ceramic art appears in all its splendor in large wall decorations composed of square tiles. Their use for wall decoration first became popular under Shah 'Abbas, although they must have been known earlier. Faïence mosaics were not eliminated by glazed square tiles, for the two forms of decoration

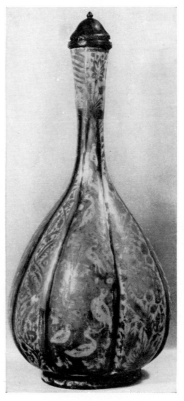

Fig. 137. Lustered Bottle, Iranian, Safavid, XVII Century

Fig. 138. Panel of Tiles from a Palace at Isfahan, Iranian, Safavid, XVII Century

were often used together on the same building, as for instance on the mosque of Shah Safi at Ardabil. Three panels of tiles are in the Metropolitan Museum (see fig. 138); others are in the Victoria and Albert Museum in London and the Louvre. They are supposed to have come from the palace of Chihil Sutun in Isfahan built by Shah 'Abbas. Dieulafoy has pointed out, however, that the Chihil Sutun had only wall paintings and that the tile panels came from one of the pavilions which surrounded the garden or the promenade Chahar Bagh and from which ladies of the court watched the life of the street and various spectacles. Most of these pavilions have disappeared, but early photographs show some of the tile decoration, which is identical with that in the Museum. The scenes are entirely pictorial in style and were copied from contemporary wall paintings created by the celebrated Riza-i-'Abbasi. They represent garden feasts in which ladies of the court are attended by young men and women dressed in rich Safavid costumes, or occasionally Dutch, as may be seen in figure 138. The colors are yellow, cobalt and turquoise blue, green, brown, and purple manganese with black outlines on a white ground. The manufacture of these wall tiles was not limited to Isfahan. Such tiles are known also to have been made in Ardabil in northwestern Iran, where, however, the decoration used was predominately floral. The manufacture of square tiles continued in the seventeenth, eighteenth, and nineteenth centuries in Isfahan and Shiraz. The color schemes and the designs, however, gradually became less pleasing and a marked decline may be seen in the work of the eighteenth century.

D. SO-CALLED KUBATCHA POTTERY

There is a type of Safavid pottery which is classified as "Kubatcha," since most of the examples were brought from Kubatcha, a village in the mountains of Daghestan, in the Caucasus. This type may be divided into two groups, one with painted black decoration under a blue or green glaze, the other with polychrome decoration under a transparent colorless glaze often stained brown. The former group is like the Timurid ware from Daghestan (see p. 206) but has additional patterns. Among them are plants and wormlike motives that resemble the conventionalized Chinese cloud bands which occur in Safavid art. The decoration of the polychrome group is richer than that of the blue and black group. Safavid landscapes with trees and plants, enlivened by the addition of human figures, animals, and birds, are the most popular subjects of this ware. In some pieces (see fig. 139) busts of men or women are placed in the center surrounded by floral scrolls. The motives are drawn freely but always with a sure sense for decorative design and are rendered in a more or less subdued color scheme which consists of white, yellow, blue, green, black, brown, and orange. The latter two colors are thickly applied, leaving a part of the design in relief. This "Kubatcha" ware, like other Safavid ceramics, must be attributed to the end of the sixteenth century and the seventeenth. Although most of this ware came from Kubatcha, it is hardly possible to regard it as a local product. It was, most probably, made in the Iranian province of Azerbaijan, where Tabriz was the most important artistic center. "Kubatcha" ware thus represents a provincial Safavid style, copying the finer ware made in Isfahan and other ceramic centers.

Fig. 139. Plate, Iranian, "Kubatcha," about 1600

8. Tulunid Pottery of Egypt (IX Century)

The debris and waste heaps of Fustat (Old Cairo) for a long time supplied us with examples of ceramic art of the Near East dating from the Coptic era to the sixteenth century. Not all these ceramics were of Egyptian manufacture; a great many of them were imported from Mesopotamia, Iran, Turkey, and Syria.

The earliest Islamic pottery from Fustat and other sites in Egypt is closely connected with the development of the ceramic art of the whole Near East, particularly of Mesopotamia and Iran. Both glazed and unglazed pieces have been found. The finest among the glazed ware are those with lustered decoration, which according to some authorities are all of local manufacture. Some go so far as to regard lusterware found in Mesopotamia and Iran as of Egyptian origin. This theory is just as extreme as that which regards most of the lustered pottery of the period of the Abbasids and Tulunids (868-904) as importations. That such pottery was made in Egypt is evident from the many wasters found in Fustat. These wasters are either of buff or of reddish earthenware and are decorated with gold luster, usually of greenish shade. They are often related in design and figure subjects to Iranian lusterware of the ninth century and were no doubt inspired by it. Some pieces show geometrical motives which are common to Iran and Mesopotamia.

Very few complete pieces of the Tulunid period are in existence. The Museum is fortunate in possessing a small vase of coarse reddish earthenware, characteristic of Fustat pottery, which is covered with an alkaline glaze. The decoration, apparently copied from a Mesopotamian piece of the ninth century, consists of concentric circles, half circles, and dots painted in gold luster.

9. Fatimid Pottery of Egypt and Syria (X-XII Century)

Under the rule of the Fatimids, the ceramic art of Egypt reached an unusually high standard. It may be divided roughly into two groups, one with engraved decoration under monochrome glazes, the other with lustered decoration. The former pieces are covered with various colored glazes such as green, blue, red-brown, and purple. This is in imitation

Fig. 140. Lustered Vase, Egypto-Arabic, Fatimid, XI Century

of Chinese ware of the Sung period, while the engraved decoration is characteristic of the Fatimid era and similar to that on the lustered ware.

The Fatimid lusterware shows a body of varying fineness, covered with a white glaze upon which the decoration is painted in gold or brown luster of great brilliancy. The rich decoration of this ware consists of figure subjects, animals, and birds on a background of arabesques. Sometimes the decoration is a purely ornamental one of arabesques or palmette scrolls, as on a fine vase in the Metropolitan Museum's collection (fig. 140). The Cairo Museum is particularly rich in fine examples, a number of them complete, of Fatimid

Fig. 141. Plate, Syrian, XIII Century

lusterware found mostly in Fustat. A great many of them bear on the bottom the names of makers, the most frequent being those of Sa'd and Muslim, whose kilns were most probably at Fustat. The work of Sa'd and his studio is related to some of the pre-Fatimid lusterware discussed above, particularly in the design of the animals. The style is characterized by a great certainty of brush and a superior decorative quality in the rendering of human figures and animals, which are placed against a background of elaborate arabesques. It represents the height of the Fatimid style of the eleventh century. Among the best-known pieces by Sa'd is a bowl in the

Kelekian collection, in the Victoria and Albert Museum, London, representing a figure holding a mosque lamp or possibly an incense burner. The work of Muslim stresses a more broad, monumental quality and shows less detail than that of Sa'd. A fine example of Muslim's work is a bowl in the Museum lent by Walter Hauser. An eagle, in gold luster, with spread-out wings covers the whole interior. This bowl and some of Sa'd's work may be assigned to the end of the tenth century. According to Wiet, an important fragment in the Arab Museum in Cairo bears the name of the caliph al Hakim (996-1021). To this period may be assigned, among other pieces, the dish with a cock in the Arab Museum and the bowl with an elephant in the collection of Ibrahim Pasha, which according to the inscription was made by Ibrahim in Misr (Egypt or Old Cairo).

Lustered pottery of the Fatimid period was made also in Syria, where a number of pieces of excellent quality were found. The Louvre possesses two bowls of Syrian origin—one, with the design of a hare, comes from a house at Marra, near Aleppo; the other, with a "lotus" pattern and debased Arabic writing, was found in Damascus. The lustered pottery of Syria, fragments of which were also found in Fustat, differs from the typical Egyptian ware. It is of creamy yellow or grayish white earthenware instead of the buff clay characteristic of Fustat pottery. Turquoise blue was the favorite color for the background. Several pieces which may be attributed to Syria are in the Museum. A complete bowl has a decoration of meaningless Kufic letters with arabesques painted in greenish luster on a purple manganese ground. A fragmentary bowl shows the characteristic Fatimid design of a bird amid arabesques.

10. Ayyubid and Mamluk Pottery of Egypt and Syria (XII-XV Century)

At the end of the twelfth century, the potters of Egypt and Syria continued to use some of the patterns and techniques of the Fatimid era. This is particularly evident in ware with monochrome glazes, often in imitation of Chinese porcelains and celadons, which were very popular in Egypt. The luster technique, the predominant method of decoration of the Fatimids, disappeared almost entirely from Egypt but continued in Syria. An important piece of Syrian manufacture is a vase in the collection of Countess de Béhague, in

Fig. 142. *Mosque Lamp, Egypto-Arabic, Mamluk, XIV Century*

Paris, decorated in gold luster on a blue ground, bearing the following inscription: "Made for Asad of Alexandria [Alexandretta] by Yusuf in Damascus." The decoration of this vase consists of Kufic writing in large letters on a background of fine scrolls and arabesques, which are characteristic of thirteenth-century ceramics found in Syria and in Fustat. This type of lustered ware continued in the fourteenth century, under the Mamluks, and was decorated with scrollwork or naturalistic birds.

By far the most common pottery made in the Near East during the thirteenth and fourteenth centuries and even later is one with a painted decoration under a transparent glaze, usually of a greenish tint but sometimes turquoise blue. Fragments of such ware were found in both Egypt and Syria, for instance, at Baalbek, Damascus, Rakka, and Rusafa. The decoration and the material of the pottery from Egypt and Syria are so similar that sometimes it is difficult to decide whether a ware was made in Egypt or imported. Signatures of potters and numerous wasters indicate that most of the pottery found at Fustat and other places is of Egyptian origin, although made by artists who came from Syria or Iran and worked in the style of their native countries. We find in the Ayyubid period imitations of the Rakka, Rusafa, and Rayy ware, which, as kiln wasters indicate, must have been made locally. In many Ayyubid pieces the highly stylized animal decoration was inspired by Saljuk art, which influenced all arts and crafts of the Near East. Mamluk pieces with painted decoration in black and blue recall the Iranian ceramic art of the late thirteenth and fourteenth centuries from Sava, Sultanabad, and Rayy. A Syrian plate in the Metropolitan Museum (fig. 141) with a decoration of plants and a bird shows clearly the Iranian influence.

Other Mamluk vases and bowls, from both Egypt and Syria, are decorated with arabesque inscriptions, often on a dotted background and arranged in bands or segments. A large vase in the Moore Collection of the Museum is a typical example of this Mamluk pottery of the fourteenth century. The main decoration consists of large Arabic inscriptions, expressing good wishes, on a foliated background. In the fourteenth century such designs are frequently combined with naturalistic plants of Chinese origin, upon which are placed birds. Patterns of this type are well known to us from Iranian ceramics of the so-called Sultanabad type. The similarity is frequently so great that Mamluk pieces are mistaken for Iranian. Often the Mamluk pieces may be recognized through their body, which is generally softer than that of contemporary Iranian pieces. As we have mentioned above, this type of Mamluk pottery was made in both Egypt and Syria, which makes it rather difficult to make

Fig. 143. Enameled Wall Tile,
Turkish, Asia Minor, XV
Century

attributions to one or the other country without actual knowledge of the provenance or signatures. The numerous fragments of Mamluk pottery from Fustat, of which there are examples in the Metropolitan Museum, bear on their bottoms names of potters working in Egypt. Among the most frequent signatures of fourteenth-century potters are those of al Ghaibi, ash Shami (the Syrian), al Ajami (the Iranian), al Ghazal, al Hurmuzi (from Hormuz, Iran), at Tawrizi (from Tabriz), and Ustad al Misri (the Egyptian). A rare piece of Mamluk ware is a mosque lamp (fig. 142) in the Moore Collection of the Museum. It is decorated with large inscriptions expressing good wishes, fine arabesques, and floral motives in white and blue reserved in the black background. The ornament is definitely Mamluk and similar to that of many pieces found in Fustat. The inscription on the bottom of the lamp gives us the name of the maker, Ibn al Ghaibi at Tawrizi, the son of the well-known Egyptian potter al Ghaibi.

A common type of Mamluk pottery of the fourteenth and fifteenth centuries consists of vessels made of red-brown clay, with a white slip covered with a yellowish, or sometimes green, transparent lead glaze. The decoration of this ware, which was used in the households of amirs, is engraved in the slip, exposing the red body of the ware. Sometimes the decoration is painted in liquid slip used alone or in combination with engraving, and the painted part of the design appears in relief. Frequently the pattern is enhanced by purple or brown manganese. Usually the decoration consists of inscriptions (sometimes with names), interlacings, official blazons similar to those seen in metalwork (see p. 149), and arabesques, and occasionally of animals and human figures. A basin in the Arab Museum in Cairo bears the name of Shihab ad Din ibn Faraji, an officer of Nasir ad Din Muhammad (1293-1340).

Mamluk pottery of various types continued to be made in the

fifteenth century, but compared with earlier pieces showed a marked decline in both technique and design.

11. Ceramic Art of Turkey

The earliest known examples of the ceramic art of Asia Minor in the Muhammadan period are employed in architectural decoration and date from the thirteenth century. The mosques at Konia, the capital of the Saljuk empire, are embellished on both the exterior and the interior with bricks or with faïence mosaics, enameled in a few colors, such as turquoise blue, cobalt blue, black, and white. The designs are purely geometrical, consisting mainly of angular interlaced bands and inscriptions. The ornament and technique are of Iranian origin, introduced by Iranian craftsmen working in Asia Minor.

Fig. 144. Plate, Turkish, Asia Minor, XV Century

At the end of the fourteenth century, under the rule of the house of 'Uthman, a new chapter in the art of Asia Minor began. Brusa,

Fig. 145. Panel of Tiles, Turkish, Asia Minor, XVI Century

the capital of the early Ottoman emperors, became an important art center. The enameled bricks, or cut mosaics, that had been popular in the earlier period were superseded for the most part by tiles, usually rectangular but sometimes hexagonal in shape, decorated in polychrome enamels or in underglaze painting. Magnificent examples of fifteenth-century tile decoration occur in the Green Mosque completed in 1423 and the Green Tomb built in 1421, of Sultan Muhammad I at Brusa, both having beautiful mihrabs. The prayer niche of the Green Mosque is decorated with arabesques and floral motives showing Chinese influence. That the mihrab was made by Iranian artists is proven by an inscription on the niche: "Work of masters from Tabriz." The color scheme is similar to that of earlier ceramics, but purple manganese, green, and yellow have been added. An example in the Museum's collection of these fifteenth-century enameled wall tiles is illustrated in figure 143. On a cobalt-blue ground within a lobed yellow arch is a decoration of arabesques in white, turquoise blue, and dark purple manganese, while in the spandrels are angularly interlaced bands in white.

The art of underglaze painting in blue and white, in imitation of Ming porcelain, was also known in Turkey and like the enameled-tile technique was introduced by Iranian potters. Some of the finest examples of tile work with blue and white decoration are in the mosque of Sultan Murad in Adrianople, built in 1433. The hexagonal tiles of the walls are decorated with plant designs which, although inspired by Timurid ornament of Iran, show a certain original style which is characteristic of the early Ottoman period.

The dated tile work permits us to establish a more accurate chronology of Turkish pottery of Anatolia prior to the sixteenth century. A group of bowls, dishes, and

Fig. 146. Mosque Lamp, Turkish, Asia Minor, Second Half of the XVI Century

mosque lamps decorated with elegant floral scrolls, Chinese cloud bands, and Kufic inscriptions may be assigned to the fifteenth century. Excellent examples of this Ottoman pottery are in the British Museum, the Louvre, and the Evkaf Museum. Two examples of this type are in the Metropolitan Museum. One is a deep bowl with

221

palmettes and cypress trees; the other, in the Altman Collection, has very fine floral decoration (fig. 144).

The most important ceramic center of Asia Minor in the sixteenth and seventeenth centuries was Isnik, although other centers, among them Kutahia, are known to have flourished. The ceramic art of Isnik, or Nicaea, attained its highest development in the second half of the sixteenth century and at the beginning of the seventeenth. The Turkish potters had become thorough masters of the art of underglaze decoration painted in cobalt blue, turquoise blue, green, and yellow, and a characteristic tomato red, which was made from a clay, the Armenian bole, applied thickly to the surface of vessels or tiles. In another group of Isnik ware the decoration is painted in cobalt and turquoise blue. Both types are splendidly represented in the Museum's collection. The decoration consists of Iranian palmettes and floral motives which are characteristic of Turkish art, such as carnations, tulips, hyacinths, and roses, arranged into various designs. The tiles of dated monuments of Constantinople permit us to assign the finest of the Isnik ceramics to the second half of the sixteenth century and the first half of the seventeenth. One of the earliest sixteenth-century pieces is a mosque lamp in the British Museum, from the mosque of 'Umar in Jerusalem, dated A.H. 956 (1549). Beautiful tile decoration may be seen in the mosque of Rustam Pasha (1560), the harem of the old palace (1574), the apartment of Murad III, and other buildings. This Turkish style of the second half of the sixteenth century is represented in the Museum by pottery and several panels of tiles in which the Iranian influence is quite apparent. In the field of one of the panels (fig. 145) large palmettes, rosettes, vine leaves, and rosebuds form an all-over pattern, while in the blue border floral scrolls are intertwined with Chinese cloud bands. In other tiles of the second half of the sixteenth century the Turkish floral mo-

Fig. 147. Plate, Turkish, Asia Minor, Early XVII Century

222

tives either predominate over the Iranian ones or are used exclusively (see plate III) but are still arranged in more or less formal patterns. The tiles permit us to date some of the vessels and mosque lamps (see fig. 146) in the second half of the sixteenth century. From the technical point of view the tiles and pottery of this period are superior to those of the seventeenth century. The designs are very carefully drawn and of great elegance.

Fig. 148. Plate, Syrian, Damascus, Early XVII Century

With the beginning of the seventeenth century the drawing of plants became gradually more naturalistic and the composition less rigid than in the sixteenth century. Fine seventeenth-century tiles are in the mosque of Sultan Ahmad (1614) in Constantinople. Isnik still held the leading place in the manufacture of tiles and pottery. In the time of Sultan Ahmad (1603-1617) there were in Isnik three hundred ceramic workshops. Numerous plates, ewers, and mosque lamps seen in various museums here and abroad should be assigned to the seventeenth century. Some of the finest ones, as the dish in figure 147, are of the first half of the seventeenth century; in later ones the design and the painting are less carefully executed.

The manufacture of ceramics continued in Turkey in the eighteenth century, but the pieces show a marked decline in both technique and design. The colors became less vigorous, the tomato red changing to brownish red.

To Kutahia in Anatolia are attributed eighteenth-century bowls, cups, coffee pots, and other dishes decorated with floral motives, occasionally with figures, as on a piece of 1719 in the Kelekian collection. The design is usually crude and among the vivid colors yellow is conspicuous. A few of the pieces bear Armenian inscriptions, and it is probable that they were made by Armenian potters of Kutahia.

B. CERAMIC ART OF SYRIA (XVI-XVIII CENTURY)

Among the Turkish ceramics of the sixteenth and seventeenth centuries may be distinguished a group in which purple manganese is substituted for the tomato red characteristic of the wares of Asia Minor. The designs on pottery of this type are in general similar to

Fig. 149. Panel of Tiles, Syrian, Damascus, XVI Century

those of Asia Minor, but frequently a greater elegance of execution may be noticed. Examples in which purple manganese occurs have usually been assigned by some to the school of Damascus, by others to Anatolia.

The attribution to Damascus is based on fine tiles in dated Damascus mosques and on excavated material which leaves little doubt that this ware was not imported from Asia Minor but was of local manufacture. Syria had had a great ceramic tradition since the Roman period and produced good pottery under the Mamluks. One rather rare group of the so-called Damascus ware is characterized by unusually fine and elegant design, with large floral motives. In a piece in the Louvre, formerly in the Koechlin collection, a peacock, unknown in Anatolian ware, is introduced into the floral design. Peacocks were popular in Syrian pottery of the fifteenth century and continued to be so in the Ottoman period.

The Museum's collection includes many Syrian tiles of the sixteenth and seventeenth centuries but only a few vessels, one of them in the Altman Collection of the Museum (fig. 148). To the second half of the sixteenth century may be assigned a mosque globe in the Altman Collection decorated with arabesques, large rosettes, and Chinese cloud bands in blue, green, black, and purple. Dating from the second half of the sixteenth century is a panel of tiles (fig. 149), decorated with a diaper pattern of floral scrolls, conventional palmettes, tulips, carnations, hyacinths, and pomegranates.

Fig. 150. Lustered Albarello, Hispano-Moresque, XV Century

In Syria, as in Asia Minor, the style of decoration became freer in the seventeenth century. The eighteenth-century ware continues the traditional color scheme, but the drawing is inferior to that of earlier pieces. A characteristic example in the Museum's collection, dated A.H. 1150 (1737/8), is a panel of tiles inscribed with the names of Allah, Muhammad, and the four Orthodox Caliphs.

12. Hispano-Moresque Pottery

The earliest known ceramics of Arabic Spain have been unearthed in the palace city of Madinat az Zahra, near Cordova. Much of the

Fig. 151. Lustered Bowl, Hispano-Moresque, XV Century

pottery so found is probably the work of native Cordova potters and may be assigned to the second half of the tenth century. The painted decoration consists of birds, floral motives, and inscriptions in green, blue, and dark brown. Fragments of lustered ware found at Madinat az Zahra and related to that of Samarra and other sites in Mesopotamia and Iran were most probably imported.

Hispano-Moresque pottery from the eleventh to the thirteenth century is still very little known. We may assume, however, that the manufacture of both lustered and painted ceramics continued in this period, judging from the fragments found in various sites. The Moorish potters of Andalusia were manufacturing well tops and large water jars with a decoration stamped or molded in relief. This type of ware is either unglazed or covered with a green glaze. An early example, dated A.H. 430 (1039), a well top from Seville with a

Fig. 152. Lustered Plate, Hispano-Moresque, XV Century

decoration in barbotine technique, is in the Archaeological Museum in Madrid. A large unglazed water jar in the Metropolitan Museum, decorated with straight and wavy bands in relief and with geometrical ornaments, may be assigned to about the thirteenth century.

An important ceramic center of Moorish Spain in the thirteenth and fourteenth centuries was Paterna, near Valencia. The great quantities of ware found there belong to several types, but the most characteristic one has a painted decoration in green and brown or purple manganese on a white ground. The decoration of the Paterna ware consists mostly of stylized animals, birds, and human figures. A fourteenth-century Paterna dish in the Havemeyer Collection of the Museum has a pattern of interlaced bands enclosing nine shields with crosses.

In the fourteenth century and the beginning of the fifteenth, the potters of Malaga and of Granada excelled in the production of large vases, tiles, and bowls with a very fine decoration in gold luster used alone or in combination with blue. Best known are the ovoid "Alhambra vases" with wing handles, which may be assigned to the fourteenth century. Their decoration is composed of arabesques, Arabic inscriptions, and stylized animals, as on the famous vase in the Alhambra at Granada. It is suggested now that the vases with gold luster only were made in Malaga, while those with decoration in gold and blue were the work of Moorish potters at Granada.

An important ceramic center in Spain from the fourteenth through the sixteenth century was Manises, in the province of Valencia. The lustered pottery produced there consists of albarelli, plates, and vases.

To the beginning of the fifteenth century is assigned a type of lusterware which perpetuates the traditions of the school of Malaga. The motives include arabesques, palmettes, and interlacings in brown luster and blue, together with simulated Arabic inscriptions derived from the word "peace" (see fig. 150). A large plate in the Moore Collection of the Museum has a pattern of rosettes in gold luster placed within interlaced bands of blue. To this Moorish decoration are often added coats of arms of Christian families of Spain, as may be seen on a plate in the collection of the Hispanic Society in New York.

During the first half of the fifteenth century Gothic elements were gradually introduced into the patterns of the Valencia lusterware. A popular type of design consists of rosette blossoms on a dotted background (see fig. 151), upon which are frequently placed graceful animals and Gothic inscriptions in blue.

To the period between 1450 and 1465 Kühnel attributes lustered plates and bowls with a large pattern of lions and birds on a background of scrollwork and large palmettes. Such palmettes are also frequently painted on the backs of lustered plates.

In the second half of the fifteenth century lustered plates and

228

vases were usually decorated with Gothic vine scrolls in blue and gold that became more formal and stylized toward the close of the century. The vine scrolls were commonly combined with coats of arms. One such plate in the Museum shows the coat of arms of the Medici family of Florence (fig. 152).

In the sixteenth century the manufacture of ceramics at Manises passed gradually into Christian hands. The designs of the fifteenth century degenerate into a dense pattern showing little connection with the Moorish tradition.

Chapter 11

GLASS AND CRYSTAL

1. Early Islamic Glass from Egypt, Syria, Mesopotamia, and Iran (VII-XII Century)

As early as the Roman period the Near East, particularly Syria and Egypt, was famous for beautiful glassware. In the Islamic period, the various techniques of decorating glass known in antiquity continued to be used in all the provinces of the Muhammadan Near East. Early Islamic glass is known to us chiefly from finds in Egypt, Syria, and Mesopotamia. The ninth-century glass from Samarra shows a continuation of Sasanian forms found in Ctesiphon and Kish. Until recently Islamic glass of Iran was very little known. The material now available comes from various sites, such as Susa, Rayy, Gurgan, and Nishapur, the latter excavated by the Metropolitan Museum. These pieces show forms and methods of decoration known from other provinces.

Early Islamic glass consists of bottles, flasks, vases, and cups for domestic use, many of them for oil and perfume. The variety of these glass vessels, made in many sizes, is so great that it would be impossible to enumerate here all the types. The majority, which date from the eighth and ninth centuries, are undecorated; the rest are decorated by various methods, usually with molded flutes, honey comb patterns, or other designs, including inscriptions. Of the latter type are cups and pear-shaped jugs found in Egypt, Syria, Mesopotamia, and Iran. A small complete jug of this type in the Metropolitan Museum has a decoration of Kufic inscriptions, and two rows of disks in relief. The body of the jug was blown into a mold consisting of two parts, a method used in the early Islamic era. From the shape and type of writing, this jug can be assigned to the eighth or ninth century. Related to the Roman, so-called Sidonian, glass, it was probably made in Syria.

Another group of early Islamic vessels has a stamped decoration, usually consisting of round medallions with disks, animals, or Kufic inscriptions. In some of these vessels the pattern is produced by double stamping or by a pinching iron, a method which seems to be an invention of the Muhammadan era and appears mostly on pieces found in Egypt. The design is usually geometrical, although conventionalized birds appear.

Decorating glass vessels with applied threads or disks, a technique known in the Roman period, was particularly popular in Syria. The applied threads form zigzags, wavy bands, and disks or drops, either in the same color as the vessels or, more frequently, in blue. The applied threads are white when the glass vessel is blue or manganese, as seen in a bottle in the Museum. Some of the vessels with applied decoration, several of which are in the Museum, are shaped in the form of animals (camels?) supporting baskets with containers. They usually come from Syria and belong to the pre-Islamic or the beginning of the Islamic era. Vessels with applied disks are also either pre-Islamic or early Islamic, for example, the bowl in the Berlin Museum which shows Kufic inscriptions as well as Sasanian motives.

An interesting group of vessels such as flasks, cups, and bowls, mostly in purple manganese, has a decoration of applied white-thread ornament which is marvered flush with the surface. These threads or rods were dragged, while still hot, with a comblike tool, a process which formed various designs such as chevron, herringbone, or fern patterns. Often Islamic pieces of this type are wrongly regarded as Roman. The characteristic feature of the Islamic ones is the greater thickness of the vessel walls, the majority being of purple manganese into which the white rods are not very deeply embedded.

Another survival of antiquity is the technique of engraving and cutting glass, either by hand or, more frequently, on the wheel. Some of the engraving on glass bottles and ewers from Egypt and Syria is rather simple, consisting of horizontal bands and wavy lines, as may be seen on two examples from Egypt in the Metropolitan Museum. Some of the ninth-century glass found in Samarra and in Iran shows an engraved decoration of high quality. Noteworthy among the pieces found at Nishapur by the Museum expedition is a portion of a blue dish with engraved decoration of vine scrolls and geometrical design in compartments. Other glass objects from Nishapur, of the ninth and tenth centuries, are beakers, flasks, and jugs with cut decoration. Among the finest pieces in the Museum is a ewer decorated with three medallions containing birds and an animal, separated by palmette scrolls and geometrical motives. The discovery of glass ingots by the expedition proves conclusively that glass was made in Nishapur.

A large group of Islamic glass of the eighth to ninth century consists of small, thick, perfume flasks, mostly prismatic, which by means of horizontal and vertical grooves and notches are cut into the shape of molar teeth. They are made of lead glass, either blue or green, and are found in all the Islamic provinces. Two such flasks in the Museum's collection come from excavations at Nishapur and are probably of Iranian origin. Such perfume containers were made also in cut crystal, several examples of which are known.

Fig. 153. *Glass Bottle, Egypto-Arabic, Fatimid, XI-XII Century*

In a number of early Islamic vessels, chiefly from Iran but also from Mesopotamia, the wheel-cut decoration consists of raised disks or of hollow medallions placed closely together to form a honeycomb pattern. In some of the Iranian pieces, such as the globular vessels, the raised and hollow cuts are combined. Cut ornament of this type, which probably had its prototype in crystal, was particularly popular in the Sasanian era and is known to us from examples in museums and from excavations of Sasanian sites in Mesopotamia, chiefly at Ctesiphon. In the Museum this wheel-cut decoration is represented by a globular bottle of about the tenth century found at Rayy, which shows two rows of hollow-cut oval disks.

The wheel-cutting of glass in the early Islamic era was not limited

232

to the above-mentioned simple forms of decoration. From Egypt, Mesopotamia, Iran, and particularly from Gurgan come pieces decorated with floral and animal patterns in relief. An important group of ninth-century fragments of crystal-clear glass with low-relief decoration was found in Samarra. These fragments of the Abbasid period may be regarded, according to Lamm, as products of Mesopotamia, probably of Baghdad, which was famous for its cut glass. They may also be considered a prototype of the cut glass and crystal of the Fatimid period, which is discussed below. In some of the early Islamic cut glass, particularly from Egypt, the relief is vigorously cut out of the background, as may be seen on a fragmentary bowl of about 900 in the Arab Museum in Cairo, which is decorated with a frieze of goats and a votive Kufic inscription in blue.

2. *Fatimid Glass and Crystal of Egypt and Syria (X-XII Century)*

Under the Fatimids the glass industry of Egypt, and to some extent that of Syria, reached a high standard. The main centers of the Egyptian industry were Fustat, Madinat al Fayum, and Alexandria, which had been the chief center of the Roman industry. Fustat seems to have been the chief center under the Fatimids, and there the various techniques used in the Tulunid period were perfected. Some of the finest and most luxurious glass was made for the use of the Fatimid court, known for its richness and splendor. The decoration of the Fatimid glass is either based on earlier designs or shows the new style features developed by contemporary Egyptian artists. To this period may be assigned two graceful bottles with molded decoration: one has a lozenge diaper in low relief; the other has a globular body and straight long neck (fig. 153) and shows many interesting technical features. This piece belongs to a small group of early Islamic glass bottles made of two parts, mold-blown separately, the lower one colorless, the upper one, including the neck, blue. The main part of the bottle is decorated with medallions containing running animals, rendered schematically in relief. A similar bottle in two colors, but with a decoration of concentric knobs in medallions, is in the collection of Mrs. W. H. Moore in New York.

All the types of early Islamic glass described above continued to be made in the Fatimid period. Glass with applied thread decoration, both in relief and pressed, was made in Egypt and Syria. To this period also belong some of the beakers with blue ribs and various vessels of green or manganese glass with pressed-in white threads, among them containers in the shape of birds, like one in the collection of Ray Winfield Smith on loan in the Metropolitan Museum.

One of the great achievements of Fatimid glassmakers of Egypt and Syria was the decoration of glass by painting with luster or enamel-like colors. Unfortunately, this type of glass is now exemplified chiefly by fragments, although several more or less complete pieces are now in the Arab Museum in Cairo, the British Museum, and the Berlin Museum. These small bowls and bottles are of greenish or manganese glass and have a decoration of scroll-work, geometrical patterns, or Kufic writing, painted in brown luster and silver luster respectively. Other rich shades of luster were used by Egyptian glassmakers of the tenth to the twelfth century—gold, copper, and various shades employed in contemporary lustered ceramics. In some of the pieces several luster colors are combined and the decoration painted on both sides. On others the decoration is painted with enamel-like colors together with gold and silver luster. In three pieces in the Museum the back of the greenish glass has a reddish brown coating, while the decoration is painted in orange and brown with luster of silver and gold. Rich effects were often produced by the use of glass pastes, usually in turquoise blue. Fragments of glass vessels of this type have a luster decoration or imitate earlier millefiori glass, as in a fragment in the Museum, which shows spots of red, green, yellow, and white and tiny pieces of gold leaf pressed into the surface. Actual gold painting was also known to Fatimid glassmakers, as may be seen on a number of pieces found in Fustat. Most of the pieces are not decorated with gold leaf but are painted in liquid gold, the details being scratched out with a needle. A fragmentary bottle in the British Museum, decorated with dancers, trees, and birds painted in gold and rendered in the style of Fatimid art, probably dates from the twelfth century. It has a Naskhi inscription, which, however, is not complete enough to make an attribution to a particular sultan possible, although Lamm has suggested 'Imad ad Din Zangi II. atabeg of Sinjar and for a time of Aleppo (1171-1197).

The cut decoration of glass vessels was brought to perfection by Fatimid glassmakers. The style of cutting and the decoration are closely related to that of objects of rock crystal, which were greatly favored by the Fatimid caliphs. Makrizi's description of the destruction of the treasures of Caliph Mustansir, in 1062, mentions a great number of both plain and decorated crystal vessels. Many fine pieces, of various sizes, came early into the possession of European courts and churches, often as reliquaries, and were regarded as great treasures. The most beautiful crystal vessels are in the Vienna Museum, in the treasury of San Marco in Venice, in the Victoria and Albert Museum, in the Palazzo Pitti in Florence, and in the Louvre.

Several of them bear the names of Fatimid caliphs, for instance, the pear-shaped ewer in San Marco with the name of al 'Aziz (976-96). The San Marco ewer, which shows two seated lions separated by an arabesque tree, is of exquisite beauty and technical perfection. The decoration is richly carved in relief with cut and engraved details. Animals and birds, singly or in groups, and arabesque devices were the most favored motives of the Fatimid crystals. The Museum possesses three small bottles, probably perfume containers, which were presented by George D. Pratt. One is a heart-shaped bottle (fig. 154) with arabesque pattern; the others are of

Fig. 154. Rock Crystal Bottle, Egypto-Arabic, X-XI Century

cylindrical shape decorated with arabesques or with Kufic inscriptions expressing good wishes to the owner.

The cut-glass vessels contemporary with the Fatimid crystals were probably less costly substitutes for the latter. In their decoration they equal the crystals but in technique are often inferior to them. A special group are the so-called Hedwig glasses (some of them being associated with the wine miracle of St. Hedwig), consisting mostly of beakers, of which about thirteen exist today in various European collections and museums, such as the Germanic Museum in Nuremberg, the Rijksmuseum in Amsterdam, the museum in

Breslau, and in the treasury of the Abbey of Oignies in Namur. There is little doubt that this group of cut glass was made in Egypt in the eleventh or twelfth century. Their animal decoration, in relief and engraved, is related to that of Fatimid crystals but is rendered in a bolder style.

3. Ayyubid and Mamluk Enameled and Gilt Glass of Syria and Egypt (XII-XV Century)

The greatest era of Muhammadan glass began at the end of the twelfth century, reaching its climax in the thirteenth century and first half of the fourteenth. The richly enameled and gilt decoration of this glass is based on earlier, particularly Fatimid, traditions, and we owe the perfection of the enameling technique to the glassmakers of Syria. Glass of Aleppo and Damascus, which became in the thirteenth and fourteenth centuries the leading centers of glass manufacture, must be classified among the finest ever produced. Although some enameled glass was made in Egypt and probably in Mesopotamia and Iran, Syria produced most of the glass of this period. Al Kazwini (about 1203-1283), in describing Aleppo, which in the thirteenth century was an important art metropolis, mentions its glass bazaar and the magnificent ware exported thence to foreign countries. An Iranian geographer, Hafiz-i-Abru, speaks of the wonderful glass of Aleppo as decorated with elegance and taste. Glass made in Damascus was also famous, especially in the time of the Mamluk sultans. Damascus craftsmen supplied the Cairo bazaars with luxurious products, and in European inventories of the fourteenth and fifteenth centuries gilded and enameled glassware is called "Damascus glass." Some of the earliest glass of this type was attributed by Lamm to Rakka, on the Euphrates, where enameled glass fragments were found. Predominant in this group are goblets with flaring rims, of which several complete ones are preserved in various European collections. The most important pieces of the group are the beaker of Charles the Great in the museum at Chartres and that of the eight priests of Douai, which may be assigned to the end of the twelfth century. Characteristic of the Rakka group are pearl motives of blue and white enamel and heavy outlines. A fragmentary cup found at Rakka and now in the Chinili Kiosk in Istanbul is decorated with figure subjects, which are rendered rather conventionally as compared with those on other Syrian glasses of the thirteenth century. Whether these glasses of the Rakka group were made there or were imported from northern Syria, they are closely connected with the development of enameled and gilt glass of Syria in the Ayyubid and Mamluk periods. The richness of the decoration and the magnificent polychromy of the vessels were admired by early travelers, pilgrims, and Crusaders, who brought back many of the fine pieces now seen in various European church treasuries and museums. More numerous than the vessels are the lamps for Cairo mosques, made to order for the Mamluk sultans and their amirs and frequently bearing their names and badges. The Metropolitan Museum possesses an important collection of thirteen lamps, ten large vessels—basins, bottles, cups, and a tray—and several small beakers and flasks which in quality is surpassed by none. In number the Metropolitan Museum's collection of mosque lamps is second only to that of the Arab Museum at Cairo.

The technique of gilding and enameling consisted of several processes. The glassmakers applied first the gilt decoration, using a pen for the outlines and a brush for larger surfaces. After the first firing, the design was outlined in red and the enamel in various colors was applied thickly according to the design. The semiopaque enamels consisted of a flux containing much lead and colored with metallic oxides. Green was obtained from oxide of copper, red from oxide of iron, yellow from antimonic acid, and white, which was entirely opaque, from oxide of tin. The blue enamel which plays such a prominent part in the decoration of this glass was made from pulverized lapis lazuli mixed with colorless glass.

The style and decoration of the enameled and gilt glass vary according to the period. In thirteenth-century pieces, both of the Ayyubid and Mamluk periods, figure subjects, animals, arabesques, and Arabic inscriptions were the most popular motives. The decoration is frequently arranged in horizontal zones of various widths, separated by narrow bands. Pieces of this period, goblets, jugs, and bottles with figure subjects, are among the most beautiful Islamic glass. Some of the figure subjects are polo players, hunting scenes, and court entertainers not unlike those seen in silver-inlaid Saljuk and Ayyubid bronzes of Mesopotamia and Syria. On some of the glass, particularly beakers and jugs, figures are drawn on a large scale, occupying the main part of the vessels; on other pieces, the figures are smaller, often being confined to narrow bands (see fig. 155).

Among the most famous examples of the former type are the goblets in the museum at Kassel and in the Louvre, a magnificent jug in the collection of Baron Edouard de Rothschild in Paris, a bottle in the Berlin Museum, and a pilgrim bottle in St. Stephan's Church in Vienna. With the exception of the pilgrim bottle, which is probably Mamluk, all these pieces may be assigned to the first half of the thirteenth century, mostly to the period of the Ayyubid sultan of Aleppo and Damascus, Malik Nasir Yusuf (1236-60), whose name appears on a long-necked bottle in the Arab Museum at Cairo. All these pieces are characterized by careful drawing and enameling of the decoration. On some of them, as the Rothschild jug, the figures appear on a blue ground with gold arabesques, which frequently form the main decoration. The front and back of the beautiful pilgrim bottle in the British Museum show a pattern of arabesques, some of them ending in animal heads, while the sides are decorated with large figures of hunters, a musician, and a drinking scene, the latter two in medallions. Arabesques and angular interlacings in gold within medallions form the sole decoration of a platter in the Moore Collection of the Metropolitan Museum, richly enameled in white, blue, red, and gold. To this type, which has geometrical designs, also belongs a candlestick in the collection of Baron Edouard de Rothschild in Paris, and a bottle in the Royal Ontario Museum in Toronto.

Under the Mamluks the Syrian glassmakers continued to manufacture fine gilt and enameled vessels. From 1260 on, in the time of Sultan Baibar, Damascus became the main center of glass production, although glass probably continued to be produced in Aleppo. Egypt, Mesopotamia, Asia Minor, Iran, and even China imported fine glass vessels from Syria. Mamluk gilt and enameled glass can be divided roughly into two groups: the early Mamluk, that is, of the second half of the thirteenth century, and the late Mamluk, chiefly of the fourteenth century. In the decoration of the early Mamluk pieces the Ayyubid tradition is quite apparent, although the style begins to show features characteristic of the new era. Two most important early Mamluk pieces are the pilgrim bottle in Vienna and the cup in the Moore Collection of the Metropolitan Museum (fig. 155). The former is decorated with palmette scrolls and large figure subjects in medallions. The Moore cup is decorated with horizontal bands containing running animals, seated musicians and drinkers, Arabic poems, and arabesques in gold, white, blue, red, yellow, green, and black. The main bands of the cup are separated by four medallions with eagles, which are most probably a badge of an unknown amir. The small figures of the entertainers are reminiscent of the decoration on thirteenth-century Mosul bronzes, for instance, the candlestick base illustrated in figure 87. In the drawing of the Moore cup, the Vienna pilgrim bottle, and related

Fig. 155. Enameled Glass Cup, Syrian, Mamluk, Second Half of the XIII Century

pieces, there is greater freedom than in the earlier enameled glass. The figures of musicians playing various instruments and the animals are perfectly executed. A noteworthy feature of this cup and other early Mamluk pieces is the predominance of gilt decoration over enameled, which is often confined to smaller surfaces than in the Ayyubid period.

The largest group of gilt and enameled glass of the Mamluk

239

period consists of mosque lamps made to the order of the sultans and amirs as donations to Cairo mosques. Many of them are inscribed with names of the sultans and their officials, permitting us to

Fig. 156. *Mosque Lamp, Enameled Glass, Syrian, Mamluk, Second Half of the XIII Century*

date them exactly. In date the mosque lamps range from the end of the thirteenth century through the fourteenth, revealing the changes of style, seen also in metalwork of the same period (see fig. 86), due to Chinese influences introduced by the Mongols. The decoration of these lamps includes, besides large inscriptions and medallions with badges, arabesques and naturalistic floral motives of Chinese origin, which gradually replaced the traditional abstract patterns. As a result of the Chinese influence we observe a great freedom in the drawing. One of the earliest lamps in the Museum's collection (fig. 156) was made for the mausoleum of the amir Aidakin al Bundukdar (died 1285), who was the commander of the arbalesters, as the badge showing two bows bound together indicates.

Two lamps of the beginning of the fourteenth century belong to a rare group made of blue glass. One of them (fig. 157) bears the name of the Mamluk sultan al Muzaffar Rukn ad Din Baibars II, who ruled from 1308 to 1309, interrupting the rule of Nasir Muhammad. The finely executed floral decoration of this lamp shows, besides the naturalistic lotus scrolls, a vine ornament which appears in a number of Mamluk lamps. The other blue mosque lamp in the Museum's collection is richly decorated with arabesques and floral patterns, with compartments formed by interlaced bands. The design and enameling are of unusually high quality, which characterizes the early period of Nasir Muhammad (1293-1340, with interruptions), represented in the Museum by several lamps. One of the finest, bearing the name of this sultan, was made for a hospice founded by Karim ad Din and situated in the cemetery of al Karafa near Cairo. Wiet identifies Karim ad Din provisionally with an intendant of the private house of the sultan, who disappeared from political life in 1323. The superior style and the elaborate gilt decoration also suggest the beginning of the fourteenth century. About contemporary with this lamp is another one in the Museum, which bears the name of the amir Shihab ad Din Ahmad Mihmandar (died 1332) and was probably made for a mosque built at his order in 1324/5. A few years later in date is a lamp made for Saif ad Din Kusun, the cupbearer of Malik an Nasir, whose badge, a red cup, appears in several medallions. Probably it was made for his mosque, erected in 1329-30. This lamp is of special interest, as it bears on the foot the name of the glassmaker, 'Ali ibn Muhammad Amaki (or ar Ramaki or az Zamaki), who also made two other lamps, one now in the Arab Museum at Cairo, the other in the Boston Museum.

Another lamp (fig. 158), inscribed with the name of Sultan Nasir Muhammad and the badge of an anonymous cupbearer, shows a type of decoration which is quite different from the usual one with bands of large inscriptions. The name and title of the sultan appear

Fig. 157. *Mosque Lamp, Enameled Glass, Syrian, Mamluk,
Beginning of the XIV Century*

in three small medallions beneath the body, while the rest of the
lamp shows a naturalistic floral decoration of large rosettes and
peonies placed between medallions with arabesques and badges.

Such floral decoration is known to us from Mamluk metalwork and became popular under Nasir Muhammad. The enameling of this piece reveals several interesting features, such as the use of gold and red outlines and the addition of pink and light blue enamel colors, which are seldom seen on earlier glass. The flower petals are

Fig. 158. Mosque Lamp, Enameled Glass, Syrian, Mamluk, First Half of the XIV Century

divided into three parts, showing two shades of red or blue and white.

Syrian glassmakers of the first half of the fourteenth century did not confine themselves to the manufacture of mosque lamps. Various vessels, such as vases, bottles, buckets, dishes, and cups of different sizes, were magnificently decorated. Their ornament is similar to that of the mosque lamps, but often representations of animals and human beings are added. A few of the vessels were made for the Rasulid sultans of Yemen, for instance, the Rothschild bottle, now in the Freer Gallery in Washington, inscribed with the name of Sultan Mujahid 'Ali (1321-63). Three important pieces of the first half of the fourteenth century are in the Metropolitan Museum.

One is the famous bottle (fig. 159) from the Kunsthistorisches Museum in Vienna, which came into the possession of the Hapsburgs in 1825. This large bottle may be considered one of the masterpieces of mediaeval Islamic glass. The gilded and enameled decoration covers almost the entire surface of the bottle. In the richness and brilliance of the enamel and the perfection of the design, it surpasses most of the Mamluk glass. On the shoulder of the bottle, interlaced bands form three large medallions which contain intricate arabesques in red and gold, with touches of white, red, and green, on a dark blue ground. The design and color of these medallions are reminiscent of the stained-glass windows of mediaeval churches. The spaces between the medallions are filled with a pattern of vine scrolls and pine cones in gold with drops in white, yellow, green, red, and blue, outlined in red. The main part of the body is decorated with a frieze of warriors on horseback, fighting each other with swords, lances, bows and arrows, and maces. The headgear of the warriors varies; some of them wear turbans, others Mongol caps and helmets. Of particular interest is the richness of color apparent in the warrior frieze. The horses are rendered in white, yellow, blue, red, green, dark brown, and aubergine. The costumes and saddles of the horsemen are in contrasting colors which contribute to the liveliness of the design. The neck of the bottle has a broad band decorated with a Chinese phoenix, whose wings spread all around the neck. The narrow bands above and below contain scrolls or bird motives. The Chinese influence and the naturalistic style of the landscape and figures indicate that the

Fig. 159. Bottle, Enameled Glass, Syrian, Mamluk, First Half
of the XIV Century

bottle dates from the beginning of the fourteenth century, probably
about 1320.

The other two fourteenth-century pieces are a cup with a high
foot, presented to the Museum in 1923 by Mr. and Mrs. V. Everit

Fig. 160. Bottle, Enameled Glass, Syrian, Mamluk, First
Half of the XIV Century

Macy and a bottle (fig. 160) formerly in the collection of Baron Robert de Rothschild in Paris. The arabesque and floral decoration of the Macy cup recalls two similar cups, one formerly in the Sarre collection and the other in the Baar collection at Leiden. All show style features which permit one to date them in the first half of the fourteenth century. Of great elegance is the Rothschild bottle, now in the Metropolitan Museum, which displays a richly enameled and gilt decoration on a blue ground. The decoration consists of heart-shaped palmettes alternating with split palmettes, which contain medallions with an eagle attacking a goose. The fine lacy ornament in gold and red shows a Mamluk floral design rendered in a very sketchy manner. On the shoulder of the body is a frieze of running animals on a blue ground; the details reveal a close observation of nature, which the Muhammadan artists learned from China. How successfully the Syrian glassmakers combined decorative quality with realistic motives is seen in the pattern of flying birds (parrots?) and arabesques, which is also found on the mosque lamps of Kusun.

Fig. 161. Glass Bottle, Iranian, XVIII Century

The style of enameled lamps and vessels developed under Nasir Muhammad continued in the second half of the fourteenth century, but the numerous dated lamps show a gradual decline in both design and technique. The Arab Museum possesses a number of lamps inscribed with the name of Sultan Malik Nasir Hasan (1347-60), some of which come from his madrasa, built in 1362. They are decorated in the traditional style or with an all-over floral pattern which covers every inch of the glass. Work of this period is exemplified in the Museum by three lamps, one of which bears the name of Amir Shaikhu and was probably made for his convent and mausoleum, built in 1355. There are several other lamps which bear his name, two of them in the Arab Museum in Cairo. A bottle, a basin, and a ewer with enameled decoration, in the Metropolitan Museum, may be assigned to the second half of the fourteenth century.

The enameled glass of the end of the fourteenth century, including mosque lamps with the name of Sultan Barkuk (1382-98), reveals a hasty execution and poverty of design and enameling; a lamp that belonged to this sultan is in the Moore Collection of the Museum. Enameling was still practiced in the fifteenth century, but the existing dated examples in the Arab Museum in Cairo show the art in full decline at this time.

4. Iranian Glass of the XVII to the XIX Century

Under Shah ʿAbbas the Great (1587-1628) a renaissance of glassmaking took place in Iran, most probably under European influence, chiefly Italian. From the *Travels* of Chardin, who visited Iran between 1664 and 1681, we learn that glass vessels were made at Shiraz and Isfahan, the former producing the best in the country. The superiority of Shiraz glass is confirmed in the writings of other travelers. In the early nineteenth century glassmaking was still "prosecuted with sufficient diligence and success," as we learn from the *Travels* (1817-20) of Sir Robert Ker Porter, who notes that window glass, bottles, and goblets made at Shiraz "though not of the most elegant sort, are vendable all over the kingdom."

Of this late Iranian glass, the Museum owns a large and representative collection—toilet glass, including bottles, ewers, and vases in various forms—mainly of the eighteenth and nineteenth centuries. The glass is white, amber, violet, green, or blue in color. Some pieces are decorated with painting and gilding; others have simple molded ornament. The painted and gilded decorations are coarsely executed as a rule, and the most attractive specimens are those that depend solely on beauty of form and the color of the glass for their effect (see fig. 161).

Chapter 12

TEXTILES

In the early Muhammadan period textiles continued to be made in the style and technique of the earlier Coptic and Sasanian weaves, but gradually a true Muhammadan style was developed, which spread over all the countries under Arab rule.

1. Abbasid and Tulunid Textiles of Egypt (VIII-X Century)

The conquest of Egypt by the Arabs in 641 wrought but little change in the life of the native Christians, or Copts. The Copts were great craftsmen, and as such were extensively employed by the Arabs in building mosques and palaces and for work in the newly established textile manufactories, called Dar at Tiraz. The term tiraz applies to bands containing inscriptions either woven or embroidered, to the garments so decorated, and to the factories where such garments were made. The institution of tiraz factories, which existed in all the provinces, was of great importance in the official life of the Muhammadan rulers of the Umayyad and Abbasid dynasties. In these shops, some of which were housed in palaces of the caliphs, were made robes of honor with tiraz bands which were presented to officials of high rank at least once a year and corresponded somewhat to our orders. The name of the ruler was mentioned in the inscriptions of the tiraz bands as a mark of his sovereignty.

The tiraz factories of Egypt were famous for their linens and silks, and Arabic textiles were exported from Egypt to other provinces such as Syria and Mesopotamia. An embroidered inscription in red silk on a linen fragment of the ninth century, found at Samarra, indicates Tinnis, near Port Said, as the place of manufacture. Tinnis, which had five thousand looms, was renowned for several kinds of fabrics, such as *kasab*, a very fine linen used for turbans; *badana*, a fabric used for the garments of the caliphs; and *bukalimun*, a fabric with changing colors, used for saddlecloths and for covering royal litters. Nasir-i-Khusrau, a Persian traveler of the eleventh century, tells us that the products of the royal tiraz at Tinnis were reserved for the sovereign of Egypt and could neither be sold nor given to anyone else. Tinnis, however, was not the only place where fabrics were woven. In Tuna, near Tinnis, were made fine linen cloth and *kiswas*, or coverings, for the Kaaba at Mecca. Every year the Abbasid caliph sent *kiswas*, made in the state tiraz by his direct order or that of his vizier, from Baghdad to Mecca. Dabik was famous for its silks. In Damietta fine white linen cloths were woven, of which the Metropolitan Museum possesses a piece dated A.H. 328 (939/40). Other manufactories are known to have existed at Alexandria and at Fustat, or Old Cairo. Several tenth-century linens of the Fustat looms are in the Museum. Arabic textiles were also made in Upper Egypt, for example, at al Ashmunain and Bahnasa. Under the Fatimids the importance of the tiraz increased even more, and the state factories at Tinnis, Alexandria, and Damietta worked chiefly for the Fatimid caliphs.

Arabic textiles of Egypt have been found at various sites. A great number come from al Azam, near Assiut; others from Erment, Drunka, Akhmim, and the rubbish heaps of Fustat. The usual technique is that of tapestry weaving with linen warp and weft of silk or wool. Some fabrics are woven entirely of silk and often brocaded with gold threads.

A. TEXTILES WITH TAPESTRY-WOVEN DECORATION IN POLYCHROME WOOL AND LINEN

The style of Coptic tapestry weaves in wool, which achieved its highest development in the sixth and seventh centuries, continued under the rule of the Arabs. Textiles made by Coptic weavers for the use of Arabs of the Abbasid and Tulunid periods show little difference from those made for the Copts (see p. 9). The gauzelike cloth of garments, mostly scarves and turbans, is often of black linen or wool decorated with tapestry-woven bands. The tiraz bands of the Abbasid era contain inscriptions in several varieties of Kufic. In a few pieces the Kufic inscriptions give us a date or the place of manufacture. A fragment of a turban in the Arab Museum in Cairo was made, according to the inscription, in 707. Another fabric in Cairo, decorated with a row of camels, bears an inscription which indicates that it was woven in a private shop in the district of Fayum. Here and in other parts of Upper Egypt existed looms which continued to weave in the Coptic tradition.

The Museum has a representative collection of such textiles. A notable piece is a large portion of a black woolen scarf or shawl (fig.

Fig. 162. *Woolen Cloth with Tapestry-woven
Decoration, Coptic, Tulunid, IX Century*

162), decorated with four bands of various widths, tapestry-woven in polychrome wool and linen. The ornament of the main band consists of medallions containing various motives and separated by highly stylized birds, in white, yellow, and black on red, and bordered by Kufic writing in white on black. Another band shows a pattern of human figures, animals, birds, and rosettes in hexagons. The extreme stylization of these figures and animals is a characteristic feature of Tulunid textiles of the ninth century. Another group of textiles of the ninth century shows an interesting mixture of meaningless Arabic writing and Coptic inscriptions of a religious character. The Copts evidently made these fabrics for their own use.

Among the tapestries found in Egypt are a number of coarse, thick fabrics which were probably used as rugs or hangings. Several interesting pieces of this type, one with large peacocks, another with Kufic inscriptions, are in the Museum.

B. TEXTILES WITH TAPESTRY-WOVEN AND EMBROIDERED DECO-
RATION IN SILK

The decoration of linen cloth woven in state manufactories was always in silk. One of the earliest known tiraz pieces is a textile, in the Islamic Museum in Berlin, inscribed with the name of the caliph Harun ar Rashid (786-809) and the name of the weaver Marwan, son of Mari. The Kufic inscriptions and geometrical pattern are

Fig. 163. Linen Cloth with Tapestry-woven Decoration, Egypto-Arabic, Fatimid, 1021-1036

tapestry-woven in polychrome silk. A similar textile in the Arab Museum in Cairo is inscribed with the name of the caliph al Amin (809-13), the son and successor of Harun, and was made in Misr.

Through the generosity of George D. Pratt the Museum now possesses a fine collection of textiles with tiraz bands and other decorations of the Abbasid period, either tapestry-woven or embroidered in silk of various colors. One of the earliest inscriptions on these textiles, which is embroidered in red silk, contains the date A.H. 282 (895) and name of the Abbasid caliph al Mu'tadid (892-902). The majority of linen textiles with inscriptions are of the tenth century, bearing the names of al Muktadir bi'llah and other caliphs. The Kufic writing of these textiles shows numerous decorative variations, some of them terminating in half palmettes (Kufic fleuri). One piece with a black inscription containing the name of the caliph al Muti' li'llah (946-74) is of special importance, as it is enriched in places with gold threads which are made of brown linen wound with narrow gilded strips of goldbeater's skin. In this tenth-century piece we have the earliest known example of the use of this type of gold thread, which was most probably of Islamic origin and not a Byzantine invention as some believe.

Although most of the textiles decorated with human figures and animals in Coptic tradition were of wool, several pieces are preserved which are tapestry-woven in silk. A fragment in the Museum

252

is decorated with medallions containing conventionalized animals and birds and with floral devices in white, yellow, blue, green, and red on a red ground. Another silk tapestry with Kufic inscriptions and an animal decoration is in the Victoria and Albert Museum, London, and may be attributed to the ninth century. Other silk tapestries of this period are in the Arab Museum, Cairo, in the Kaiser Friedrich Museum, Berlin, and in the Brussels Museum.

2. Fatimid Textiles of Egypt (Late X-XII Century)

Magnificent textiles were produced in the Fatimid period, even surpassing those of the Abbasid period. The cloth made of linen and

silk became extremely fine and was greatly admired by travelers; one source tells us that the texture of Cairene fabrics was so fine that a whole robe could be passed through a finger ring. In the arrangement of inscriptions and ornament the Fatimid weavers followed the scheme developed under the Abbasids. A broad band with geometrical or animal decoration (see fig. 163) is flanked by inscriptions. The Kufic writing at first followed the Abbasid prototype, as may be seen on a linen in the Museum inscribed with the name of the Fatimid caliph al 'Aziz bi'llah (976-96). The tall, elegant letters of this inscription are in yellow silk

Fig. 164. Silk Tapestry Weave, Egypto-Arabic, Fatimid, XI Century

outlined in blue. In another piece of the same period, the inscription is in yellow silk on a blue ground. The ripe Fatimid period developed new types of Kufic letters, so-called Kufic fleuri, in which some of the letters end in palmette scrolls.

The Fatimid style of decoration is exemplified in the Museum's collection by a number of fine pieces. Among the early dated textiles is a portion of a linen cloth (fig. 163) inscribed with the name of the Fatimid ruler az Zahir (1021-36). Each of the two bands of decoration shows a row of medallions alternately red and dark blue, containing birds and griffins. One of the bands is bordered by

Fig. 165. Linen Cloth with Tapestry-woven Decoration, Egypto-
Arabic, Fatimid, XI Century

two inscriptions in red with blue scrolls. A richer type of Fatimid textile decoration is illustrated in figure 164. Here five broad bands in golden yellow, light and dark blue, and red are decorated with hares in small compartments formed by interlaced bands and with birds in circles.

A fine example of luxurious Fatimid weave is a portion of a linen cloth (fig. 165); it is decorated with horizontal bands, the central one with pairs of falcons, which with palmettes form an intermittent scroll on a green ground. The pattern is tapestry-woven in silk and gold threads of gilded goldbeater's skin. The style of the pattern is characteristic of the period of the caliph al Mustansir, who reigned from 1036 to 1094. Such fine fabrics decorated all over with gold tapestry may be identified with garments called *badana* made at Tinnis for the exclusive use of the caliph.

The Fatimid textiles of the twelfth century followed the style of the eleventh century, with Naskhi or round characters replacing the Kufic. Often the cursive writing is ingeniously combined with arabesque motives, as seen on two sleeve bands in the Museum bearing the name of the caliph 'Abd al Majid al Hafiz (1130-49). The quality of the decoration of many of these twelfth-century textiles is as good as that of eleventh-century pieces. The Museum owns several fine examples. Among them is a portion of a blue linen cloth with a polychrome silk decoration showing several ornamental bands and a large yellow medallion with a pair of gazelles separated by a tree.

3. Abbasid and Fatimid Textiles with Painted and Printed Decoration

Of great technical interest are linen textiles on which inscriptions or decorations are painted or stamped. In six textiles in the Museum the decoration is drawn with a reed pen in dark brown ink and partly gilded. One of the Abbasid pieces shows a rectangular panel, with an inscription and arabesques recalling the chapter headings of ninth-century Korans (see p. 67). Such inscriptions, sometimes painted in liquid gold, are probably identification marks of Egyptian weaving shops. Noteworthy also are several cotton textiles, dyed in the so-called chiné or ikat technique, which have elaborate Kufic inscriptions painted in gold and outlined in black. One of the pieces, in the Cairo Museum, bears the name of a Rassid prince of Yemen of the tenth century. These pieces are similar to cotton textiles with embroidered inscriptions, several of which contain names of Abbasid caliphs of the ninth and tenth centuries, having been made in the tiraz of San'a in Yemen. Among the textiles with painted decoration is a noteworthy piece of the early Fatimid period. The decoration of birds, arabesques, and Kufic inscription in polychrome recalls some of the tapestry-woven textiles.

The technique of stamping and printing patterns on textiles, used earlier by the Copts, was developed and improved in the Islamic period in Egypt, whence it later spread to Europe, particularly to Germany. The Arabic weavers used wooden stamps for their printed textiles. Frequently the decoration is an all-over pattern similar to that on a piece in the Museum, consisting of arabesques printed in gold. A rare and unusually fine linen fabric of the tenth century (fig. 166) has an all-over pattern of lions stamped in brown and gold within squares and intervening spaces. Here the artist used six different stamps, four for printing the lions, one for the brown background of the squares, and one for the disks bordering the squares. Such elaborately stamped fabrics were probably substitutes for the more costly cloths, which were tapestry-woven or embroidered in gold threads.

Fig. 166. Linen Fabric with Stamped Decoration, Egypto-Arabic, Fatimid, X Century

4. Ayyubid and Mamluk Textiles (Late XII-XIV Century)

In the Ayyubid and Mamluk periods the tapestry technique inherited from the Fatimids was still practiced, but to a lesser extent than earlier. An important Mamluk tapestry-woven textile in the Metropolitan Museum (fig. 167) has been presented by V. Everit Macy.

The peony palmettes and naturalistic leaves are similar in style to the ornament on Mamluk metalwork of the early fourteenth century. The colors are white, tan, light brown, light blue, and black; gold and silver are also liberally used.

The embroideries of the Ayyubid and Mamluk periods are simple compared with the magnificent Fatimid embroideries in polychrome silk or gold thread. A group of polychrome embroideries in a running or chain stitch, with Naskhi or Kufic inscriptions, may be assigned to the twelfth century. Dating from the twelfth and thirteenth centuries are other embroideries in polychrome silk showing pairs of animals or birds separated by trees. A linen cushion cover of the thirteenth century in the Victoria and Albert Museum is embroidered with lozenges enclosing seated human figures, lions, peacocks, birds, and other motives. Two pieces of similar type in the Cooper Union Museum in New York are decorated with arboreal motives and illegible inscriptions.

In embroideries of the Mamluk period the designs are angular

Fig. 167. Silk Tapestry Weave, Egypto-Arabic, Mamluk, about 1300

in character, owing to the technique employed. It is a running stitch in steps, sometimes called the Holbein stitch. Often the stitches follow the direction of the weft, giving the appearance of weaving.

Printing of textiles continued in the Mamluk period. The thirteenth- and fourteenth-century examples are usually decorated with lozenge diapers with rosettes and floral scrolls in blue, red, or brown.

257

5. Silk Weaves from Egypt and Syria

In the silk stuffs now to be considered, the entire fabric is woven with a shuttle on a drawloom, in distinction to textiles with tapestry-woven decoration, in which the weft threads of the pattern are introduced with a bobbin or needle.

The early Islamic woven textiles, in both wool and silk, continued at first in the style of East Christian and Sasanian weaves (see p. 18). Several such textiles, some of them in the Metropolitan Museum,

Fig. 168. Silk Weave, Syrian, VIII-IX Century

have Arabic writing in Kufic script and therefore, in spite of their pre-Islamic pattern, must be assigned to the eighth or ninth century. Several silk weaves of the end of the eighth or the beginning of the ninth century, in buff on a green ground, similar in style to the textiles found at Akhmim, may be attributed to Syrian looms, which existed in Damascus and probably also in Antioch. The interesting silk weave in figure 168 shows an Islamic version of a Sasanian motive of a palmette tree. The palmettes within almond-shaped compartments also recall early Christian jewelry from Cyprus (see p. 9), which was doubtless of Syrian origin. The angular outlines of the design and the scroll of the medallion border are both features of the early Islamic era. The continuation of Sasanian motives in the Umayyad and early Abbasid periods outside of Iran was particularly strong in Syria and Mesopotamia.

Probably of the Fatimid period is a woven silk fabric in the Brussels Museum, decorated with rows of confronted birds separated by palmette devices and bearing on their wings Arabic inscriptions expressing good wishes. The coloring is unusual, as the fabric is divided into horizontal bands of blue, purple, yellow, and red with-

Fig. 169. Silk Weave, Syrian, Ayyubid, XIII Century

out any relation to the design. In style this fabric recalls some of the lustered ceramics of the eleventh or twelfth century found at Fustat, and it may be similarly dated. It is quite possible that the silk was woven in Egypt.

Probably Ayyubid and of Syrian origin is a silk textile in the Metropolitan Museum (fig. 169), woven in buff on a green ground. The design consists of pairs of birds and griffins within compartments formed by wavy bands. The birds and griffins are separated by palmette trees, which are seen in Saljuk textiles from Iran. The Saljuk style is also evident in the highly decorative rendering of the griffins and the palmette trees, so that at first glance the silk might be regarded as Saljuk. However, as several large portions of the same silk were found at al Azam in Egypt, it is more probable that it was made in Syria in the beginning of the thirteenth century, under strong Saljuk influence.

To the second half of the thirteenth century is assigned a silk textile in buff and green, in the Victoria and Albert Museum, with

Fig. 170. Silk Weave, Syrian, Mamluk, Early XIV Century

pairs of birds within roundels. This early Mamluk piece may also be regarded as a product of Syrian looms.

Textiles in the Chinese style belong to the fourteenth and fifteenth centuries. A number of silk fabrics from church treasuries, now in the Kunstgewerbe Museum of Berlin and the Victoria and Albert Museum, London, bear the name and titles of Nasir ad Din Muhummad ibn Kalaun, the Mamluk sultan of Egypt and Syria, who reigned from 1293 to 1340. The patterns of these fabrics were influenced by Chinese textiles, which were known at that time in the Near East.

To the period of Ibn Kalaun may be assigned an important silk weave in the Metropolitan Museum (fig. 170). The decoration in buff on a brown ground is arranged in horizontal bands and consists of a traditional Islamic design with floral motives borrowed from China.

The titles of Mamluk sultans of Egypt and Syria occur also on several brocades. A well-known piece in Saint Mary's Church at Danzig is woven with flat strips of gilded leather on a black silk ground and has pairs of parrots and Chinese dragons inscribed with the title "an Nasir." The inscription presumably refers to Nasir ad Din Muhammad ibn Kalaun. Other important brocades in the Chinese style are a chasuble and a cope in the same church, and two dalmatics in Regensburg Cathedral bearing the name of the maker, "Master 'Abd al 'Aziz." These brocades have been attributed by Falke and Kendrick to the looms of China or Central Asia, but an Egyptian origin is not excluded.

6. Iranian Textiles of the VIII to the X Century

Tiraz manufactories were established all over the Islamic world. A great number are known to have existed in Iran, and the textiles manufactured there were exported to other provinces, some of them having been found in Egypt. The Arab Museum in Cairo owns dated Abbasid pieces of the ninth and tenth centuries with inscriptions indicating the place of manufacture as Merv and Bishapur. A fragment of a linen cloth in the Metropolitan Museum has an embroidered inscription which tells us that the piece was made in Nishapur in A.H. 266 (879/80). The textiles with inscriptions follow the style of tiraz bands of other provinces.

Iranian woven silks of the early Islamic era are based on Sasanian tradition. To the period between the seventh and ninth centuries may be ascribed the sudarium of Saint Victor and a fabric with a design of elephants, both in the Treasury of Sens Cathedral. A large piece of the latter textile is also in the Cooper Union Museum in New York. These silk fabrics, reminiscent in style and color scheme of Sasanian textiles, were probably woven in western Iran.

A distinctive group of Iranian silk textiles of the early Muhammadan era is characterized by angularly rendered animals and birds. The best known specimens are the sudarium of Saint Columba, ornamented with lions, in the Vatican; a similar stuff at Nancy; and two fabrics at Sens, one with peacocks and another with horses. Two Iranian silk textiles are in the Metropolitan Museum, one with a pair of ducks within circles, the other (fig. 171) decorated

with pairs of horses within circles and birds in intervening spaces. The pattern of this latter piece is rendered in white, yellow, green, and lilac on a red ground. Similar textiles were unearthed by Sir Aurel Stein in the caves of the Thousand Buddhas at Tun-huang in Chinese Turkestan. Stein is of the opinion that they were woven in Sogdiana, western Turkestan. From literary sources we know that looms existed at Samarkand, and this group of textiles was probably woven there.

Fig. 171. Silk Weave, Iranian, VIII-IX Century

A silk fabric from the Church of Saint Josse-sur-Mer (Pas-de-Calais), now in the Louvre, was woven in Khurasan, the chief centers of which were Merv and Nishapur. It is decorated with large confronted elephants, bordered by rows of small camels and peacocks. The Kufic inscription gives the name of Amir Mansur Bukhtagin of Khurasan, who died in 960, thus dating the piece in the tenth century.

7. Saljuk Textiles of Iran, Mesopotamia, and Asia Minor (XI-XIII Century)

The invasion of Iran by the Turkish Saljuks in 1037 greatly influenced the art of weaving. That there was an important revival of arts and crafts under the Saljuks and their successors, who ruled over Iran, Mesopotamia, Syria, and Asia Minor, is evident from many silk weaves long known in various collections and some recently found in Iran, especially at Rayy, a famous weaving center. Though the influence of the Sasanian style may still be seen in the patterns of the early Saljuk pieces, it was gradually supplanted by a style in which arabesque motives of Islamic origin are combined with linear scrolls and palmette forms. Saljuk textiles may be divided into several groups. Those of the early eleventh century are still related in style to Iranian textiles of the eighth to tenth centuries. In the ripe Saljuk period, however, the design, hitherto more or less angularly treated, develops a style characteristic of Saljuk art in general: beautiful patterns with elegant and flowing outlines. This may be seen on a silk weave in the Metropolitan Museum, in which the pattern of animals and arabesques is woven in buff and brown, and in a number of other pieces in European and American collections, most of which are of the twelfth century, and a few of the thirteenth. Also of this type are a green and white silk fabric with confronted griffins, in the Kunstgewerbe Museum in Berlin, and a red and green silk with lions, in the Saint Servatius Church in Maastricht. A black and white stuff with pairs of eagles, said to have come from Tabriz and now in Berlin, may be dated in the thirteenth century.

Literary evidence indicates that at an early period silk fabrics were woven in Baghdad, where the Abbasid caliphs transported a group of weavers from Shushtar. About ten textiles of the first half of the tenth century are known which are inscribed with the name of the tiraz of Baghdad (Madinat as Salam). Marco Polo, writing in the thirteenth century, mentions silk fabrics and gold brocades woven in Baghdad and Mosul. In the Colegiata de San Isidoro at León, Spain, there is a silk fabric with a design of birds, elephants, and various other animals, Iranian in style, and bearing a Kufic inscription which shows that it was woven in Baghdad, probably in the eleventh century. Silk fabrics were also manufactured in the Saljuk empire in Asia Minor. A thirteenth-century gold brocade in the museum at Lyons is decorated with lions and inscriptions containing the name of Sultan Kai-Kubad of Konia (either Kai-Kubad I [1219-1237] or Kai-Kubad II [1249-1257]).

8. Mongol and Timurid Textiles of Iran (XIV-XV Century)

Very few Iranian textiles can be assigned with certainty to the fourteenth or fifteenth century. The ornament of textiles of this period was strongly Chinese in character. Under the rule of the Mongols, the demand for Chinese fabrics was so great in Iran that Chinese motives were imitated by native weavers. In Mongol and Timurid miniatures are represented fabrics in the Chinese style which are decorated with the dragon, phoenix, *kilin*, and floral ornaments such as the peony and the lotus. Occasionally these motives are combined with purely Islamic ones.

Several brocades attributed to Iran by Falke are most likely of Spanish origin. The Metropolitan Museum possesses a rare silk brocade which may be assigned to the end of the fifteenth century (fig. 172). Here arabesques form an ogival diaper, each compart-

Fig. 172. Silk Brocade, Iranian, End of the XV Century

ment containing floral scrolls with blossoms, naturalistic leaves, and peony palmettes in black and silver on an olive-green ground. The elegance of the design and the color scheme are related to Timurid decoration.

9. Safavid Textiles of Iran (XVI-XVIII Century)

With the Safavids begins the golden era of Iranian weaving. Safavid silks may be divided into three groups: plain silk weaves, silk brocades, and silk velvets. Such fabrics were used for garments of the princes and nobles, hangings, and covers, and often served as gifts from the shahs to those whom they wished to honor. The decoration consists of figure subjects, animals, birds, and floral motives. The scenes are taken for the most part from the great Iranian epics, such as the *Shah-nama*, or from the romantic poems

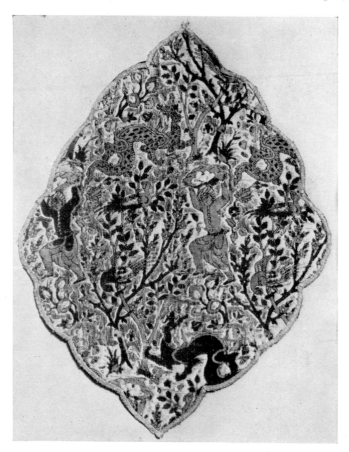

Fig. 173. *Velvet Panel, Iranian, Safavid, XVI Century*

of Nizami, while some depict Iranian nobles hunting or enjoying the pleasures of life in their gardens.

A beautiful example of a polychrome sixteenth-century Iranian silk is illustrated in plate IV. The repeat design shows an Iranian youth with a bottle and a cup, standing in a rocky landscape among cypresses, cherry trees, animals, and birds. Also of the sixteenth

Fig. 174. *Velvet Carpet (Detail), Iranian, Safavid, about 1600*

century is a magnificent velvet (fig. 173), the gift of V. Everit
Macy, which served, with other panels now in several American
museums, for the interior decoration of a tent used by Kara Mus-
tapha Pasha in 1683 during the second siege of Vienna. The design represents Iskandar (Alexander) killing a dragon with a rock.
The colors are wine red, light green, dark blue, light and dark
tan, and black on a gold background consisting of flat gilded
silver strips. In the Armory of Moscow there is a coat of silk brocade decorated with the same subject, woven in polychrome silk
on a blue background. A fragment of another sixteenth-century
brocade in the Metropolitan Museum represents a seated man to
whom an attendant offers fruit; it is woven in rich colors on a
white background. The Cooper Union Museum in New York
possesses two fine silks relating the story of Laila and Majnun.
One shows Laila, in a litter on the back of a camel, looking down
on Majnun, who is surrounded by animals. This piece is of special
importance, as it bears the signature of the maker, Ghiyath. The
other fragment depicts Laila approaching Majnun, who is holding
a gazelle. A noteworthy silk of the sixteenth century, in Ros-

enborg Castle at Copenhagen, is decorated with very large figures (about 20 inches in height) of a prince and his attendant. Many of the figures in these silks resemble those in contemporary miniature paintings.

Other Safavid textiles of the sixteenth century are ornamented only with floral designs, either naturalistic or stylized. Figures in Iranian miniatures of the same period often wear garments made from silk brocades of this type. A panel of silk velvet[1] in the Museum's collection is decorated with palmette devices within ogival compartments, combined with tulip and rosette motives on a gold background.

Under Shah 'Abbas the Great (1587-1628), a noble patron of all the arts, the weaving of costly fabrics, brocades and velvets, continued to be practiced with great skill. In addition to the long-established

Fig. 175. Velvet, Iranian, Safavid, XVII Century

looms of Yazd and Kashan, Shah 'Abbas founded other manufactories, especially in Isfahan, where luxurious fabrics and those for daily use were woven. The Metropolitan Museum possesses two small dated fragments of a silk fabric of the Shah 'Abbas period, inscribed: "1008 [1599-1600] made by Husain." Names of other sixteenth- and seventeenth-century weavers are known: Ghiyath, 'Abd Allah, Ibn Muhammad, Muizz ad Din, son of Ghiyath, and Saifi-i-'Abbasi. The fragments show all the characteristics of this period, such as subdued colors and a more realistic

[1] From the same tent decoration as the velvet shown in figure 173.

drawing of figures and draperies than were favored in the period of Shah Tahmasp. The velvets and gold brocades produced in the time of Shah 'Abbas are among the most sumptuous fabrics ever produced, and the Museum has an especially fine collection of textiles of the late sixteenth and the seventeenth century.

A masterpiece from the Iranian looms of the Shah 'Abbas period is a large carpet of brocaded silk velvet (fig. 174) now in the Museum collection. It was formerly in the possession of the royal house of Saxony, to which it had belonged since 1683, being captured during the siege of Vienna. The design consists of two large, eight-pointed medallions and of segments of similar figures. The field, as well as the medallions, is richly ornamented with delicate flower and stem motives, chiefly in red and green on a gold ground, while the border design in pastel shades is placed against a silver ground. This beautiful velvet carpet was probably made at the Isfahan looms and may be assigned to about 1600. A fine example of a seventeenth-century velvet in the Museum (fig. 175) shows plants growing out of rocks and Chinese clouds and butterflies in soft colors on a gold ground.

New floral motives, naturalistic in style, became popular in the beginning of the seventeenth century. An unusually fine brocade,

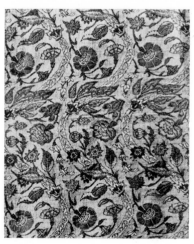

Fig. 176. Silk Brocade, Iranian, Safavid, Beginning of the XVII Century

part of a coat (fig. 176), is a masterpiece of design and color. It has a decoration of carnations, roses, and irises woven in soft and delicate colors blending harmoniously with the gold background.

An integral part of the Iranian costume of the Shah 'Abbas period and later was the sash, the use of which spread from Iran to East Europe. Several complete sashes and fragments are in the Museum. The finest one (fig. 177) was presented by the late George D. Pratt.

Fig. 177. Sash (Detail), Iranian, Safavid, First Half of the
XVII Century

10. Iranian Embroideries and Printed Cottons (XVII-XIX Century)

In the Museum are many examples of Iranian embroidery dating
from the seventeenth, eighteenth, and nineteenth centuries and
showing a variety of stitches. There is a seventeenth-century embroidery with figure subjects, animals, and floral motives in many
brilliant colors on a black background, as well as embroideries with
dense floral patterns of the type used for women's trousers
(*nakshe*). Also included is a group of Caucasian embroideries,
mostly with geometrical patterns. Patchwork made from cloth of
many colors was popular in the eighteenth and nineteenth centuries and was often padded with papier-mâché and outlined with
couched silk and silver thread. This work was done chiefly at Resht
and Isfahan.

The Museum's textile collection includes several examples of
the block-printed cotton hangings known as *kalamkar*, which were

made in Isfahan, Hamadan, and Yazd. Most of them date from the nineteenth century.

11. *Turkish Textiles and Embroideries (XVI-XIX Century)*

The majority of Turkish textiles of the Ottoman period consists of brocades and velvets. A few pieces have been assigned to the late fifteenth century by analogy with costumes worn by figures in Italian paintings of that period, particularly those by Gentile Bellini (1429-1507). Brusa, the early capital of the Ottoman Turks, was the chief center of Turkish weaving, although other cities in Asia Minor, such as Scutari and Hereke, were known for their fine textiles.

The patterns of Turkish brocades and velvets are less varied than those of Iranian textiles. The designs were limited to floral patterns, thus following more strictly the tradition of the Prophet prohibiting representations of living creatures. Although influenced by

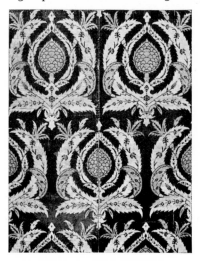

Fig. 178. Velvet, Turkish, XVI Century

Iranian and Italian art, the Turks evolved a style of their own, which is familiar to us from the ceramics made at the kilns of Isnik (see p. 222). From Iran Turkish artists borrowed the floral scroll with palmette devices, from Italy the pomegranate and other motives found in Venetian velvets of the fifteenth century. Velvets made in Brusa are sometimes taken for Italian, although they may be recognized as Turkish by their patterns and their less elaborate technique.

Turkish velvets, of which the Museum possesses a representative collection, have in general a much bolder design than Turkish brocades, being used mostly for hangings and cushion covers. In the sixteenth-century velvets the ground is usually red and the pattern is in gold, often with the addition of silver threads. A mixture of Italian and Turkish design is seen in a large velvet in the Museum (fig. 178) decorated with a repeat pattern of devices formed of cones and lanceolate leaves overlaid with sprays of carnations, roses, and hyacinths. These flowers, which are characteristic of sixteenth-century Turkish velvets and brocades, also appear in a complete cover with an ogival diaper in the field. The latter design is also typically Turkish. A number of velvet cushion covers dating from the seventeenth to the nineteenth century show a gradual decline in drawing and craftsmanship.

Fig. 179. *Silk Brocade, Turkish, XVI Century*

Turkish brocades of the sixteenth and seventeenth centuries are among the finest products of oriental weaving. Less rich in color than contemporary Iranian textiles, they are nevertheless equally fine in design and technique, often even superior. The most characteristic pattern of Turkish brocades consists of a diaper forming ogival compartments which contain sprays of carnations, tulips, hyacinths, roses, and other flowers. The color scheme is usually limited to two or three colors, such as gold and red or red, blue, and gold. The ground is usually red but sometimes blue, green, or purple. The brocades are similar in style to the velvets, although the former show a more elaborate design. Patterns with pomegranates (fig.

271

Fig. 180. *Coat of Gold Brocade, Turkish, XVI Century*

179), influenced by Italian textiles, date from the sixteenth century. Most of the Turkish brocades were used for garments, several of which are preserved in museums in Istanbul and elsewhere. A complete coat of heavy gold brocade is in the Metropolitan Museum (fig. 180). The rich pattern in red, blue, and green may be assigned to the late sixteenth century. In the seventeenth century the treatment of the floral motives became more realistic and the geometrical patterns were frequently replaced by branches (fig. 181), from which grow various blossoms.

Embroideries were produced both in Asia Minor and in European Turkey. The embroideries of Asia Minor often recall Brusa velvets and brocades in their designs, in which floral motives, either stylized or naturalistic, are conspicuous. The early examples, which date from the seventeenth and eighteenth centuries, are embroidered in a darning stitch on linen (fig. 182) or in couched work on silk.

A well-known group of Turkish embroideries consists of kerchiefs and towels, some of them used for ceremonial purposes only.

Fig. 181. *Gold Brocade, Turkish, XVII Century*

Although most of them date from the nineteenth century, there are some from the eighteenth. These pieces are embroidered in a double darning stitch in silk and silver-gilt threads. Floral designs, such as roses, are the most popular ones, although motives such as the mosque and cypress were frequently used.

12. *Islamic Textiles of Spain and Sicily*

The Arab conquest of Spain in 711 introduced the arts and crafts of the Near East into Europe. Spanish textiles were mentioned in the papal inventories as early as the ninth century, and Idrisi, the Arab historian (1099-1154), recorded that there were eight hundred looms at Almería in Andalusia for the weaving of costly silk stuffs. Textiles were also woven in Murcia, Seville, Granada, and Malaga. In the Royal Academy of History at Madrid is preserved a fabric decorated with a tapestry-woven band in light blue, dark blue, and red, with octagons containing geometrically stylized animals, birds, and human figures. It is inscribed in Arabic with the name of Hisham II, Caliph of Cordova (976-1009). The design, which is undoubtedly of Egypto-Arabic origin, resembles some of the patterns on contemporary Hispano-Moresque ivory caskets.

An interesting fabric with tapestry-woven decoration in colored silk is in the Cooper Union Museum in New York. Within interlaced circles are pairs of figures drinking. Here again the similarity of the figures to those on Spanish ivory caskets of the eleventh century is striking and indicates that the piece must belong to the same period. Similar in style is a fragment of gold brocade (fig.

Fig. 182. Embroidery, Turkish, Asia Minor, XVII Century

183) in the Metropolitan Museum with a design of musicians holding tambourines. The colors are light brown, red, blue, green, and gold on a gold background. The fabric is of particular interest because the figure subjects may be assigned to the twelfth or thirteenth century.

An important group of Andalusian textiles of the eleventh to twelfth century is characterized by a bold pattern of figures, birds, and animals. The best-known pieces are those with the representations of the legendary lion-strangler and others with pairs of sphinxes, which are today in the Episcopal Museum at Vich, the Kunstgewerbe Museum in Berlin, and the Cooper Union Museum in New York. They have a distinctive color scheme, being woven in red, green, and gold.

Another group of Hispano-Moresque textiles is identified with the help of a brocade in Berlin, which originally protected a document in the cathedral of Salamanca and belongs to the period of Fernando II, King of León (1158-88). In this type of textile, which continued to be woven in the thirteenth century, appear pairs of griffins or birds in circular medallions, usually in red-brown, cream white, and gold, and sometimes in other colors. The Museum possesses three such brocades, which can be dated to the end of the twelfth century and the beginning of the thirteenth. Other brocades of the thirteenth century are decorated with geometrical patterns, in which gold threads are profusely used. A fragment in the Museum formed part of the cope of Don Felipe (died 1274), now in the Archaeological Museum of Madrid. It is woven in tan and gold in a pattern of interlacing bands which form six-pointed stars. A thirteenth-century fragment of a brocade in the Museum is decorated with interlaced curved and straight lines within small squares and is probably from the cope of Saint Valerius, in the cathedral at Lérida.

To Spain are attributed certain gold brocades showing both Iranian and Chinese influence. The designs are characterized by scrollwork combined with figures of animals in gold on a blue background. Two such fabrics are in the Metropolitan Museum. In one, the scrollwork and lotus palmettes enclose a pair of hares; the other shows palmette scrolls with birds drinking from a fountain. They are probably of the early fourteenth century and are closely related in both style and technique to other Spanish textiles.

Fig. 183. Gold Brocade, Hispano-Moresque, XII-XIII Century

Other fourteenth- and fifteenth-century textiles of Spain are decorated in the so-called Alhambra style. The ornament consists of interlaced bands, polygons, inscriptions, and arabesques in vivid colors. Excellent specimens of such textiles, probably woven at Granada, may be seen in the Museum. One of our fabrics (fig. 184) bears an Arabic inscription in yellow and red reading "Glory to our Lord the Sultan." The Hispano-Moresque style did not lose favor until well into the sixteenth century.

Silk fabrics are known to have been woven in Sicily under Arabic rule in the tenth and eleventh centuries, but no existing specimens can be attributed to the Sicilian looms of that period. Under the

Normans, who perpetuated the customs and manners of the Arabs, the art of weaving was highly developed. After the oriental fashion, the Norman kings established in the twelfth century at Palermo royal manufactories (tiraz) which produced woven and embroidered silk fabrics of high quality. Magnificent dated examples in the State Treasury at Vienna, such as the imperial mantle and alb, were made in Palermo. The former, dated A.H. 528 (1134) and embroidered in gold with pearls on a red background, has a pattern with a repeat motive of a camel attacked by a lion. The alb was made under the Norman king, William II, in 1181, and shows a beautiful border of griffins and palmette trees in gold on a purple background. To these manufactories is also assigned the brocade still at Palermo from the burial robe of the Emperor Henry VI (died 1198) and other similar fabrics.

Fig. 184. Silk Weave, Hispano-Moresque, XIV-XV Century

13. Indian Textiles

The beginnings of textile arts in India may be traced back to remote antiquity, the weaving of fine cotton muslins being among the ancient Indian crafts which have survived until the present day. Mughal textiles were under court control and show a mixture of Iranian and Hindu motives. India also adopted from Iran many weaving techniques and, as in rug knotting, often surpassed her teachers. Mughal velvets are very rare and belong mostly to the period of Shah Jahan (1628-58); the decoration consists mainly of naturalistic floral designs or plants similar to those used in the rugs of the same period (see p. 306).

The weaving of silk brocades in India was highly developed in the Mughal period. Many centers of weaving are known, among the most famous being Lahore, Aurangabad in the Deccan, Chanderi in Gwalior, Benares, and Ahmedabad. These Indian brocades, all showing sumptuous designs, rich color schemes, and a lavish use of gold, were made into garments for men and women. The beautiful saris, oudhnis, and sashes must be classified among the finest weaving in the world. Several such garments may be seen in the Metropolitan Museum.

Embroidery was a popular art in India, being applied to cotton turbans, coats, sashes, and cushions. Among fine examples of Mughal embroideries in the Museum is the upper portion of a Mughal court robe embroidered in chain and outline stitch with floral sprays in delicate shades of green, yellow, and red. Another fine piece of the seventeenth century is a quilted red cotton hanging decorated with a plant design resembling irises growing out of a vase.

Among the Indian textiles best known to Americans are the Kashmir shawls, which usually date from the eighteenth century. Some of them are woven, others are embroidered, and the characteristic designs are dense floral patterns and cone-shaped motives derived from Iranian art.

Two methods of decorating fabrics are of ancient Indian origin. These are block printing and resist dyeing, which in the Mughal period were brought to a high degree of perfection and combined with painting. The Museum possesses several fine specimens of seventeenth- and eighteenth-century printed and painted cottons, well known in England and America under the names of palampores and pintados. Such cottons, made mostly at Masulipatam, are decorated with figure subjects or trees of life. Early examples of pintados are several cushion covers with figures of men and women dressed in Iranian and Hindu costumes (fig. 185). According to inventory notes written on the back, they may be dated to about the middle of the seventeenth century. Printing and painting

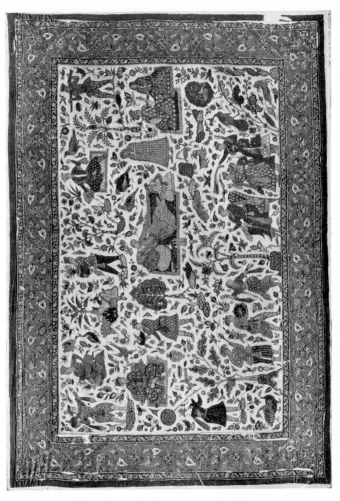

Fig. 185. *Painted Cotton, Indian, XVII Century*

were also applied to cotton garments, for instance, the Museum's magnificent court robe, which is decorated with a repeat design of blossoms in pink and gold.

Chapter 13

RUGS

1. Early Islamic Pile Rugs from Egypt (VIII-XII Century)

Fragments of rugs found or excavated at Fustat (Old Cairo) in Egypt have furnished us with important material for the history of the origin of rug knotting. Among the fragments in the Arab Museum in Cairo are two pieces with Kufic inscriptions, one of which bears a date, either A.H. 102 (720/1) or A.H. 202 (817/8). A third fragment, also found in Egypt, with Kufic inscriptions similar to those on the Cairo pieces, is in the Textile Museum in Washington, D.C. These fragments, together with several others in Swedish collections, which have been published by Lamm, must be regarded as examples of Abbasid pile rugs. As in most of the pre-Islamic rugs from Central Asia and in Spanish rugs, the knots are tied around single warp threads. Another interesting fragment from Fustat is in the Metropolitan Museum (fig. 186). It shows a dentelated ornament, a band of triangles, and disks in blue, yellow, green, and brown, on a red background, bordered by a band of Kufic characters in yellow on a dark blue ground. The knots, like those in the fragments described above, are tied around one warp. The Kufic characters are of a more developed type than those in the Abbasid pieces. This fragment should be assigned to the Fatimid period, that is, to the eleventh or twelfth century. Whether all these fragments from Fustat were made in Egypt or were imported from other provinces, such as Mesopotamia or Iran, is as yet difficult to determine. Some authorities favor an Egyptian origin for the pieces with Kufic inscriptions in the Arab Museum. That rugs were made in Egypt in the Fatimid period is evident from literary sources; Ya'kubi praises Kermes rugs of Siut; Makrizi mentions among the rugs used in the Fatimid palace the so-called Kalimun rugs and a type of rug made of reeds and embroidered in silver and gold. A fine Abbasid reed mat of the tenth century, made in Tiberias, Palestine, is in the Metropolitan Museum.

2. Saljuk Rugs of Asia Minor (XIII Century)

The Saljuks of Asia Minor were famous in the thirteenth century for their fine rugs; Marco Polo, who visited Asia Minor about 1270, tells us that the finest and most beautiful rugs in the world were made in Turcomania by Greek and Armenian craftsmen. An important group of Saljuk rugs, from the mosque 'Ala ad Din at Konia, is now in the Evkaf Museum at Istanbul. They were made sometime during the thirteenth century, probably for the mosque, which was built in A.H. 616 (1219/20). The decoration of these rugs consists of geometrical all-over patterns, including interlacings and rows of octagons or oval medallions, bordered by Kufic writing. The popular colors are yellow, red, dark blue, and light blue. These rugs from Konia are the earliest known to show the true Ghiordes knot so characteristic of Turkish rugs. Related to the Konia rugs are several discovered in the mosque at Beyshehir in Anatolia. Some of them, with an all-over design of arabesques and palmette devices treated in angular fashion, may be regarded as prototypes of Anatolian rugs of the seventeenth and eighteenth centuries.

3. Anatolian or Caucasian Rugs of the XIV and XV Centuries

In Italian paintings of the fourteenth and fifteenth centuries we often find representations of rugs with angularly stylized birds or animals within rectangular or octagonal compartments. These animal rugs were very popular in Italy and were imported from Asia Minor through Genoa and Venice. Erdman, who published a study of these rugs, recognizes four types. There are only three fragmentary specimens of these animal rugs known. The earliest one, a small fragment found in Fustat and assigned to the fourteenth century, is now in the Museum. Knotted in the Ghiordes technique, it is decorated with a single bird in tan, green, and red within a blue-green octagon. Other

Fig. 186. Fragment of Rug from Fustat, Egypto-Arabic, XI-XII Century

rugs with single birds within compartments, recalling the design of tiled pavements, are known from several fourteenth-century paintings, for instance, The Marriage of the Virgin by Niccolò da Buonaccorso in the National Gallery, London, and the fresco of the Annunciation in the church of Santissima Annunziata, Florence. To the fifteenth century belong a portion of a rug in the Historical Museum at Stockholm and another piece in the Berlin Museum. The fragment in Stockholm, found in the church at Marby, shows two complete compartments with confronted birds rendered in geometrical style and separated by a palmette tree. The piece in Berlin has two fields with octagons containing an interesting representation of a fight between a dragon and a phoenix, a device borrowed from China. A pattern resembling that of the Berlin rug appears in a fresco by Domenico di Bartolo in the hospital of Santa Maria della Scala at Siena, representing the Marriage of the Foundlings, painted between 1440 and 1444. These animal rugs may be attributed to eastern Asia Minor or the southern Caucasus, the home of the so-called dragon rugs, sometimes known as "Armenian" (see p. 318).

4. Mongol and Timurid Rugs (XIV-XV Century)

Although rugs are represented in Iranian miniatures of the fourteenth and fifteenth centuries, there are no existing specimens of Iranian manufacture that may surely be assigned to this early period. Some rugs have been so dated, but on insufficient grounds. The rugs represented in Mongol and Timurid miniatures show geometrical patterns consisting of octagonal diapers, interlacings, and Kufic writing. Interesting rugs, often suggesting the so-called Holbein rugs of Asia Minor, are represented in the Shah-nama of 1429 in the Teheran Museum.

Judging from representations of rugs in miniature paintings of the end of the fifteenth century, particularly those by Bihzad and his school, a change in rug design took place. Under the influence of Timurid illuminations, geometrical patterns were almost entirely replaced by arabesques and floral scrolls placed in lobed medallions and compartments. In several miniature paintings by Bihzad, for instance, in the Bustan in Cairo, dated A.H. 893 (1487), are depicted rugs which may be regarded as prototypes of some of the sixteenth-century rugs of the Tabriz school.

Fig. 187. Medallion Rug (Detail), Iranian, Timurid, End of the
XV Century

There is still a difference of opinion as to the dating of some of
the early Iranian rugs, but it is certain that the vast majority of
those seen in private collections and in museums are not earlier
than the sixteenth century. A few specimens, however, may have

been woven at the end of the fifteenth century in Tabriz during the reign of the Turkoman dynasty. To this period may be assigned a rug in the Ballard Collection of the Metropolitan Museum, decorated in the center with a sixteen-pointed, star-shaped medallion with stems and palmettes on blue and red grounds (fig. 187). The main field is covered with interlaced arabesques and floral scrolls bearing small palmettes on a salmon-red background. The stylized design and the unusual color scheme point to an early date.

5. Safavid Rugs of Iran (XVI-XVII Century)

The finest Iranian rugs known to us were woven in the sixteenth century under the Safavid dynasty. During this period, particularly in the reigns of Shah Isma'il (1502-24) and Shah Tahmasp (1524-76), Tabriz became one of the greatest centers of Iranian arts and crafts, including rug weaving. Among the other centers of rug manufacture were Kashan, Hamadan, Shushtar, and Herat. The finest rugs were made in court manufactories.

Both rugs and textiles in this century were influenced by the Safavid style of miniature painting and illumination. The greatest achievement of the rug designers was the development of a plant ornament consisting of floral scrolls with blossoms and palmettes, frequently interlaced with arabesques and intertwined with undulating cloud bands derived from Chinese designs. Poets were frequently inspired by the beauty of royal carpets, comparing them with a "wild white rose" or "a garden full of tulips and roses." Every Iranian rug shows a well-balanced composition of intricate floral scrolls and arabesques forming a background for various other decorative elements.

Iranian rugs are generally classified into groups on the basis of their designs rather than the localities in which they were woven, as our knowledge of the latter still remains more or less hypothetical.

A. MEDALLION AND ANIMAL RUGS OF THE XVI CENTURY

Medallion and animal rugs are characterized by central medallions of various shapes, with cartouches and pendants attached, and quarter sections of medallions in the corners. The decoration consists

Fig. 188. Medallion Rug (Detail), Iranian, Safavid,
Early XVI Century

of arabesques and floral motives, to which animal and hunting
scenes are sometimes added. Several fine early sixteenth-century
medallion rugs are in America. Two well-known examples are in
the Metropolitan Museum, one in the Altman Collection (fig. 188)
and the other in the Blumenthal Collection; other fine specimens

are in the collections of Myron C. Taylor and J. Paul Getty. The Altman rug shows a central medallion with a cartouche and a shieldlike pendant above and below. The rose-colored ground is filled with arabesques and fine floral scrolls. The floral ornament and the color scheme of this rug are richer than those in the Ballard rug shown in figure 187. The floral motives, derived from the Chinese lotus and peony, are generally stylized, but sometimes a more naturalistic trend is noticeable.

With the help of a few dated rugs, we are able to establish a

Fig. 189. *Compartment Rug (Detail), Iranian, Safavid, XVI Century*

chronology of Safavid rugs. The earliest so far known is the medallion rug with hunting scenes, in the Poldi-Pezzoli Museum in
Milan, inscribed with the date A.H. 929 (1522/3)[1] and the name
of the maker, Ghiyath ad Din Jami. This important rug has a central medallion in red decorated with floral scrolls and birds. The
blue field shows hunting scenes on a ground of angular floral scrolls
and arabesques. The angular treatment of the floral motives recalls
the patterns of the medallion rugs of figures 187 and 188, and of the
magnificent medallion rug with animal decoration in the collection
of J. Paul Getty, which has Timurid elements in the design and
was probably made about the same time as the Milan hunting rug,
that is in the reign of Shah Isma'il (1502-24).

One of the greatest masterpieces of Safavid rug knotting is the
famous compartment rug (fig. 189) in the Metropolitan Museum,
which combines elegance of design and richness of color. Instead
of the usual central medallion the field shows nine small ones in
dark blue, containing the Chinese motive of a fight between a
mythical dragon and phoenix. Each medallion has eight radiating
escutcheons, red, blue, and green in succession, with arabesques
or flying ducks. Small lobed medallions with four running lions
on a blue ground join units of the pattern into a diaper. The intervening spaces are patterned with arabesques, floral scrolls, and
Chinese cloud bands, in blue, orange, and red on a white background. The border is also of great beauty; here, on a brilliant red
ground, richly decorated with floral scrolls, appear arabesques and
wormlike Chinese cloud bands within cartouches of cobalt blue
and fighting phoenixes and dragons enclosed by medallions. The
color combinations of the pattern are always so chosen as to blend
harmoniously with the tone of the background. Characteristic of
this rug is the abundance of Chinese motives, which play an important role in ornamentation of the Safavid period. However, since
the design retains many Timurid features, the rug was probably
made at the court manufactory at Tabriz in the time of Shah
Isma'il or early in the reign of Shah Tahmasp.

The style of design developed under Shah Tahmasp is best
known from a famous medallion rug from the tomb mosque of
Shaikh Safi at Ardabil, now in the Victoria and Albert Museum in

[1] Sarre and others favor the reading of the date as A.H. 949 (1542/3).

286

London. According to the inscription, it was made or ordered by Maksud of Kashan as an offering to the holy shrine and finished in 1539. The intricate floral pattern is here rendered more naturalistically than in the rugs described above. An important prayer rug (fig. 190) from the Fletcher Collection in the Museum also belongs to the Tabriz school. It is decorated with floral scrolls, arabesques, and Koranic inscriptions along the border and in the small compartments of the main field. The design and color scheme recall those of the animal rug (fig. 192) from the tomb mosque at Ardabil.

There are other medallion rugs that are decorated not only with floral and arabesque ornament but also with animals and human figures. An early example is the rug already referred to in the Poldi-Pezzoli Museum, the animal and medallion rug in the collection of J. Paul Getty, a mate to it in the Kaiser Friedrich Museum in Berlin, and a similar rug in the collection of Count Boucqoi in Vienna. To about the middle of the sixteenth century may be assigned the medallion and animal rugs in the Poldi-Pezzoli Museum, the Stieglitz Museum in Leningrad, the Musée des Arts Décoratifs in Paris, the collection of Prince Schwarzenberg in Vienna, and the splendid rug with large Chinese vase motives in the Victoria and Albert Museum in London. To this group belongs also a magnificent rug presented to the Metropolitan Museum by George F. Baker, Jr. It has a rich floral and animal decoration within a medallion. The main field is red and is intricately patterned with naturalistic palmette scrolls and a symmetrical composition of animals, single or in combat. Several parts are brocaded in gold and silver. The design and workmanship of this rug, which was probably woven in one of the court manufactories at Tabriz, are of superb quality.

Of great interest are two identical rugs with central medallions (fig. 191) in the Metropolitan Museum's collection, containing representations of human figures in blue, green, and red costumes, playing upon instruments or holding animals. Trees in rich colors on a yellow ground form the background. The rest of the main field is decorated with floral scrolls bearing palmettes and with animals in many colors on a claret-red background. The dark green border contains floral scrolls with palmettes and birds. Among the realistically drawn animals are leopards pursuing deer, tigers fighting with dragons, lions attacking the Chinese *kilin*, and bears pursuing a goat. In the intervening spaces are a few large palmettes with the strongly serrated outlines so often seen in the so-called Herat rugs

Fig. 190. *Prayer Rug, Iranian, Safavid, XVI Century*

(see fig. 195). These large palmettes, together with the smaller ones, predominate in the beautiful borders of these rugs, which may be assigned to the second half of the sixteenth century.

B. WOOLEN RUGS WITH ANIMAL DECORATION

Woolen rugs with animal decoration have an all-over floral pattern in which figures of animals, single or in pairs, are introduced. Of

Fig. 191. Medallion Rug (Detail), Iranian, Safavid, XVI Century

great beauty is a woolen rug (fig. 192) owned by the Museum that comes from the tomb mosque of Shaikh Safi at Ardabil. A companion to this rug is now in the Rockefeller collection in New

York. The pattern shows a repeat motive of a lion and a tiger attacking a Chinese *kilin* and other animal motives disposed sym-

Fig. 192. Animal Rug from Ardabil (Detail), Iranian, Safavid,
XVI Century

metrically. Against a claret-red background, the figures are ingeniously combined with floral scrolls bearing rosettes and peony palmettes in rich and harmonious colors. The design was originally enhanced by silver threads, which are still preserved in part. The border has a simple, dignified design of arabesques interlaced with floral scrolls and Chinese cloud bands on a dark blue background.

Fig. 193. Silk Rug (Detail), Iranian, Safavid, XVI Century

The style of this remarkable animal rug relates it to a number of rugs of the middle of the sixteenth century, attributed to the school of Tabriz.

C. SILK RUGS OF THE XVI CENTURY

Luxurious medallion rugs in silk and metal threads were products of the court manufactories and were made only for the use of the court or as gifts to foreign rulers. Among the presents brought by the Iranian ambassador to Constantinople on the occasion of the accession to the throne of Selim II (1566) are mentioned twenty large and many small carpets of silk and gold, decorated with birds, animals, and flowers. Only four large silk rugs of the sixteenth century are known today: the famous imperial hunting rug in Vienna, the hunting rug in the collection of Baron Maurice de Rothschild, Paris, a rug in Stockholm in the collection of the royal house of Sweden, and the Branicki carpet in Warsaw. The most magnificent example of Iranian rug weaving is the rug in Vienna, knotted in colored silk and enriched with gold. The salmon-pink main field shows horsemen, in costumes of the early Safavid period, hunting various animals, the landscape being indicated by plants. This famous rug was probably made in the middle of the sixteenth century in one of Shah Tahmasp's court manufactories. The subject and style recall the miniature paintings of Sultan Muhammad, who probably designed it.

Fortunately a far greater number of small silk rugs have survived and may be seen in museums and private collections here and abroad. Three examples in the Altman Collection of the Metropolitan Museum represent different types of small silk rugs, revealing a great richness of color. In the center of one (fig. 193) is a quatre-foil medallion with arabesques and floral scrolls in green and silver on a dark blue ground. The main field is decorated with floral scrolls bearing peony palmettes and Chinese motives in rich colors on a claret-red ground. The border, originally black, has blue-green bands with palmettes. In the second rug, the central medallion is encircled by a band of palmettes. The third rug in the Altman Collection (fig. 194) represents another type of silk rug. Six rows of animals—panthers, tigers, lions, dragons, deer, jackals, lion-*kilins*, foxes, and running hares—single or in combat, are placed in a mountainous landscape with flowering plants, trees, and birds, on a ground of vivid and lustrous crimson. The blue-green border has a pattern of palmettes and pairs of pheasants in various colors.

These small silk rugs have been generally attributed to Kashan looms, which were famous for their velvets and brocades. Their

Fig. 194. Silk Animal Rug (Detail), Iranian,
Safavid, XVI Century

texture is often so fine—some of them having 800 knots to the square inch—that it approaches that of Iranian velvets.

A popular type of Iranian rug is characterized by an all-over pattern of floral scrolls combined with palmettes and Chinese cloud bands. Such rugs, of which many examples are in museums and private

Fig. 195. Rug (Detail), Iranian, Safavid, XVI Century

collections, are often wrongly called Isfahans but are properly associated with Herat in eastern Iran. Rugs of this type are represented in paintings by Dutch and Spanish masters of the late sixteenth and seventeenth centuries. Olearius, who visited Iran about 1637 with the embassy of the Duke of Holstein-Gottorp, states that the handsomest carpets of Iran were then made at Herat in Khurasan. The reputation of Khurasan for the excellence of its rug manufactories is also established by other evidence. It seems probable, therefore, that these rugs were produced in the sixteenth and seventeenth centuries at Herat, the principal rug-weaving center of the province. The Herat rugs may be divided into two distinct groups, a sixteenth-century group and a seventeenth-century one. Rugs of the former group (see fig. 195) show an intricate floral pattern with characteristic fan-shaped palmettes having serrated

Fig. 196. Rug (Detail), Iranian, Safavid, XVII Century

outlines. Such floral patterns appear in a group of animal rugs already attributed to Herat looms (p. 288). The ground color of the field of these rugs is a vivid red, the border green or dark blue.

In the seventeenth-century rugs of the Herat type the design follows that of the sixteenth century but becomes bolder, the palmettes are larger (see fig. 196), and, in addition, long, curved leaves appear. In the seventeenth-century group, which are well known commercially as "Isfahans," the designs are less elegant and the color schemes less harmonious, often showing purplish tints unknown in earlier examples. Rugs of this type were exported to India, where they served as models in manufactories established by Akbar (see p. 303).

An eighteenth- or early nineteenth-century floral rug in the Ballard Collection of the Metropolitan Museum has a trellis pattern with large palmettes on a dark-blue ground. Such rugs are known to the trade as Shah 'Abbases or Jushagans, and are related in point of design both to the rugs of Herat and to the so-called vase rugs discussed later on. The latter were probably woven at Jushagan in central Iran, where a rug industry flourished until the middle of the nineteenth century.

E. VASE RUGS

A distinct group of sixteenth- and seventeenth-century rugs with floral patterns takes its name from the vases introduced into the decoration. A technical peculiarity of the vase rugs is their double warp. There are two varieties of vase rugs. One of them, represented by the fine specimen in the Ottoman Museum in Istanbul, is decorated with a lozenge diaper of lanceolate leaves which encloses four small palmettes and vases placed against a background of different colors. This polychrome effect is present in a similar rug formerly owned by Clarence H. Mackay, which together with the Istanbul vase rug, may be assigned to the late sixteenth century. The second type of vase rug (see fig. 197) has a trellis design overlaid with large palmette devices and vase motives on a red or white ground. On a basis of style this type must be assigned to the beginning of the seventeenth century.

Related to the vase rugs are certain floral rugs, which, without showing actual vases in their design, have all the other characteristics of vase rugs. In this category belongs a strikingly beautiful rug in the collection of Horace Havemeyer (on loan in the Metropolitan Museum). The field is divided into compartments of various brilliant colors filled with palmettes, one of which suggests a

Fig. 197. Vase Rug (Detail), Iranian, First Half
of the XVII Century

vase motive. This unique rug may be dated at the end of the sixteenth century.

The place of manufacture of vase rugs is still a matter of speculation. For some time they were attributed to Kirman in southern Iran. Lately they have been assigned tentatively to Jushagan looms near Isfahan, although there is still insufficient evidence for such an attribution.

For a long time a group of luxurious silk rugs with floral patterns, brocaded with gold and silver thread, some of them actually bearing Polish coats of arms, were wrongly regarded as of Polish manufacture. Bode and Martin were the first to call attention to their purely Iranian character, which is clearly demonstrated by comparison with other Iranian rugs of the sixteenth and seventeenth centuries. It is quite certain that rugs of this type were manufactured in Iran during the first half of the seventeenth century, in court manufactories at Isfahan and Kashan, for the use of the court at Isfahan and as gifts of the shah. They were also made for European rulers; Polish sources tell us that in the seventeenth century the kings of Poland sent Armenian merchants chiefly to Isfahan and Kashan to order rugs of silk and gold thread. Such silk rugs were made in the time of Shah 'Abbas (1587-1628), Shah Safi (1628-42), and Shah 'Abbas II (1642-66). Most of the "Polish" silk rugs are probably of the time of the latter two shahs. To the Shah 'Abbas period belong rugs presented by Iranian embassies to Venice in 1603, 1613, and 1623. Assigned to this period are two important rugs with arabesques and floral scrolls, respectively, in the Lichtenstein collection in Vienna and that of the late Mrs. Rainey Rogers in New York.

"Polish" rugs may be divided into two groups, those knotted in silk only and those of silk brocaded with silver and silver-gilt threads. The latter show delicate color schemes with pastel shades predominating. The Metropolitan Museum possesses four such rugs of different quality and in various states of preservation. A fine specimen (fig. 198) in the Altman Collection is decorated with a rich pattern of arabesques, floral scrolls, and palmettes in light yellow, blue, and rose on a silver and gold ground in the main field, and in light blue and gray in other compartments. The border shows the long, serrated leaves which occur in the so-called Herat rugs and palmettes in light colors on an emerald-green ground.

Fig. 198. Silk Rug, Iranian (So-called Polish), Safavid,
First Half of the XVII Century

G. TREE AND GARDEN RUGS

Gardens played an important part in the daily life of Iran. Iranian
painters took delight in depicting them in miniatures, and garden

designs were incorporated early into the Safavid rugs. One of the earliest known and rarest examples of a landscape rug is in the Joseph Lees Williams Memorial Collection in Williamstown. The design consists of large cypresses, shrubs, and flowering trees on a red background. The coloring and the angular stylization of the design recall rugs of the early sixteenth century.

Another example of a tree rug, in this case dating from the second half of the sixteenth century, is in the Metropolitan Museum. In the center of the design is a small pond with fishes, surrounded by four flowering trees; birds perch on the branches or fly around near by. The claret-red field has a balanced design of naturalistic trees and palmettes. The tree motive is used also in a beautiful sixteenth-century prayer rug in the Altman Collection.

Another interesting group of Iranian rugs is distinguished by schematic representations of gardens divided into rectangular plots with trees and shrubs separated by canals. In part they are reminiscences of the mythical rug, the "Spring of Chosroes," described by Arabic writers. The earliest known example, with gold and silver threads, is in the Figdor collection in Vienna and may be assigned to the Shah 'Abbas period (1587-1628). To the same time belongs a magnificent large garden rug discovered in 1937 in a storeroom of the palace at Amber and now on exhibition in the Jaipur Museum. This rug bears several entry labels, the earliest being dated the 12th of Safar, 1042 (August 29, 1632), which indicates that it was made before that date. The rich decoration recalls that of the Figdor rug, which is doubtless contemporary.

The majority of these garden rugs must be assigned to the eighteenth century and were probably made in northwestern Iran or the Caucasus. Two of the latter type (see fig. 199) are in the Metropolitan Museum's collection.

H. TAPESTRY-WOVEN SILK RUGS

A number of Iranian silk rugs of the seventeenth century are not knotted but tapestry-woven with characteristic interlocked warp threads, thus avoiding the slits found in Turkish *kilims*. The designs of these rugs are similar to those of the knotted ones. We find medallion rugs with floral scrolls, arabesques, and cloud bands, which often form a background for animal decoration or figure

Fig. 199. Garden Rug, Iranian or Caucasian, XVIII Century

subjects. There are two varieties of such tapestry-woven rugs, one with a rich polychromy, the other with more subdued color schemes. Both types are represented in the Metropolitan Museum. The typical pattern of these Iranian *kilims* is shown in figure 200.

301

Fig. 200. Tapestry-Woven Silk Rug, Iranian, Safavid,
XVII Century

This rug, formerly in the possession of the royal house of Saxony,
is tapestry-woven in vivid colors with the addition of gold brocad-
ing. Most rugs of this type must be assigned to the first half of the

seventeenth century, on the basis of style and documentary evidence.

In the Residenz Museum in Munich there are several important tapestries. Two, one with hunting scenes in vivid colors, another with a Polish coat of arms, were part of the dowry of a Polish princess, Anna Katherina Kostanza, on her marriage to the Elector Palatine Philip Wilhelm in the year 1642. With regard to the place of manufacture of these tapestries, interesting information is supplied by a Polish scholar, Mankowski, who found documents, one dated 1601, which tell us the cost of tapestry-woven rugs bought in Kashan, where they were made to order for Sigismund III, King of Poland. Thus Kashan, famous for its fine textiles and rugs, must be regarded as one of the centers in which tapestries of the seventeenth century, particularly those with rich colors, were woven. Isfahan was probably another place where tapestry-woven rugs were made.

6. Mughal Rugs of India

Like the Mughal school of painting, Mughal rug weaving was of Iranian origin. According to the historian Abu'l-Fazl, the emperor Akbar (1556-1605) "caused carpets to be made of wonderful variety and charming textures; he has appointed experienced workmen who have produced many masterpieces. The carpets of Iran and Turan are no more thought of, although merchants still import carpets from Jushagan (between Kashan and Isfahan), Khuzistan (in which province Tustar is the chief town), Kirman and Sabzavar (in Khurasan). All kinds of carpet weavers have settled here, and drive a flourishing trade. These are found in every town, especially in Agra, Fathpur and Lahore."

The rugs woven in India at this time, to judge from representations of rugs in miniature paintings, were much influenced by Iranian models. Hindu weavers, working in the state manufactories of Akbar and Jahangir (1605-28), under the guidance of Iranians, copied the floral rugs of Iran. A number of such Mughal rugs exist today in museums and private collections, particularly in the collection of the Maharajah of Jaipur, and are known as Indian "Isfahans." These rugs, often wrongly regarded as Iranian, may be recognized by their color schemes, which include reddish brown and a deep orange unknown in Iranian "Isfahans."

303

Gradually, the Hindu weavers introduced into rug design naturalistic plants, flowers, and figure subjects. The design of these Mughal rugs shows considerably more freedom of composition than that of the Iranian rugs which served as their models. This may be seen in several pictorial rugs, one in the Widener collection in the National Gallery, Washington, the other in the Museum of Fine Arts, Boston.

Fig. 201. Rug (Detail), Indian, about 1600

Fig. 202. Rug (Detail), Indian, XVII Century

A magnificent example of an early Mughal rug, dating from about 1600, is illustrated in figure 201. This large rug, which, together with the one described below, came from the collection of Lord Sackville and is now in the Metropolitan Museum, is patterned with trees and shrubs interspersed with animals. The design is derived from Iranian rugs but is distinguished by a greater freedom

305

of composition, a more realistic representation of landscape, and a peculiar color scheme in which madder red is conspicuous.

Another great rug in the Museum's collection, measuring thirty feet in length, has a balanced design of floral scrolls, large serrated leaves, and palmettes on a red background. The border is composed of medallions and cartouches with palmettes and Chinese cloud bands. The design shows clearly the influence of the so-called Herat and Kirman rugs, but the deep coloring and some of the floral motives are purely Indian in character. Many details recall the famous Indian rug in the possession of the Girdlers' Company, London, which was made, according to records, in the imperial factory at Lahore for the master Robert Bell, who presented it to the Girdlers' Company in 1634. The Museum rug is either contemporary with the Girdlers' Company rug or somewhat earlier.

The Mughal style is more evident in the rug illustrated in figure 202, which may be assigned to the period of Shah Jahan. Although the design was inspired by a Herat rug, it has been essentially modified by the introduction of Hindu floral motives. The main field shows a balanced arrangement of small medallions connected by stems bearing large leaves, palmettes, lilies, and other flowers in beautiful colors on a claret-red ground. The border, with its naturalistic flowering plants on a blue-green ground, is purely Indian. The fine woolen pile has an almost silken luster, and the color scheme, more Indian than Iranian, is enriched by many delicate nuances. Realistic plants like those in the border of this rug are often the sole decoration of rugs made for Shah Jahan and his courtiers. Numerous rugs of his period are in the collection of the Maharajah of Jaipur and were originally made for the palace at Amber, built about 1630.

Another popular variety of Mughal rug, also made in the time of Shah Jahan and represented by numerous rugs in the Jaipur collection, shows a trellis framework containing realistic plants. Several fragmentary rugs of this type are in the Altman Collection of the Museum. In one of them the trellis is composed of numerous delicate scrolls enclosing palmettes and floral scrolls on a dark claret-red ground.

In technical perfection the Indian weavers of the time of Shah Jahan often surpassed their Iranian masters. The trellis rug mentioned has 702 knots to the square inch; another woolen fragment in the Altman Collection has 1,258. Silk rugs were also woven in India, some of them being so closely knotted that their texture resembles that of velvets. A fragment of such a silk rug in the Altman Collection, decorated with a realistic landscape, has the unusual number of 2,552 knots to the square inch.

Fig. 203. Rug, Turkish, XVI Century

7. Turkish Rugs

Turkish rugs may be divided into two main groups: rugs made at court manufactories and rugs made by peasants, who were sometimes organized on a semi-industrial basis. As previously stated, rug knotting was introduced into Asia Minor by the Saljuks. Their style, which we have characterized as a geometric one, was continued in the fourteenth- and fifteenth-century animal rugs of Asia Minor and may be found later in all the Turkish peasant rugs dating from the sixteenth to the nineteenth century.

A. TURKISH COURT RUGS

A group of floral rugs of various sizes, including prayer rugs, long associated with Damascus, is now properly assigned to Turkish looms. Several good examples are in the Metropolitan Museum (see fig. 203). These rugs are decorated with elegant floral scrolls peculiar to Turkey, bearing palmettes, curving lanceolate leaves, and blossoms among which appear hyacinths, tulips, and carnations, familiar to us from the sixteenth- and seventeenth-century ceramics (p. 222) from Isnik and Kutahia in Asia Minor. Rugs of this type may be regarded as the work of the Turkish court looms established by Sultan Sulaiman in Constantinople or not far from there at Brusa in Asia Minor. There are, however, marked differences in the quality of the floral rugs, and some of the coarser ones, with more vivid colors, must have been made in private manufactories. Both types are well represented in the Museum. Red is featured as the ground color of both the field and the borders, upon which the design appears in yellow, green, red, and blue, outlined in white. Judging from the style of the design, the earliest ones may be dated at the end of the sixteenth century, when the best rugs of this class were made; others are of the seventeenth century.

To the group of Turkish court rugs also belongs a number of prayer rugs, a splendid example (fig. 204) of which is in the Ballard Collection of the Museum. This rug has an unusually fine texture and a brilliant color scheme. The border design with its turquoise-blue ground is contemporary with that of Isnik pottery of about 1600. Such prayer rugs are of great interest to students, as they are the prototypes of the eighteenth-century Anatolian prayer rugs of the Ghiordes and Kula varieties (see fig. 209).

B. SO-CALLED DAMASCUS RUGS WITH GEOMETRICAL PATTERNS

Related in color and material to the Turkish floral rugs discussed

above is a group of sixteenth-century rugs with geometrical patterns
(fig. 205), sometimes called "Damascus." The field has a tilelike
pattern of geometrical compartments, filled with arabesques, scrollwork, trees, and candelabra motives in red, yellow, blue, and green.

Fig. 204. Prayer Rug, Turkish, about 1600

The ground of the field is red, of the border and compartments
yellow-green or blue. As in the Turkish floral rugs, the colors vary
from deep to lighter shades. The finest collection of these geometrical "Damascus" rugs, one of them in silk, is in the Museum for Art
and Industry in Vienna.

From time to time other localities besides Damascus have been suggested as the place of origin of these rugs, including Morocco, Asia Minor, and Egypt. Sarre suggested Cairo as the manufacturing center because of stylistic similarities to Mamluk ornament. Although the latter attribution has been more or less generally ac-

Fig. 205. Rug (Detail), Probably Egyptian, Cairo, XVI Century

Fig. 206. Rug, Turkish, Asia Minor, Ushak, XVII Century

cepted, there is still a tendency for authorities to assign them to the same Turkish looms as the floral rugs, which were doubtless made in either Constantinople or Asia Minor.

C. USHAK RUGS AND OTHER VARIETIES FROM ASIA MINOR

Several types of Turkish rugs, examples of which exist in various

Fig. 207. Rug, Turkish, Asia Minor, XVI-XVII Century

sizes, are attributed to Ushak in Anatolia. One type has a decoration consisting of several large stars and floral scrolls and arabesques, rendered angularly in blue, yellow, and green, usually on a red ground. Rugs of this type, imported into Europe probably by the Venetians, frequently appear in sixteenth- and seventeenth-century paintings of the Italian, Dutch, and Spanish schools. Two such Ushaks in the collection of the Earl of Dalkeith are dated 1584 and 1585 respectively. Another type has either a large central medallion or several small ones as the chief feature of the decoration (see fig. 206).

Related to the star and medallion Ushaks is a group of prayer rugs with floral patterns characterized by severity of design and often with a prayer niche in the field. Several examples are in the Ballard Collection.

An interesting variety of Asia Minor rug, related to both the Ushak and the "Holbein" rugs, has an all-over pattern of angular arabesques in yellow and blue on a red ground (see fig. 207). These rugs are depicted in Italian and Dutch paintings of the sixteenth and seventeenth centuries. Their borders of simulated Kufic writing, in yellow and red on green, are identical with those of the Holbein variety. In a few later rugs of this type, the borders are identical with some of the Ushaks.

Another variety of Asia Minor rug related to the Ushaks is the so-called bird rug, which is patterned with arabesques and floral scrolls on a white background; one motive composed of two arabesque palmettes suggests a bird, but the similarity seems to have been entirely unintentional.

D. SO-CALLED HOLBEIN RUGS

An interesting type of Asia Minor rug is the so-called Holbein rug, which appears in German and Italian paintings of the fifteenth and sixteenth centuries, particularly in those by Hans Holbein. The ornament is based on much earlier Saljuk patterns. A characteristic feature is the purely geometric pattern, usually consisting of small squares and medallion-like units formed by interlacings and arabesques. The borders show interlacings derived from Kufic writing. Red and blue predominate among the colors, which are vigorous.

E. GHIORDES PRAYER RUGS

The largest group of Anatolian prayer rugs (fig. 208) is attributed to Ghiordes looms. The distinctive feature of these is a representation of the niche, or mihrab, which indicates in the mosque the direction of Mecca, toward which the Muhammadan faces at the time

Fig. 208. Prayer Rug, Turkish, Ghiordes, XVIII Century

of prayer. The arch takes various shapes and is at times supported by two columns or pilasters. Sometimes a mosque lamp, which may be transformed into an ornamental device, is shown suspended from the apex of the arch. The floral motives are rendered schematically and are confined to several species, such as carnations, hyacinths, tulips, and roses, derived from the court rugs (see fig. 204). One of the chief attractions of the Ghiordes rugs is the harmonious

Fig. 209. Prayer Rug, Turkish, Ghiordes or Kula, XVIII Century

color composition of red and blue, with the addition of white and yellow. Ghiordes rugs are not earlier than the eighteenth century. There is one in our collection dated A.H. 1210 (1795/6).

315

Fig. 210. Prayer Rug, Dated 1795/6,
Turkish, Ladik

F. KULA RUGS

Very similar rugs were made at Kula, not far from Ghiordes. Sometimes it is difficult to make a distinction between the rugs made
in the two towns, as they are almost identical in design (see figs.
208 and 209), but there are differences. In the Kula rugs the prayer
niches frequently have all-over patterns of small floral motives,
while the borders are often divided into a number of narrow stripes.
Occasionally in one of the stripes appears a floral scroll with curling
leaves, changing color at intervals. The absence of a cross panel be-

316

low the field and the predominance of yellow and blue are also regarded as characteristic of Kula rugs.

G. LADIK RUGS

An attractive group of Anatolian prayer rugs was woven in the neighborhood of Ladik (Laodicea). This type has peculiar features which easily distinguish it from others. The panel above or below the niche is decorated with pointed arches like arrowheads, from which issue stalks of lilies. A typical Ladik border shows a design of lilies alternating with rosettes. Ladik rugs do not appear before

Fig. 211. Prayer Rug, Turkish, Bergama, XVII Century

the middle of the eighteenth century. The Metropolitan Museum possesses a specimen (fig. 210) which bears the date A.H. 1210 (1795/6).

A type of Asia Minor rug frequently found in churches in Hungary and Transylvania, and known as Siebenbürgen or Transylvanian, was probably made in the district of Bergama. Such rugs have fields decorated with stylized floral scrolls and one or two mosque lamps in brilliant red, blue, yellow, and green. They are often represented in paintings of the seventeenth century and the beginning of the eighteenth. The earliest examples date from the seventeenth century.

8. Caucasian Rugs

At an early period the nomads of the Caucasus, the country between the Black Sea and the Caspian, developed their own style of design in rug weaving. This is characterized by boldness of pattern and contrasting color schemes. Many patterns of Caucasian rugs are based on traditional designs, but in the rugs made in the country's eastern section, which was for some time under Iranian rule, the influence of Iranian design is quite apparent. Most Caucasian rugs belong to the nineteenth century. An earlier group, the so-called dragon rugs, is related to later Kubas and Kazaks.

These rugs, which have frequently been called "Armenian," show a lozenge diaper of serrated leaves enclosing palmettes and dragons, some of them in combat with phoenixes. Their style is bold and angular, almost archaic. Their colors are bright and contrasting, contributing to the highly decorative effect. The animal decoration of these dragon rugs is based on an earlier animal style, with the addition of Chinese elements. It is possible that animal rugs represented in paintings of the fourteenth and fifteenth centuries were the predecessors of dragon rugs. Doubtless the floral decoration is of Iranian origin. Some Caucasian rugs, for instance,

Fig. 212. Dragon Rug (Detail), Caucasian, XVII Century

the magnificent floral one formerly in the mosque at Nigde in Asia
Minor and now in a private collection in New York are reminiscent
of Iranian vase rugs in both color and design. One of these "Ar-

menian" rugs is in the Davis Collection of the Museum. It is decorated with a pattern of stepped bands and stylized animals in bright
colors and may be assigned to the seventeenth century.

The production of dragon and related floral rugs very likely began
at the end of the sixteenth century and lasted through the eighteenth. In the earliest group, probably of the sixteenth century, the
design of the dragons and animals is most complete, as in the rug
in the Berlin Museum and one in a private collection in New York.
But in the pieces from the next century, of which the Metropolitan
Museum possesses two fine specimens (see fig. 212), the animal
design is more stylized, and finally in the eighteenth-century pieces
the identity of the dragon is lost entirely.

The original attribution of these rugs to Armenia was challenged
first by Jacoby, who presented good reasons for assigning them and
related floral rugs to the region of Kuba, which is in the south-
eastern Caucasus. But recently an Armenian scholar, Sakisian, has
given excellent support to the Armenian theory. These two opin-
ions are not mutually exclusive, if we consider the term Armenian
in a national rather than a geographical sense. As the Kuba region
is populated also by Armenians, it is not impossible that they were
the makers of these rugs.

B. CAUCASIAN RUGS OF THE XVIII TO THE XIX CENTURY

Rugs made by Caucasian nomads from the end of the eighteenth
century through the nineteenth are divided into groups according
to the place of their manufacture. As it is impossible to discuss here
all the varieties of Caucasian rugs, we shall limit ourselves to the
main and best-known types, which are well represented in the
Metropolitan Museum. The largest and most striking group of rugs
are from the southwestern Caucasus and are known as Kazaks.
They are characterized by a high, lustrous pile and a bold geometrical design in vivid colors; in the patterns of some we can discover
the derivation of the so-called dragon rugs.

The rugs made in the eastern part of the Caucasus show certain
differences from those of the western region. The knotting is finer,
the pile is short and less lustrous, the colors are less vivid than in the
Kazaks. Among the best-known rugs of this region are the Shirvans
and Kubas. The most interesting ones are those with floral patterns,

which reveal Iranian influence in both color and design. In the earlier Kuba pieces, of about 1800, the large palmettes are connected by stems; in the later ones the stems disappear. An interesting feature of the Shirvans and Kubas is the survival of simulated Kufic writing in the borders, which is also seen in early rugs from Asia Minor. To Baku is assigned a group of Shirvan prayer rugs. One in the Museum's collection, decorated with a repeat pattern of cone-shaped motives, bears the date A.H. 1223 (1808/9).

The eastern Caucasus, particularly Kuba and Derbend, was the home of smooth-faced rugs woven without a pile and known as Sumakhs. The technique is related to tapestry weaving but is more complicated. The rugs made in Kuba were the finer ones. Their geometrical patterns are related to both the western and the eastern Caucasian rugs. In another variety of rug in Sumakh technique, called Sile, the patterns show large, angular S-forms.

9. Turkoman Rugs

The wandering Turkoman tribes of Turkestan and Central Asia have long been skilled weavers of rugs, which serve a variety of purposes in the life of these tent-dwelling people. Turkoman rugs thus include not only floor coverings but also saddle bags, camel collars, tent bags, and borders for the tent entrance. Most Turkoman rugs are not earlier than the nineteenth century. The principal district in which these rugs were produced corresponds roughly to the regions of West Turkestan and Chinese Turkestan. It extends from the Caspian Sea eastward to Bukhara, northward to the Aral Sea, and southward to the boundary of Iran, including Afghanistan and Baluchistan. The Turkoman rugs were made by various nomad tribes whose names designate the different types of rugs. The patterns of these rugs are strongly geometrical and vary among the tribes. A familiar group are the rugs of the Tekke Turkomans, sometimes wrongly called Bukharas. They are usually of fine texture and show an all-over pattern of octagons and the gull or rose motive, called also "the flying eagle." The color is a brownish red, with white and dark blue.

The rugs of Afghanistan and Baluchistan are not unlike other Transcaspian rugs, but are inferior in texture, color, and design. The Bukhara rugs (so-called Beshirs), made mostly by Uzbegs in the region between Herat and Samarkand, have patterns which show geometrical designs with the addition of motives borrowed from Iranian rugs. Their color scheme, with a bright yellow, is more vivid than that of other Turkoman rugs.

In the design of rugs from East Turkestan Chinese influence is strongly evident. Rugs woven in the vicinity of Kashgar, but sometimes called Samarkands, show a mixture of Turkoman and Chinese elements. A characteristic feature of these rugs is the polychrome border of Chinese cloud motives.

10. Moorish Rugs of Spain

With the Arab conquest, Spain was brought into close relation with the arts and crafts of the East. That rugs were woven in Spain in the twelfth and thirteenth centuries is known from literary sources, but no existing rugs can be assigned to an earlier period than the fourteenth century. To this period may belong a so-called synagogue rug in Berlin decorated with an elaborate candelabrum whose arms end in "Thora" shrines.

Several fifteenth-century rugs bear coats of arms that may be identified and dated. The arms are displayed upon a field ornamented with a repeat pattern of octagons enclosing geometrical motives, human figures, and birds, angular in design and woven in many vivid colors. The borders are divided into several bands of Kufic inscriptions, geometrical patterns, and grotesque figures. A well-known heraldic rug of the first half of the fifteenth century with the arms of the Henriquez family is in the Williams collection.

A rare type of Moorish rug may be assigned to the same period as the heraldic rugs; this type, with geometrical patterns of stars within octagons, may be regarded as the Moorish version of the fifteenth-century "Holbein" rugs. An example in the Metropolitan Museum is reproduced in figure 213. The design and color scheme of these rugs, probably the products of Alcázar, are characteristic of the Moorish style of decoration. An interesting rug in the Ballard Collection of the Museum with conventionalized bird and floral motives exemplifies another variety of Hispano-Moresque rugs of the late fifteenth century.

Although Western motives predominated in sixteenth-century Spanish rugs, in some of them we find Moorish elements as well.

Fig. 213. Rug (Detail), Hispano-Moresque, XV Century

In others, exemplified by a rug in the Ballard Collection, we can see Turkish influence. The main field has an arabesque pattern familiar to us from the Ushak rugs of Asia Minor, while the border shows renaissance scroll motives. The colors are two shades of blue and white on yellow, a combination frequently seen in sixteenth-century Spanish rugs.

Chronology

For a complete list of Muhammadan dynasties see: Stanley Lane-Poole, *The Mohammadan Dynasties* (London, 1893), and E. de Zambaur, *Manuel de généalogie et de chronologie pour l'histoire de l'Islam* (Hanover, 1927).

THE CALIPHATE

A. D.

632– 661 The Orthodox Caliphs
    632– 634 Abu Bakr
        The capital at Medina
    634– 644 'Umar
        Conquest of Syria, Mesopotamia, Iran
          and Egypt
    644– 656 'Uthman
    656– 661 'Ali
        The capital at Kufa

661– 749 Umayyad Caliphs
    661– 680 Mu'awiya I
        The capital at Damascus
    680– 683 Yazid I
    744– 749 Marwan II

749–1258 Abbasid Caliphs
    754– 775 Mansur
        Beginning of the decline of the caliph-
          ate in 755
        Foundation of Baghdad, the new capi-
          tal of the Abbasid caliphs, in 762
    786– 809 Harun ar Rashid
        Foundation of Rakka, a second resi-
          dence, in 795
    833– 841 Mu'tasim
        The Abbasid capital removed from
          Baghdad to Samarra, a newly
          founded city, in 836

847– 861   Mutawakkil
                In 858 the residence transferred for a
                short time to Damascus
870– 892   Mu'tamid
                Samarra abandoned in 892
                The residence transferred to Baghdad
                again in 892
892– 902   Mu'tadid
1242–1258   Musta'sim
                Conquest of Baghdad by Hulagu, the
                Il-khan of Iran, in 1258, and the end
                of the eastern caliphate of the Ab-
                basids

SPAIN

710– 713   Arab conquest of Spain
713– 756   Governors appointed by the Umayyad caliphs
756–1031   Umayyads of Cordova
          912– 961   Abd ar Rahman III
                      The title of caliph adopted by this ruler
                      in 929
          961– 976   Hakam II
          976–1009   Hisham II
1010–1091   Minor dynasties of Malaga, Algeciras, Seville, Granada,
                Cordova, Toledo, Valencia, and Saragossa
1056–1148   Almoravides (Berber dynasty, rulers of Morocco and
                part of Algeria)
1130–1269   Almohades of North Africa
1232–1492   Nasrids of Jaen and Granada
                Granada captured by Ferdinand and Isabella of
                Castile in 1492

SICILY

827– 902   Conquest of Sicily by the Aghlabids of Tunis
909–1071   Fatimids of Syria and Egypt
                Conquest of Sicily by the Normans in 1071

NORTH AFRICA

669– 800   Governors appointed by the caliphs

789– 985	Idrisids of Morocco
800– 909	Aghlabids of Tunis
909– 972	Fatimids
	The capital at Mahdiya
972–1148	Zayrids of Tunis
	The capital at Kairwan
1007–1152	Hammadids of Algeria
	The capital at Kalat Beni Hammad
1056–1147	Almoravides of Morocco and part of Algeria and Spain
1130–1269	Almohades
1228–1534	Hafsids of Tunis

EGYPT

641	Arab conquest of Egypt
661– 868	Governors appointed by the Umayyad and Abbasid caliphs
868– 904	Tulunids (a dynasty of Turkish origin)
	The capital at Katai, near Fustat
935– 969	Ikhshidids
969–1171	Fatimids (a Shiʻa dynasty, rulers in North Africa since 909)
	Foundation of a new residence and capital, Kahira, or Cairo, in 969
	996–1021 Hakim
	1036–1094 Mustansir
1169–1250	Ayyubids
	1169–1193 Nasir Salah ad Din (Saladin)
	1238–1240 Abu Bakr II
	1240–1249 Salih Ayyub
1250–1516	Mamluk Sultans (slaves of Turko-Circassian origin)
	1250–1390 Bahri Mamluks
	1280–1290 Mansur Saif ad Din Kalaun
	1293–1340 Nasir ad Din Muhammad ibn Kalaun (reigned three times)
	1347–1360 Malik Nasir Hasan
	1382–1516 Burji Mamluks
	1468–1496 Kait-Bey
1516–1805	Ottoman Sultans of Turkey

328

1229–1454 Rasulids
1446–1516 Tahirids

638– 640 Arab conquest of Khuzistan and Shushtar
642 Overthrow of the Sasanid dynasty at the battle of Nihavand
661– 819 Governors appointed by the Umayyad and Abbasid caliphs
819–1055 Iranian Dynasties
    819–1004 Samanids in Transoxiana and Iran
    820– 874 Tahirids in Khurasan
    864–1032 Alids in Tabaristan (Mazandaran)
    868– 903 Saffarids
    932–1055 Buwayhids in southern Iran and Iraq
1037–1194 Saljuks (the descendants and followers of Saljuk, a Turkish chieftain)
    1037–1157 Great Saljuks
        The capital at Isfahan
        1037–1063 Tughril Beg
            Proclaimed king after the capture of Nishapur
        1041–1187 Saljuks of Kirman
1077–1231 Shahs of Khwarizm (Khiva)
1206–1251 Great Khans
    1206–1227 Chingiz Khan (a chieftain of clans from eastern Central Asia)
1256–1353 Il-Khans of Iran
    The summer residence at Tabriz
    1256–1265 Hulagu
    1282–1284 Ahmad Khan
        Embraced Islam in 1282
    1295–1304 Ghazan
    1304–1316 Uljaitu
1314–1393 Muzaffarids of Fars, Kirman, and Kurdistan
1370–1500 Timurids
    1370–1404 Timur, or Tamerlane (a descendant of Chingiz Khan)
        The capital at Samarkand

Campaigns in Iran, 1380–1387

1404–1447 Shah Rukh
The capital at Herat
1378–1469 Kara-Kuyunli of Azerbaijan and Armenia (Turkomans of the Black Sheep)
The capital at Tabriz
1437–1467 Jahan Shah
1378–1502 Ak-Kuyunli of Azerbaijan (Turkomans of the White Sheep)
1428–1599 Shaibanids of Transoxiana (Uzbeg sultans)
1502–1736 Safavids
1502–1524 Isma'il I
The capital at Tabriz
Capture of Herat in 1510
Battle of Chaldiran near Tabriz against the Turks in 1514
1524–1576 Tahmasp I
The residence transferred to Kazvin in 1549
1587–1628 'Abbas I
The capital at Isfahan
1628–1642 Safi
1642–1666 'Abbas II

ASIA MINOR AND TURKEY

1077–1327 Saljuks of Rum
The capital at Konia
1300–1924 Ottoman Sultans
1299–1326 'Uthman
Europe invaded by the Turks in 1308
Surrender of Brusa to the Ottoman Turks in 1326
1326–1360 Urkhan
The capital at Brusa
1360–1389 Murad I
The capital transferred to Adrianople in 1365
1389–1403 Bayazid I
1403–1421 Muhammad I

1451–1481   Muhammad II
          Capture of Constantinople in 1453;
          Constantinople the capital
1481–1512   Bayazid II
1512–1520   Selim I
1520–1566   Sulaiman I
1623–1640   Murad IV

INDIA AND AFGHANISTAN

711   Arab conquest of Sind
962–1186   Ghaznavids
     The capital at Ghazna
     962– 963   Alptigin (founder of the dynasty; formerly
          a Turkish slave at the Samanid court)
     977– 997   Sabaktigin
          Defeat of the Rajputs
     998–1030   Mahmud
          Conquest of Gujarat in 1024
     1099–1114   Mas'ud III
1100–1215   Ghorids of Afghanistan and Hindustan
1206–1555   Sultans of Dehli
1391–1572   Kings of Gujarat
1526–1858   Mughal Emperors
     1526–1530   Babur (a descendant of Timur)
          The residence at Agra
     1530–1556   Humayun
          Refugee in Iran, 1540–1555
     1556–1605   Akbar
          The residence at Fathpur-Sikri 1569–
          1584; afterwards at Lahore
     1605–1628   Jahangir
          The residence at Lahore
     1628–1658   Shah Jahan
     1658–1707   Aurangzib

ᘔ𝒾𝒷𝓁𝒾ℴℊ𝓇𝒶𝓅𝒽𝓎

PRE-ISLAMIC ART

A. EAST CHRISTIAN ART OF EGYPT, SYRIA, AND MESOPOTAMIA

Butler, Howard Crosby. *Architecture and Other Arts* (Publications of an American Archaeological Expedition to Syria in 1899-1900 . . ., part 2). New York, 1903.

——— *Syria*, div. II: *Architecture*, sect. A: *Southern Syria*, and sect. B: *Northern Syria* (Publications of the Princeton University Expeditions to Syria in 1904-5 and 1909). 2 vols. Leyden, 1919, 1920.

——— *Early Churches in Syria, Fourth to Seventh Centuries* . . ., edited and completed by E. Baldwin Smith. [Princeton] 1929.

Chassinat, Émile. *Fouilles à Baouît* (Mémoires . . . de l'Institut français d'archéologie orientale du Caire, vol. 13 [sculpture]). Cairo, 1911.

Clédat, Jean. *Le Monastère et la nécropole de Baouît* (Mémoires . . . de l'Institut français d'archéologie orientale du Caire, vol. 12 [paintings]). Cairo, 1904.

Crum, W. E. *Coptic Monuments* (Catalogue général des antiquités égyptiennes du Musée du Caire, nos. 8001-8741). Cairo, 1902.

Dimand, M. S. *Die Ornamentik der ägyptischen Wollwirkereien* . . . . Leipzig, 1924.

——— "Coptic Tunics in The Metropolitan Museum of Art," *Metropolitan Museum Studies*, vol. II (1930), pp. 239-252.

——— "An Early Cut-Pile Rug from Egypt," *ibid.*, vol. IV (1932-1933), pp. 151-161.

Duthuit, Georges. *La Sculpture copte* . . . . Paris, 1931.

Grüneisen, W. de. *Les Caracteristiques de l'art copte.* Florence, 1922.

Kendrick, A. F. *Catalogue of Textiles from Burying-Grounds in Egypt* (Victoria and Albert Museum, Department of Textiles). 3 vols. London, 1920-1922.

Pfister, R. *Tissues coptes du Musée du Louvre.* Paris, 1932.

——— *Textiles de Palmyre découverts par le Service des Antiquités du Haut-commissariat de la République Française dans la nécropole de Palmyre.* Paris, 1934.

——— *Nouveaux Textiles de Palmyre* . . . . Paris, 1937.

Quibell, J. E. *Excavations at Saqqara* (1907-8), with sections by Herbert Thompson and W. Spiegelberg. Cairo, 1909.

———————— *Excavations at Saqqara (1908-9, 1909-10): The Monastery of Apa Jeremias*. Cairo, 1912.

Strzygowski, Josef. *Koptische Kunst* (Catalogue général des antiquités égyptiennes du Musée du Caire, nos. 7001-7394 and 8742-9200). Vienna, 1904.

Wulff, Oskar. *Altchristliche und Mittelalterliche . . . Bildwerke*, part 1: *Altchristliche Bildwerke* (Beschreibung der Bildwerke der christlichen Epochen, vol. III). Berlin, 1909.

Wulff, O., and Volbach, W. F. *Spätantike und koptische Stoffe aus ägyptischen Grabfunden in den Staatlichen Museen* . . . . Berlin, 1926.

B. PARTHIAN AND SASANIAN ART

Andrae, Walter. *Hatra, nach Aufnahmen von Mitgliedern der Assur-Expedition der Deutschen Orient-Gesellschaft*, parts 1 and 2. Leipzig, 1908, 1912.

Baltrusaïtis, Jurgis. "Sāsānian Stucco," *A Survey of Persian Art . . .*, edited by Arthur Upham Pope, vol. I, pp. 601-645, vol. IV, pls. 171-178. London and New York, 1938.

Dalton, O. M. *The Treasure of the Oxus* . . . (British Museum). 2nd edition. London, 1926.

Dimand, M. S. "Sasanian Wall Decoration in Stucco," *Bulletin of The Metropolitan Museum of Art*, vol. XXVI (1931), pp. 193-195.

———————— "Parthian and Sasanian Art," *ibid.*, vol. XXVIII (1933), pp. 79-81.

———————— "A Sasanian Silver Dish," *ibid.*, vol. XXIX (1934), pp. 74-77.

Erdmann, Kurt. "Die sasanidischen Jagdschalen," *Jahrbuch der preuszischen Kunstsammlungen*, vol. LVII (1936), pp. 193-232.

Ettinghausen, Richard. "Parthian and Sāsānian Pottery," *A Survey of Persian Art . . .*, edited by Arthur Upham Pope, vol. I, pp. 646-680, vol. IV, pls. 179-196. London and New York, 1938.

Herzfeld, Ernst. *Am Tor von Asien* . . . . Berlin, 1920.

[Kühnel, Ernst, and Wachtsmuth, Friedrich]. *Die Ausgrabungen der zweiten Ktesiphon-Expedition (Winter 1931/32)* (Staatliche Museen in Berlin; Metropolitan Museum of Art, New York). Berlin, 1933. (Summary in English by M. S. Dimand.)

Orbeli, J. "Sāsānian and Early Islamic Metalwork," *A Survey of Persian Art . . .*, edited by Arthur Upham Pope, vol. I, pp. 716-770, vol. IV, pls. 203-250. London and New York, 1938.

Orbeli, J., and Trever, C. *Orfèvrerie sasanide: objets en or, argent et bronze* (Musée de l'Ermitage). Moscow and Leningrad, 1935.

Pfister, R. "Gobelins sassanides du Musée de Lyon," *Revue des arts asiatiques* (Annales du Musée Guimet), vol. VI (1929-1930), pp. 1-23.

———————— "Les Premières Soies sassanides," *Études d'orientalisme publiées par le Musée Guimet . . .*, vol. II, pp. 461-479. Paris, 1932.

Reuther, Oscar. *Die Ausgrabungen der Deutschen Ktesiphon-Expedition im Winter 1928/9* (Staatliche Museen in Berlin, Islamische Kunstabteilung). Berlin, 1929.

Rostovtzeff, M. I. "Dura and the Problem of Parthian Art," *Yale Classical Studies*, vol. v (1935), pp. 157-304.

Sarre, Friedrich. *Die Kunst des alten Persien.* Berlin, 1922.

─────── "Parthian Art," *A Survey of Persian Art* . . ., edited by Arthur Upham Pope, vol. i, pp. 406-410, vol. iv, pls. 128-145. London and New York, 1938.

─────── "Sāsānian Stone Sculpture," *ibid.,* vol. i, pp. 593-600, vol. iv, pls. 154-168. London and New York, 1938.

Sarre, Friedrich, and Herzfeld, Ernst. *Iranische Felsreliefs* . . . . Berlin, 1910.

Trever, C. *Nouveaux Plats sasanides de l'Ermitage.* Moscow and Leningrad, 1937.

ISLAMIC ART[1]

GENERAL WORKS

Bahgat Bey, Aly, and Gabriel, Albert. *Fouilles d'al Fousṭāṭ* (Musée de l'Art Arabe du Caire). Cairo, 1921.

Briggs, Martin S. *Muhammadan Architecture in Egypt and Palestine.* Oxford, 1924.

Creswell, K. A. C. *Early Muslim Architecture: Umayyads, Early 'Abbāsids and Ṭūlūnids.* 2 vols. Oxford, 1932, 1940.

Devonshire, Mrs. R. L. *Some Cairo Mosques and Their Founders.* London, 1921.

Diez, Ernst. *Churasanische Baudenkmäler.* Berlin, 1918.

─────── *Die Kunst der islamischen Völker.* Berlin, 1917.

Dimand, M. S. "Studies in Islamic Ornament, I: Some Aspects of Omaiyad and Early 'Abbāsid Ornament," *Ars Islamica*, vol. iv (1937), pp. 293-337.

Gabriel, Albert. *Monuments turcs d'Anatolie.* 2 vols. Paris, 1931, 1934.

Glück, Heinrich, and Diez, Ernst. *Die Kunst des Islam.* Berlin, 1925.

Godard, André. "Les Anciennes Mosquées de l'Īrān," *Athār-É Īrān*, vol. i (1936), pp. 187-210.

Gurlitt, Cornelius. *Die Baukunst Konstantinopels.* Berlin, 1912.

[1] For more complete bibliographies, see Ernst Kühnel, "Kritische Bibliographie: Islamische Kunst 1914-1927," *Der Islam*, vol. xvii (1928), pp. 133-248; L. A. Mayer, *Annual Bibliography of Islamic Art and Archaeology*, vol. i: 1935, vol. ii: 1936 (Jerusalem, 1937, 1938).

Hauser, Walter; Upton, Joseph M.; and Wilkinson, Charles K. "The Īrānian Expedition," *Bulletin of The Metropolitan Museum of Art*, vol. xxxii (1937), Oct., sect. ii; vol. xxxiii (1938), Nov., sect. ii; vol. xxxvii (1942), pp. 81-119.

Hautecoeur, Louis, and Wiet, Gaston. *Les Mosquées du Caire.* 2 vols. Paris, 1932.

Herzfeld, Ernst. *Erster vorläufiger Bericht über die Ausgrabungen von Samarra.* Berlin, 1912.

———— "Mschattâ, Hîra und Bâdiya," *Jahrbuch der preuszischen Kunstsammlungen*, vol. xlii (1921), pp. 104-146.

Jaussen, [A. J.], and Savignac. *Mission archéologique en Arabie*, vol. iii: *Les Châteaux arabes de Qeṣeir 'Amra, Ḥarâneh et Ṭûba.* Paris, 1922.

Kühnel, Ernst. *Maurische Kunst.* Berlin, 1924.

———— *Islamische Kleinkunst.* Berlin, 1925.

———— "Die islamische Kunst," *Handbuch der Kunstgeschichte*, edited by Anton Springer, vol. vi, pp. 373-548. Leipzig, 1929.

Lane-Poole, Stanley. *The Art of the Saracens in Egypt.* London, 1886.

Marçais, Georges. *Manuel d'art musulman: L'Architecture—Tunisie, Algérie, Maroc, Espagne, Sicile.* 2 vols. Paris, 1926-1927.

Migeon, Gaston. *Exposition des arts musulmans au Musée des Arts Décoratifs.* Paris [1903].

———— *L'Orient musulman* (Musée du Louvre, Documents d'art). 2 vols. [Paris, 1922].

———— *Manuel d'art musulman: Arts plastiques et industriels.* 2 vols. 2nd edition. Paris, 1927.

Prisse d'Avennes, [A.C.T.E.]. *L'Art arabe d'après les monuments du Kaire . . . .* Paris, 1877.

Ricard, Prosper. *Pour Comprendre l'Art musulman dans l'Afrique du Nord et en Espagne.* Paris, 1924.

Saladin, Henri. *La Mosquée de Sidi Okba à Kairouan* (Les Monuments historiques de la Tunisie, part 2, vol. 1). Paris, 1899.

———— *Manuel d'art musulman: L'Architecture.* 2 vols. Paris, 1907.

Sarre, Friedrich. *Erzeugnisse islamischer Kunst*, part ii: *Seldschukische Kleinkunst* (Sarre Collection). Leipzig, 1909.

———— *Denkmäler persische Baukunst . . . .* 2 vols. Berlin, 1910.

———— *Der Kiosk von Konia.* Berlin, 1936.

Sarre, Friedrich, and Herzfeld, Ernst. *Archäologische Reise im Euphrat- und Tigris-Gebiet.* 4 vols. Berlin, 1911-1920.

335

Sarre, Friedrich, and Martin, F. R. (ed.). *Die Ausstellung von Meisterwerken muhammedanischer Kunst in München 1910*. 3 vols. Munich, 1912.

[Smirnov, Y. I. (ed.)]. *Oriental Silver [Argenterie orientale]* (Imperial Archaeological Commission). St. Petersburg, 1909. (In Russian.)

Strzygowski, Josef. *Altai-Iran und Völkerwanderung* . . . . Leipzig, 1917.

Terrasse, Henri. *L'Art hispano-mauresque des origines au XIIIe siècle.* Paris, 1932.

Wiet, Gaston. *Album du Musée Arabe du Caire* (Publications du Musée Arabe du Caire). Cairo, 1930.

——————— *L'Exposition persane de 1931* (Publications du Musée Arabe du Caire). Cairo, 1933.

PAINTING

Arnold, Sir Thomas. *Painting in Islam* . . . . Oxford, 1928.

——————— *Bihzād and His Paintings in the Zafar-nāmah MS.* London, 1930.

——————— *The Library of A. Chester Beatty: a Catalogue of the Indian Miniatures, Oriental Manuscripts 1-18*, revised and edited by J. V. S. Wilkinson. 3 vols. [London] 1936.

Arnold, Sir Thomas W., and Grohmann, Adolf. *The Islamic Book* . . . . [Paris] 1929.

Binyon, Laurence. *The Court Painters of the Grand Moguls*, with a historical introduction and notes by T. W. Arnold. London, 1921.

Binyon, Laurence; Wilkinson, J. V. S.; and Gray, Basil. *Persian Miniature Painting, Including a Critical and Descriptive Catalogue of the Miniatures Exhibited at Burlington House, January-March, 1931.* London, 1933.

Blochet, Edgard. *Les Peintures des manuscrits orientaux de la Bibliothèque Nationale.* 2nd edition. Paris, 1925.

——————— *Les Enluminures des manuscrits orientaux, turcs, arabes, persans, de la Bibliothèque Nationale.* Paris, 1926.

——————— *Musulman Painting, XIIth-XVIIth Century*, translated by Cicely M. Binyon, with an introduction by Sir E. Denison Ross. London [1929].

Brown, Percy. *Indian Painting under the Mughals, A.D. 1550 to A.D. 1750.* Oxford, 1924.

Clarke, C. Stanley. *Indian Drawings: Twelve Mogul Paintings of the School of Humāyūn (16th Century) Illustrating the Romance of Amīr Hamzah* (Victoria and Albert Museum Portfolios, I). London, 1921.

Coomaraswamy, Ananda K. *Rajput Painting* . . . . London, 1916.

——————— *Les Miniatures orientales de la collection Goloubew au Museum of Fine Arts de Boston.* Paris and Brussels, 1929.

336

Dimand, M. S. "Notes on Persian Miniatures of the Timurid Period in the Metropolitan Museum," *Eastern Art*, vol. I (1928), pp. 23-31.

———— *A Guide to an Exhibition of Islamic Miniature Painting and Book Illumination . . . 1933-1934* (The Metropolitan Museum of Art). New York [1933].

Edhem, Fehmi, and Stchoukine, Ivan. *Les Manuscrits orientaux illustrés de la Bibliothèque de l'Université de Stamboul.* Paris, 1933.

Giuzalian, L. T., and Diakonov, M. M. *Iranian Miniatures in Manuscripts of the Shāhnāma from Leningrad Collections* (The Hermitage). Moscow and Leningrad, 1935. (In Russian.)

Glück, Heinrich. *Die indischen Miniaturen des Haemzae-Romanes im Öster-reichischen Museum für Kunst und Industrie in Wien und in anderen Sammlungen.* Vienna [1925].

Glück, Heinrich, and Strzygowski, Josef. *Die indischen Miniaturen im Schlosse Schönbrunn.* Vienna, 1923.

Goetz, Hermann. *Geschichte der indischen Miniatur-Malerei.* Berlin and Leipzig, 1934.

Herzfeld, Ernst. *Die Malereien von Samarra* (Die Ausgrabungen von Samarra, vol. III). Berlin, 1927.

Huart, Clément. *Les Calligraphes et les miniaturistes de l'Orient musulman.* Paris, 1908.

Kühnel, Ernst. *Miniaturmalerei im islamischen Orient.* 2nd edition. Berlin, 1922.

———— "Die Baysonghur-Handschrift der islamischen Kunstabteilung," *Jahrbuch der preuszischen Kunstsammlungen*, vol. LII (1931), pp. 133-152.

Kühnel, Ernst, and Goetz, Hermann. *Indian Book Painting from Jahāngir's Album in the State Library in Berlin.* London, 1926.

Lorey, Eustache de. "La Peinture musulmane: L'École de Bagdad," *Gazette des beaux-arts*, vol. X (1933), pp. 1-13.

———— "L'École de Tabriz," *Revue des arts asiatiques* (Annales du Musée Guimet), vol. IX (1935), pp. 27-39.

Marteau, Georges, and Vever, Henri. *Miniatures persanes . . . exposées au Musée des Arts Décoratifs Juin-Octobre 1912.* 2 vols. Paris, 1913.

Martin, F. R. *The Miniature Painting and Painters of Persia, India and Turkey from the 8th to the 18th Century.* 2 vols. London, 1912.

———— *The Nizami MS. from the Library of the Shah of Persia, Now in the Metropolitan Museum at New York.* Vienna, 1927.

[Musil, Alois]. *Kusejr 'Amra.* 2 vols. Vienna, 1907.

337

Sakisian, Arménag. "Les Miniaturistes persans Behzad et Kassim Ali," *Gazette des beaux-arts*, vol. II (1920), pp. 215-233.

──────── *La Miniature persane du XIIe au XVIIe siècle*. Paris and Brussels, 1929.

Sarre, Friedrich, and Mittwoch, Eugen. *Zeichnungen von Riza Abbasi*. Munich, 1914.

Schulz, Philipp Walter. *Die persisch-islamische Miniaturmalerei* . . . . 2 vols. Leipzig, 1914.

Stchoukine, Ivan. *Les Miniatures indiennes de l'époque des grands moghols au Musée du Louvre*. Paris, 1929.

──────── *La Peinture indienne à l'époque des grands moghols*. Paris, 1929.

──────── *Les Miniatures persanes* (Musée National du Louvre). Paris, 1932.

──────── *La Peinture iranienne sous les derniers 'Abbâsides et les Il-Khâns*. Bruges, 1936.

Upton, Joseph M. "A Manuscript of 'The Book of the Fixed Stars' by 'Abd ar-Raḥmān aṣ-Ṣūfī," *Metropolitan Museum Studies*, vol. IV (1932-1933), pp. 179-197.

Wilkinson, J. V. S. *The Shāh-Nāmah of Firdausī* . . ., with an introduction on the paintings [from a MS. in the Royal Asiatic Society] by Laurence Binyon. London, 1931.

BOOKBINDING

Aga-Oglu, Mehmet. *Persian Bookbindings of the Fifteenth Century*. Ann Arbor, 1935.

Gratzl, Emil. *Islamische Bucheinbände des 14. bis 19. Jahrhunderts aus den Handschriften der Bayerischen Staatsbibliothek*. Leipzig, 1924.

Sakisian, Arménag. "La Reliure persane du XIVe au XVIIe siècle," *Actes du XIe congrès de l'histoire de l'art*, vol. I, pp. 343-348. Paris, 1921.

──────── "La Reliure turque du XVe au XIXe siècle," *Revue de l'art ancien et moderne*, vol. LI (1927), pp. 277-284, vol. LII (1927), pp. 141-154.

──────── "La Reliure dans la Perse occidentale, sous les mongols, au XIVe et au début du XVe siècle," *Ars Islamica*, vol. I (1934), pp. 80-91.

──────── "La Reliure persane au XVe siècle sous les turcomans," *Artibus Asiae*, vol. VII (1937), pp. 210-223.

Sarre, Friedrich. *Islamische Bucheinbände*. Berlin [1923].

SCULPTURE IN STONE AND STUCCO

Bashkiroff, A. S. *The Art of Daghestan: Carved Stones*. Moscow, 1931.

Berchem, Max van, and Strzygowski, Josef. *Amida* . . . . Heidelberg, 1910.

Dimand, M. S. "Three Syrian Capitals of the Eighth Century," *Bulletin of The Metropolitan Museum of Art*, vol. xxxi (1936), pp. 155-157.

——————— "A Stone Relief from the Caucasus," *ibid.*, vol. xxxiii (1938), pp. 260-262.

——————— "Samanid Stucco Decoration from Nishapur," *Journal of the American Oriental Society*, vol. 58 (1938), pp. 258-261.

Flury, Samuel. *Die Ornamente der Hakim- und Ashar-Moschee* . . . . Heidelberg, 1912.

——————— "Samarra und die Ornamentik der Moschee des Ibn Tūlūn," *Der Islam*, vol. iv (1913), pp. 421-432.

——————— "La Mosquée de Nāyin," *Syria*, vol. xi (1930), pp. 43-58.

Hawary, Hassan, and Rached, Hussein. *Stèles funéraires* (Catalogue général du Musée Arabe du Caire), vols. i and iii. Cairo, 1932, 1939.

Herzfeld, Ernst. *Der Wandschmuck der Bauten von Samarra und seine Ornamentik* (Die Ausgrabungen von Samarra, vol. i). Berlin, 1923.

Riefstahl, Rudolf M. "Persian Islamic Stucco Sculptures," *The Art Bulletin*, vol. xiii (1931), pp. 439-463.

Sarre, Friedrich. "Makam 'Ali am Euphrat: ein islamisches Baudenkmal des X. Jahrhunderts," *Jahrbuch der Königlich preuszischen Kuntsammlungen*, vol. xxix (1908), pp. 63-76.

——————— "Figürliche persische Stuckplastik in der islamischen Kunstabteilung," *Amtliche Berichte aus den Königlichen Kunstsammlungen*, vol. xxxv (1913-1914), pp. 181-189.

Smith, Myron Bement, and Herzfeld, Ernst. *Imām Zāde Karrār at Buzūn: a Dated Seldjūk Ruin.* Berlin, 1935. (Reprinted from *Archaeologischen Mitteilungen aus Iran*, vol. vii [1935], nos. 2, 3.)

Strzygowski, Josef. "Mschatta, II: Kunstwissenschaftliche Untersuchung," *Jahrbuch der Königlich preuszischen Kunstsammlungen*, vol. xxv (1904), pp. 225-373.

Upton, Joseph M. "A Persian Marble Tombstone," *Bulletin of The Metropolitan Museum of Art*, vol. xxvi (1931), pp. 163-164.

——————— "Persian Sculptures of the Fourteenth Century," *ibid.*, vol. xxvii (1932), p. 210.

Viollet, Henry, and Flury, Samuel. "Un Monument des premiers siècles de l'Hégire en Perse: . . . la mosquée de Nâyin," *Syria*, vol. ii (1921), pp. 226-234 and 305-316.

Wiet, Gaston. *Stèles funéraires* (Catalogue général du Musée Arabe du Caire), vols. ii and iv-vi. Cairo, 1936-1939.

339

Christie, A. H. "Fatimid Wood-Carvings in the Victoria and Albert Museum," *The Burlington Magazine*, vol. XLVI (1925), pp. 184-187.

Deniké, Boris. "Quelques Monuments de bois sculpté au Turkestān occidental," *Ars Islamica*, vol. II (1935), pp. 69-83.

Dimand, M. S. "A Dated Koran-Stand," *Bulletin of The Metropolitan Museum of Art*, vol. XXII (1927), pp. 115-117.

————— "An Arabic Woodcarving of the Eighth Century," *ibid.*, vol. XXVI (1931), pp. 271-275.

————— "Arabic Woodcarvings of the Ninth Century," *ibid.*, vol. XXVII (1932), pp. 135-137.

————— "Dated Persian Doors of the Fifteenth Century," *ibid.*, vol. XXXI (1936), pp. 78-80.

Herz-Pacha, Max. "Boiseries fatimites aux sculptures figurales," *Orientalisches Archiv*, vol. III (1912-1913), pp. 169-174.

Lamm, Carl Johan. "Fatimid Woodwork, Its Style and Chronology," *Bulletin de l'Institut d'Égypte*, vol. XVIII (1935-1936), pp. 59-91.

Martin, F. R. *Thüren aus Turkestan*. Stockholm, 1897.

Pauty, Edmond. *Bois sculptés d'églises coptes (époque fatimide)* (Publications du Musée Arabe du Caire). Cairo, 1930.

————— *Les Bois sculptés jusqu'à l'époque ayyoubide* (Catalogue général du Musée Arabe du Caire). Cairo, 1931.

Riefstahl, Rudolf M. "A Seljuq Koran Stand with Lacquer-Painted Decoration in the Museum of Konya," *The Art Bulletin*, vol. XV (1933), pp. 361-373.

Weill, Jean David. *Les Bois à épigraphes*, [vol. I]: *Jusqu'à l'époque mamlouke*, and vol. II: *Époques mamlouke et ottomane* (Catalogue général du Musée Arabe du Caire). Cairo, 1931, 1936.

IVORIES

Cott, Perry Blythe. *Siculo-Arabic Ivories*. [Princeton] 1939.

Diez, Ernst. "Bemalte Elfenbeinkästchen und Pyxiden der islamischen Kunst," *Jahrbuch der Königlich preuszischen Kunstsammlungen*, vol. XXXI (1910), pp. 231-244.

Dimand, M. S. "An Egypto-Arabic Panel with Mosaic Decoration," *Bulletin of The Metropolitan Museum of Art*, vol. XXXIII (1938), pp. 78-79.

Ferrandis, José. *Marfiles y azabaches españoles*. Barcelona and Buenos Aires [1928].

Kühnel, Ernst. "Sizilien und die islamische Elfenbeinmalerei," *Zeitschrift für bildende Kunst*, vol. XXV (1914), pp. 162-170.

Berchem, Max van. "Notes d'archéologie orientale, III: Études sur les cuivres damasquinés et les verres émaillés," *Journal asiatique*, series 10, vol. III (1904), pp. 5-96.

Dean, Bashford. *Handbook of Arms and Armor, European and Oriental* . . . (The Metropolitan Museum of Art). 4th edition. New York, 1930.

Dimand, M. S. "Near Eastern Metalwork," *Bulletin of The Metropolitan Museum of Art*, vol. XXI (1926), pp. 193-199.

———— "Unpublished Metalwork of the Rasūlid Sultans of Yemen," *Metropolitan Museum Studies*, vol. III (1930-1931), pp. 229-237.

———— "A Silver Inlaid Bronze Canteen with Christian Subjects in the Eumorfopoulos Collection," *Ars Islamica*, vol. I (1934), pp. 17-21.

Harari, Ralph. "Metalwork after the Early Islamic Period," *A Survey of Persian Art* . . ., edited by Arthur Upham Pope, vol. III, pp. 2466-2529, vol. VI, pls. 1236-1396. London and New York, 1939.

Kühnel, Ernst. "Die Metallarbeiten auf der mohammedanischen Ausstellung in München 1910," *Kunst und Kunsthandwerk*, vol. XIII (1910), pp. 504-512.

———— "Zwei Mosulbronzen und ihr Meister," *Jahrbuch der preuszischen Kunstsammlungen*, vol. LX (1939), pp. 1-20.

Martin, F. R. *Ältere Kupferarbeiten aus dem Orient*. Stockholm, 1902.

Migeon, Gaston. "Les Cuivres arabes: Le Vase Barberini au Louvre," and "Le 'Baptistère de Saint Louis' au Louvre," *Gazette des beaux-arts*, vol. XXII (1899), pp. 462-474, vol. XXIII (1900), pp. 119-131.

Sarre, Friedrich. "Ein orientalisches Metallbecken des XIII Jahrhunderts im Königlichen Museum für Völkerkunde zu Berlin," *Jahrbuch der Königlich preuszischen Kunstsammlungen*, vol. XXV (1904), pp. 49-71.

———— "Bronzeplastik in Vogelform: ein sasanidisch-frühislamisches Räuchergefäsz," *Jahrbuch der preuszischen Kunstsammlungen*, vol. LI (1930), pp. 159-164.

———— "Die Bronzekanne des Kalifen Marwān II im Arabischen Museum in Kairo," *Ars Islamica*, vol. I (1934), pp. 10-15.

Sarre, Friedrich, and Berchem, Max van. "Das Metallbecken des Atabeks Lulu von Mosul . . .," *Münchner Jahrbuch der bildenden Kunst*, 1907, pp. 18-37.

Veselovski, N. I. *A Bronze Cauldron from Herat Dated* A.H. 559 (Bobrinski Collection) (Materials on Russian Archaeology . . ., no. 33). St. Petersburg, 1910. (In Russian.)

Wiet, Gaston. *Objets en cuivre* (Catalogue général du Musée Arabe du Caire). Cairo, 1932.

Abel, Armand. *Gaibī et les grands faïenciers égyptiens d'époque mamlouke* . . . (Publications du Musée Arabe du Caire). Cairo, 1930.

Bahgat Bey, Aly, and Massoul, Félix. *La Céramique musulmane de l'Égypte* (Publications du Musée Arabe du Caire). Cairo, 1930.

Crane, Mary E. "A Fourteenth-Century Mihrab from Isfahan," *Ars Islamica*, vol. VII (1940), pp. 96-100.

Dimand, M. S. "A Dated Persian Jug from Sultanabad," *The Burlington Magazine*, vol. XLIV (1924), pp. 246-251.

————— *Loan Exhibition of Ceramic Art of the Near East* (The Metropolitan Museum of Art). New York, 1931.

————— *Islamic Pottery of the Near East* . . . (The Metropolitan Museum of Art). New York, 1941.

Ettinghausen, Richard. "Evidence for the Identification of Kāshān Pottery," *Ars Islamica*, vol. III (1936), pp. 44-75.

————— "The Ceramic Art in Islamic Times: Dated Faience," *A Survey of Persian Art* . . ., edited by Arthur Upham Pope, vol. II, pp. 1667-1696, vol. V, pls. 555-811. London and New York, 1938, 1939.

Frothingham, Alice Wilson. *Catalogue of Hispano-Moresque Pottery in the Collection of the Hispanic Society of America*. New York, 1936.

Godard, Yedda A. "Pièces datées de céramique de Kāshān à décor lustré," *Athār-É Īrān*, vol. II (1937), pp. 309-337.

Hobson, R. L. *A Guide to the Islamic Pottery of the Near East* (British Museum). [London] 1932.

————— "The Ceramic Art in Islamic Times: Techniques," *A Survey of Persian Art* . . ., edited by Arthur Upham Pope, vol. II, pp. 1697-1702, vol. V, pls. 555-811. London and New York, 1938, 1939.

Kelekian, Dikran K. *The Kelekian Collection of Persian and Analogous Potteries* . . . . Paris, 1910.

Koechlin, Raymond. *Les Céramiques musulmanes de Suse au Musée du Louvre.* Paris, 1928.

————— *L'Art de l'Islam: La Céramique* (Musée des Arts Décoratifs, Documents d'art [vol. 1]). [Paris, n.d.]

Kühnel, Ernst. "Datierte persische Fayencen," *Jahrbuch der asiatischen Kunst*, vol. I (1924), pp. 42-52.

————— "Dated Persian Lustred Pottery," *Eastern Art*, vol. III (1931), pp. 221-236.

Lane, Arthur. *A Guide to the Collection of Tiles* (Victoria and Albert Museum, Department of Ceramics). London, 1939.

———————— "The So-called 'Kubachi' Wares of Persia," *The Burlington Magazine*, vol. LXXV (1939), pp. 156-162.

Marçais, Georges. *Les Poteries et faïences de la Qal'a des Benî Hammâd (XIe siècle)* . . . . Constantine, 1913.

———————— *Les Faïences à reflets métalliques de la grande mosquée de Kairouan.* Paris, 1928.

Migeon, Gaston. "Nouvelles Découvertes sur la céramique de Damas," *Revue de l'art ancien et moderne*, vol. XLIV (1923), pp. 383-386.

Migeon, Gaston, and Sakisian, Arménag. "Les Faïences d'Asie-Mineure du XIIIe au XVIe siècle," *Revue de l'art ancien et moderne*, vol. XLIII (1923), pp. 241-252 and 353-364.

———————— "Les Faïences d'Asie-Mineure du XVe au XVIIIe siècle," *ibid.*, vol. XLIV (1923), pp. 125-141.

Olmer, Pierre. *Les Filtres de gargoulettes* (Catalogue général du Musée Arabe du Caire). Cairo, 1932.

Pézard, Maurice. *La Céramique archaïque de l'Islam et ses origines.* 2 vols. Paris, 1920.

Pope, Arthur Upham. "The Ceramic Art in Islamic Times: The History," *A Survey of Persian Art* . . ., edited by Arthur Upham Pope, vol. II, pp. 1446-1666, vol. V, pls. 555-811. London and New York, 1938, 1939.

Raymund, Alexander. *Alttürkische Keramik in Kleinasien und Konstantinopel.* Munich, 1922.

Riefstahl, Rudolf M. "Early Turkish Tile Revetments in Edirne," *Ars Islamica*, vol. IV (1937), pp. 249-281.

Ritter, H.; Ruska, J.; Sarre, F.; and Winderlich, R. *Orientalische Steinbücher und persische Fayencetechnik* (Istanbuler Mitteilungen, no. 3). Istanbul, 1935.

Rivière, Henri. *La Céramique dans l'art musulman* . . . . 2 vols. Paris, 1913.

Sarre, Friedrich. "Die spanisch-maurischen Lüsterfayencen des Mittelalters und ihre Herstellung in Malaga," *Jahrbuch der Königlich preussischen Kunstsammlungen*, vol. XXIV (1903), pp. 103-130.

———————— "Islamische Tongefäsze aus Mesopotamien," *ibid.*, vol. XXVI (1905), pp. 69-88.

———————— *Die Keramik von Samarra* (Die Ausgrabungen von Samarra, vol. II). Berlin, 1925.

Sarre, Friedrich, and Kühnel, Ernst. "Zwei persische Gebetnischen aus lüstrierten Fliesen," *Berliner Museen: Berichte aus den preussischen Kunstsammlungen*, vol. XLIX (1928), pp. 126-131.

Wallis, Henry. *Persian Ceramic Art* . . .: *The Thirteenth Century Lustred Vases* (The Godman Collection). London, 1891.

Dimand, M. S. "A Syrian Enameled Glass Bottle of the XIV Century," *Bulletin of The Metropolitan Museum of Art*, vol. XXXI (1936), pp. 105-108.

Kühnel, Ernst. "Frühislamische Gläser mit aufgelegtem Dekor," *Amtliche Berichte aus den Königlichen Kunstsammlungen*, vol. XXXV (1913-1914), pp. 11-16.

Lamm, Carl Johan. *Das Glas von Samarra* (Die Ausgrabungen von Samarra, vol. IV). Berlin, 1928.

————— *Mittelalterliche Gläser und Steinschnittarbeiten aus dem Nahen Osten.* 2 vols. Berlin, 1929, 1930.

————— *Glass from Iran in the National Museum, Stockholm.* London [1935].

————— "Glass and Hard Stone Vessels," *A Survey of Persian Art . . .*, edited by Arthur Upham Pope, vol. III, pp. 2592-2606, vol. VI, pls. 1438-1459. London and New York, 1939.

Longhurst, M. H. "Some Crystals of the Fatimid Period," *The Burlington Magazine*, vol. XLVIII (1926), pp. 149-155.

Schmidt, Robert. "Die Hedwigsgläser und die verwandten fatimidischen Glas- und Kristallschnittarbeiten," *Jahrbuch der Schlesischen Museen*, n.s. vol. VI (1912), pp. 53-78.

Schmoranz, Gustav. *Altorientalische Glas-Gefässe* . . . . Vienna, 1898.

Wiet, Gaston, *Lampes et bouteilles en verre émaillé* (Catalogue général du Musée Arabe du Caire). Cairo, 1929.

TEXTILES

[Ashton, Leigh]. *Brief Guide to the Persian Embroideries* (Victoria and Albert Museum, Department of Textiles). London, 1937.

Breck, Joseph. "Four Seventeenth-Century Pintadoes," *Metropolitan Museum Studies*, vol. I (1928-1929), pp. 3-15.

Dimand, M. S. "Persian Velvets of the Sixteenth Century," *Bulletin of The Metropolitan Museum of Art*, vol. XXII (1927), pp. 108-111.

————— "A Persian Velvet Carpet," *ibid.*, vol. XXII (1927), pp. 247-251.

————— "Coptic and Egypto-Arabic Textiles," *ibid.*, vol. XXVI (1931), pp. 89-91.

————— "A Recent Gift of Egypto-Arabic Textiles," *ibid.*, vol. XXVII (1932), pp. 92-96.

Falke, Otto von. *Kunstgeschichte der Seidenweberei.* 2 vols. Berlin, 1913.

Kendrick, A. F. *Catalogue of Muhammadan Textiles of the Medieval Period* (Victoria and Albert Museum, Department of Textiles). London, 1924.

Kendrick, A. F., and Arnold, T. W. "Persian Stuffs with Figure Subjects," *The Burlington Magazine*, vol. XXXVII (1920), pp. 237-244.

Kühnel, Ernst. *Islamische Stoffe aus ägyptischen Gräbern in der islamischen Kunstabteilung und in der Stoffsammlung des Schlossmuseums.* Berlin, 1927.

Lamm, Carl Johan. *Cotton in Mediaeval Textiles of the Near East.* Paris, 1937.

Martin, F. R. *Figurale persische Stoffe aus dem Zeitraum 1550-1650.* Stockholm, 1899.

——— *Die persischen Prachtstoffe im Schlosse Rosenborg in Kopenhagen.* Stockholm, 1901.

Pfister, Rudolf. "Matériaux pour servir au classement des textiles égyptiens postérieurs à la conquête arabe," *Revue des arts asiatiques* (Annales du Musée Guimet), vol. X (1936), pp. 1-16.

——— *Les Toiles imprimées de Fostat et l'Hindoustan.* Paris, 1938.

Reath, Nancy Andrews, and Sachs, Eleanor B. *Persian Textiles and Their Technique from the Sixth to the Eighteenth Centuries, Including a System for General Textile Classification.* New Haven, 1937.

Schmidt, J. Heinrich. "Persische Seidenstoffe der Seldjūḳenzeit," *Ars Islamica,* vol. II (1935), pp. 84-91.

——— "Persische Stoffe mit Signaturen von Ghiyâs," *Jahrbuch der kunsthistorischen Sammlungen in Wien,* vol. VII (1935), pp. 219-227.

Victoria and Albert Museum, Department of Textiles. *Brief Guide to the Turkish Woven Fabrics.* 2nd edition. London, 1931.

——— *Brief Guide to the Persian Woven Fabrics.* London, 1937.

Wace, A. J. B. "The Dating of Turkish Velvets," *The Burlington Magazine,* vol. LXIV (1934), pp. 164-170.

——— *Mediterranean and Near Eastern Embroideries from the Collection of Mrs. F. H. Cook.* 2 vols. London, 1935.

[Wiet, Gaston]. *Exposition des tapisseries et tissus du Musée Arabe du Caire (de VIIᵉ au XVIIᵉ siècle), Période musulmane* (Musée des Gobelins). Paris [1935].

——— "Tissus et tapisseries du Musée Arabe du Caire," *Syria,* vol. XVI (1935), pp. 278-290.

RUGS

Bode, Wilhelm. *Antique Rugs from the Near East.* 3rd revised edition, with contributions by Ernst Kühnel. New York, 1922.

Bogolubov, A. *Tapis de l'Asie centrale . . . .* St. Petersburg, 1908.

Breck, Joseph, and Morris, Frances. *The James F. Ballard Collection of Oriental Rugs* (The Metropolitan Museum of Art). New York, 1923.

Dilley, Arthur Urbane. *Oriental Rugs and Carpets* . . . . New York and London, 1931.

Dimand, M. S. "Medallion Carpets," *The Art Bulletin*, vol. vi (1924), pp. 82-84.

———— *Loan Exhibition of Persian Rugs of the So-called Polish Type* (The Metropolitan Museum of Art). New York, 1930.

———— *A Guide to an Exhibition of Oriental Rugs and Textiles* (The Metropolitan Museum of Art). New York, 1935.

———— "A Persian Garden Carpet in the Jaipur Museum," *Ars Islamica*, vol. vii (1940), pp. 93-96.

Erdmann, Kurt. "Orientalische Tierteppiche auf Bildern des XIV. und XV. Jahrhunderts," *Jahrbuch der preuszischen Kunstsammlungen*, vol. l (1929), pp. 261-298.

———— "Later Caucasian Dragon Carpets," *Apollo*, vol. xxii (1935), pp. 21-25.

———— "Kairener Teppiche, I: Europäische und islamische Quellen des 15.-18. Jahrhunderts," and "II: Mamluken- und Osmanenteppiche," *Ars Islamica*, vol. v (1938), pp. 179-206, vol. vii (1940), pp. 55-81.

Grote-Hasenbalg, Werner. *Der Orientteppich: seine Geschichte und seine Kultur*. 3 vols. Berlin, 1922.

Hendley, T. H. *Asian Carpets: XVI. and XVII. Century Designs from the Jaipur Palaces* . . . . London, 1905.

Jacoby, Heinrich. "Materials Used in the Making of Carpets," *A Survey of Persian Art* . . ., edited by Arthur Upham Pope, vol. iii, pp. 2456-2465, vol. vi, pls. 1107-1275. London and New York, 1939.

[Kendrick, A. F.]. *Guide to the Collection of Carpets* (Victoria and Albert Museum, Department of Textiles). 3rd edition, revised by C. E. C. Tattersall. London, 1931.

Kendrick, A. F., and Tattersall, C. E. C. *Fine Carpets in the Victoria and Albert Museum*. London, 1924.

Lamm, Carl Johan. "The Marby Rug and Some Fragments of Carpets Found in Egypt," *Svenska Orientsällskapets Årsbok*, 1937, pp. 51-130.

Martin, F. R. *A History of Oriental Carpets before 1800*. Vienna, 1908.

Neugebauer, R., and Troll, Siegfried. *Handbuch der orientalischen Teppichkunde*. Leipzig, 1930.

Pope, Arthur Upham. "The Myth of the Armenian Dragon Carpets," *Jahrbuch der asiatischen Kunst*, vol. ii (1925), pp. 147-159.

———— "Un Tappeto persiano del 1521 nel Museo Poldi-Pezzoli," *Dedalo*, vol. viii (1927), pp. 82-108.

——————— "The Art of Carpet Making, A: History," and "C: The Technique of Persian Carpet Weaving," *A Survey of Persian Art* . . ., edited by Arthur Upham Pope, vol. III, pp. 2257-2430, pp. 2437-2455, vol. VI, pls. 1107-1275. London and New York, 1939.

Riefstahl, Rudolf M. "Primitive Rugs of the 'Konya' Type in the Mosque of Beyshehir," *The Art Bulletin*, vol. XIII (1931), pp. 177-220.

Sakisian, Arménag. "Les Tapis à dragons et leur origine arménienne," *Syria*, vol. IX (1928), pp. 238-256.

——————— "Les Tapis arméniens du XVe au XIXe siècle," *La Revue de l'art ancien et moderne*, vol. LXIV (1933), pp. 21-36.

Sarre, Friedrich. "Mittelalterliche Knüpfteppiche kleinasiatischer und spanischer Herkunft," *Kunst und Kunsthandwerk*, vol. X (1907), pp. 503-526.

——————— "Die ägyptischen Teppiche," *Jahrbuch der asiatischen Kunst*, vol. I (1924), pp. 19-23.

Sarre, Friedrich, and Falkenberg, Th. "Ein frühes Knüpfteppich-Fragment aus Chinesisch-Turkistan," *Berliner Museen: Berichte aus den preuszischen Kunstsammlungen*, vol. XLII (1921), pp. 110-114.

Sarre, Friedrich, and Trenkwald, Hermann. *Old Oriental Carpets*, translated by A. F. Kendrick. 2 vols. Vienna and London, 1926-1929.

Schmutzler, Emil. *Altorientalische Teppiche in Siebenbürgen*. Leipzig, 1933.

Tattersall, C. E. C. *Notes on Carpet-Knotting and Weaving* (Victoria and Albert Museum, Department of Textiles). 2nd edition. London, 1927.

——————— *The Carpets of Persia* . . . . London, 1931.

Thomson, William George. "Hispano-Moresque Carpets," *The Burlington Magazine*, vol. XVIII (1910), pp. 100-111.

Troll, Siegfried. "Damaskus-Teppiche," *Ars Islamica*, vol. IV (1937), pp. 201-231.

Van de Put, Albert. "Some Fifteenth-Century Spanish Carpets," *The Burlington Magazine*, vol. XIX (1911), pp. 344-350, vol. XLV (1924), pp. 119-120.

ADDITIONAL BIBLIOGRAPHY

Ashton, Sir Leigh. *The Art of India and Pakistan*, London, 1947-1948. Sculpture, K. de B. Codrington; Bronzes and Textiles, John Irwin; Painting, Basil Gray. New York, preface date 1949

Bahrami, Mehdi. *Gurgan faiences*, Cairo, 1949

Barrett, Douglas. *Islamic Metalwork in the British Museum*, London, 1949

Berk, Nouroullah. *La Peinture turque*, Ankara, 1950

Creswell, K. A. C. *Muslim Architecture of Egypt: I. Ikshids and Fatimids, A.D. 939-1171*, Oxford, 1952

Dimand, M. S. "An Exhibition of Islamic and Indian Paintings," *Bulletin of The Metropolitan Museum of Art,* vol. xiv (1955), pp. 85-102

——— *Persian Miniature Painting,* Milan, 1956

Erdmann, Kurt. *Die Kunst Irans zur Zeit der Sasaniden,* Berlin, 1943

——— *Der orientalische Knüpfteppich,* Tübingen, 1955

Gomez-Moreno, Manuel. *El Panteon real de las Huelgas de Burgos,* Madrid, 1946

Gray, Basil, and Godard, André. *Iran: Persian Miniatures,* Paris, 1956

Kühnel, Ernst. *Catalogue of Dated Tiraz Fabrics: Umayyad, Abbasid, Fatimid* (The Textile Museum), Washington, 1952

——— *Catalogue of Spanish Rugs: 12th Century to 19th Century* (The Textile Museum), Washington, 1953

Kühnel, Ernst. "Die Kunst Persiens unter den Buyiden," *Zeitschrift der deutschen Morgenländischen Gesellschaft,* vol. 106, part 1, Berlin (1956)

Lane, Arthur. *Early Islamic Pottery: Mesopotamian, Egypt and Persia,* London, 1947

——— *Later Islamic Pottery: Persia, Syria, Egypt and Turkey,* London, 1957

Mayer, L. A. *Mamluk Costume,* Geneva, 1952

Monneret de Villard, Ugo. *Le Pitture musulmane al Soffito della Capella Palatina in Palermo,* Rome, 1950

Öz, Tahsin. *Turkish Textiles and Velvets,* vol. i, XIV-XVI Centuries, Ankara, 1950, vol. ii (in Turkish), XVII-XIX Centuries, Istanbul, 1951

Rice, D. S. *Le Baptistère de Saint Louis,* Paris, 1951

——— *The Wade Cup in the Cleveland Museum of Art,* Paris, 1955

Stchoukine, Ivan. *Peintures des manuscrits timurides,* Paris, 1954

For more complete bibliographies, see K. A. C. Creswell, *A Bibliography of Glass and Rock Crystal in Islam,* Cairo, 1952; "A Bibliography of Painting in Islam," *Art Islamique,* vol. i, Le Caire (1953); Richard Ettinghausen, "Literature in Islamic Art, 1939 to 1945," part 1: *Ars Islamica,* vols. xiii-xiv (1949), pp. 150-179, part 2: vols. xv-xvi (1951), pp. 151-211.

ADDENDUM

Since 1944, when the second edition of A Handbook of Muhammadan Art was issued, the Metropolitan Museum's collection of Islamic art has been enriched by many important acquisitions through bequests, gifts, and purchases. Some of the gaps in the collection have been filled, making it even more representative than it was in the past. Among the important gifts and bequests are those of Horace Havemeyer, consisting of 102 pieces of Islamic pottery and other objects. As a result of these gifts the Museum today possesses one of the richest collections of Rakka pottery in America, perhaps anywhere. An additional gift of seventeen pieces of ceramics and glass from the Leberthon Collection was made by Mr. and Mrs. A. Wallace Chauncey. A collection of fourteen pieces of Persian pottery with painted decoration from the Mortimer Schiff collection was acquired, partly as a gift from The Schiff Foundation. In this group are several famous pieces, some of them illustrating the story of Bahram Gur and his mistress Azada. In the field of miniature painting, a notable acquisition was the album of Shah Jahan with forty miniature paintings by famous Mughal court artists. This album was purchased in part with funds donated by The Kevorkian Foundation. Twenty-eight important miniature paintings were bequeathed by Cora Timken Burnett. Through the generosity of Mr. John D. Rockefeller, Jr., the Museum's rug collection has been enriched by six Persian silk rugs of the early seventeenth century, which are among the finest in existence. An important sixteenth-century Persian rug, known as the Anhalt carpet, was presented to the Museum by the Samuel H. Kress Foundation. Through the generosity of Joseph V. McMullan the Museum received additional outstanding examples which add greatly to the importance of its collection of Oriental rugs. Of the hundreds of objects acquired in the period from 1944 until the present, only thirty-seven of the utmost importance have been selected for additional illustrations in this new edition of the Handbook.

Fig. 214. Silver bowl with a bust of a Zoroastrian priest, chased and applied. Iranian, Sasanian period, III-IV century A.D. One of four silver bowls found near Kasr-i Shirin on the road to Kermanshah

Fig. 215. Bronze ewer with cast and carved decoration of palmettes and lotus buds, originally inlaid with copper. Iranian, Sasanian period, V-VI century A.D. From the collection of Prince Orloff. The ewer is one of the finest examples of Sasanian bronzes in existence

Fig. 216. Silk weave with decoration of roosters and palmettes. Iranian, Sasanian period, VI century A.D.

Fig. 217. Men Treading Grapes. Miniature painting from a MS. of the Materia Medica of Dioscorides, dated Rajab A.H. 621 (July-August 1224). Mesopotamian, Baghdad school

Fig. 218. Design for a mechanical cup for drinking parties. (When wine is poured into the silver cup the bird turns and whistles.) Illustration from a MS. of al-Jazari's Automata, a book of mechanical inventions and devices. The manuscript is dated; end of Ramadan A.H. 715 (end of December 1315). Arabic, Mamluk school, probably Cairo. From the Kevorkian collection

355

Fig. 219. Abu al-Mijhan and Sa'ad Wakkas before a Ruler. Miniature painting
from a MS. of the Khavar-nama by Ibn Husam. Iranian, Turkoman school,
about 1480

Fig. 220. Preparation of Food for a Feast. Miniature painting in the style of Bihzad, probably from a MS of the Diwan by Hafiz. Iranian, Herat school, end of the XV century

Fig. 221. ABOVE: *A Sick Horse and His Master. Tinted brush drawing in the style of Ustad Muhammadi. Iranian, Safavid school, end of the XVI century. Gift of George D. Pratt*

Fig. 222. LOWER LEFT: *Portrait of a Youth. Miniature painting by Aka Riza. Iranian, Safavid school, end of the XVI century*

Fig. 223. LOWER RIGHT: *Two Lovers Embracing. Miniature painting by Riza-i-'Abbasi with the inscription: Drawn by the humble Riza-i-'Abbasi, in good fortune, year A.H. 1039, completed on the 8th day of Shawwal (May 21, 1630). Iranian, Safavid school*

Fig. 224. Kwaja Jahan Regards a Youth Fallen from a Tree While Bird Nesting.
Miniature painting by Aka Riza, from an album of Shah Jahan. Indian, Mughal,
school of Jahangir (1605-1628). From the Kevorkian collection

Fig. 225. Emperor Jahangir and His Father Akbar the Great. Miniature paint-ing by Balchand, from an album of Shah Jahan. Indian, Mughal, school of Jahangir (1605-1628). From the Kevorkian collection

Fig. 226. Great Hornbill. Miniature painting by Ustad Mansur, from an album of Shah Jahan. Indian, Mughal, school of Jahangir (1605-1628). From the Kevorkian collection

362

Fig. 227. Portrait of Rup Singh Sar Rai Chanda. Miniature painting by Govardhan, from an album of Shah Jahan. Indian, Mughal, school of Shah Jahan (1628-1658). From the Kevorkian collection

Fig. 228. Shah Jahan on Horseback. Miniature painting by Bhag, from an album of Shah Jahan. Indian, Mughal, school of Shah Jahan (1628-1658). From the Kevorkian collection

Fig. 230. Illuminated title page from a Koran, with the name of the calligrapher and the date: Ahmad ibn al Suhruwardi al Bakri, Baghdad, in the months of the year 707 A.H. (1307-1308). Iranian, Mongol period

Fig. 229. Bronze tray inlaid with silver. Iranian, Saljuk period, early XIII century

Fig. 231. ABOVE: Bronze incense burner in the shape of a feline, with engraved and openwork decoration, inscribed with the name of the owner, the maker, and the date: Ordered by the Amir, Saif ad-Dunya, wa'd-Din, Muhammad al-Mawardi, made by Ja'far ibn Muhammad ibn 'Ali, in the year 577 A.H. (1181-1182). Iranian, Saljuk period; found at Kariz, Khurasan

Fig. 232. UPPER RIGHT: Earthenware dish with relief decoration, covered with a yellow lead glaze with splashes of green. Mesopotamian, Abbasid period, IX century

Fig. 233. LOWER RIGHT: Earthenware vase with lustered decoration. Iranian, IX-X century, found at Gurgan. The design of the bird shows all the characteristics of Iranian style

Fig. 236. ABOVE: Bahram Gur Hunting Deer, Accompanied by His Harpist Azada. Earthenware bowl with painted overglaze decoration. Iranian, Kashan, early XIII century. Rogers Fund and gift of The Schiff Foundation

Fig. 234. UPPER LEFT: Earthenware dish with painted decoration of arabesques and Kufic inscriptions. Iranian, Samanid period, X century; found at Nishapur

Fig. 235. LOWER LEFT: Earthenware bowl with lustered decoration. Iranian, Rayy, Saljuk period, about 1200. H. O. Havemeyer collection

Fig. 237. ABOVE: Earthenware jug with lustered decoration.
Mesopotamian, Rakka, XII century. Gift of Horace Havemeyer

Fig. 238. UPPER RIGHT: Earthenware bowl with painted decoration of two peacocks in black under a turquoise blue glaze.
Mesopotamian, Rakka, XII century. The H. O. Havemeyer
collection. This bowl is one of the finest Rakka pieces known

Fig. 239. LOWER RIGHT: Saljuk Prince on Horseback. Earthenware bowl with painted and gilded overglaze decoration, partly
in relief. Iranian, Kashan, early XIII century

Fig. 240. ABOVE: Earthenware jar with relief decoration, inscribed with the date A.H. 681 (1282-1283). Iranian, probably Kashan, Mongol period, XIII century. The H. O. Havemeyer collection

Fig. 241. UPPER RIGHT: Earthenware bowl with lustered decoration. Arabic, Fatimid period, early XI century; found at Fustat

Fig. 242. LOWER RIGHT: Silk weave. Iranian, Buyid period, X-XI century

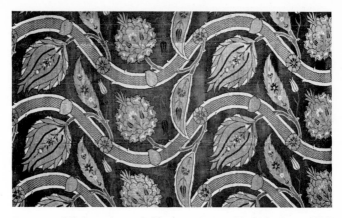

Fig. 243. *Silk brocade, probably from a coat. Turkish, Brusa, XVI century*

Fig. 244. *Silk weave, probably from a coat. Iranian, Safavid, period of Shah Tahmasp (1524-1576)*

Fig. 245. Velvet brocade,
probably from a coat.
Iranian, Safavid, period
of Shah Tahmasp
(1524-1576)

375

Fig. 246. Medallion rug. Iranian, Tabriz court manufactory, Safavid period, second half of the XVI century. From the collection of the Dukes of Anhalt, captured at the siege of Vienna in 1683. Gift of the Samuel H. Kress Foundation

Fig. 247. Cartouche rug with floral decoration. Iranian, Jushagan or Kerman, end of the XVI century. The H. O. Havemeyer collection. This piece is related to the vase rugs (see Fig. 197)

Fig. 248. Medallion silk rug brocaded with metal thread. Iranian (so-called Polish), probably Kashan court manufactory, first half of the XVII century. The European coat of arms has not been identified. From the collection of Prince Ladislas Czartoryski. Gift of John D. Rockefeller, Jr.

Fig. 249. Cartouche silk rug with metal thread. Iranian, probably Kashan court manufactory, first half of the XVII century. Gift of John D. Rockefeller, Jr.

Fig. 250. Floral and arabesque rug. Caucasian, XVII century; from the Mosque at Nigde, Asia Minor. Gift of Joseph V. McMullan